INCREMENTAL
SOFTWARE
ARCHITECTURE

INCREMENTAL SOFTWARE ARCHITECTURE

A METHOD FOR SAVING FAILING IT IMPLEMENTATIONS

Michael Bell

WILEY

Published by John Wiley & Sons, Inc., Hoboken, New Jersey.
Published simultaneously in Canada.

For general information on our other products and services or for technical support, please contact our Customer Care Department within the United States at (800) 762-2974, outside the United States at (317) 572-3993 or fax (317) 572-4002.

Wiley publishes in a variety of print and electronic formats and by print-on-demand. Some material included with standard print versions of this book may not be included in e-books or in print-on-demand. If this book refers to media such as a CD or DVD that is not included in the version you purchased, you may download this material at http://booksupport.wiley.com. For more information about Wiley products, visit www.wiley.com.

Library of Congress Cataloging-in-Publication Data is Available:

978-1-119-11764-3 (hardback)
978-1-119-21368-0 (ePDF)
978-1-119-21369-7 (ePUB)

Cover design: Wiley
Cover image: © iStock.com/Grotmarsel

Printed in the United States of America

10 9 8 7 6 5 4 3 2 1

To Lisa Nathan, for our 30-year-old friendship that has never faded.

CONTENTS

ACKNOWLEDGMENTS   ix

ABOUT THE AUTHOR   xi

CHAPTER 1   The Need for Incremental Software Architecture   1

PART ONE—Why Do Enterprise Systems Fail?   11

CHAPTER 2   What Is a Failing Enterprise System? Is It Management's Fault?   13

CHAPTER 3   Technological System-Level Failures   23

PART TWO—End-State Architecture Discovery and Analysis   35

CHAPTER 4   System Fabric Discovery and Analysis   39

CHAPTER 5   Application Discovery   55

CHAPTER 6   Application Mapping   67

PART THREE— End-State Architecture Decomposition   83

CHAPTER 7   End-State Architecture Structural Decomposition through Classification   85

CHAPTER 8   Business Analysis Drives End-State Architecture Structural Decomposition   103

CHAPTER 9   Technical Analysis Drives End-State Architecture Structural Decomposition   119

CHAPTER 10   Business Views Drive End-State Architecture Decomposition   145

CHAPTER 11   Environment Behavior Drives End-State Architecture Decomposition   161

PART FOUR—End-State Architecture Verification   179

CHAPTER **12** Design Substantiation   181

CHAPTER **13** Introduction to End-State Architecture Stress Testing   197

CHAPTER **14** End-State Architecture Stress Testing Driven by Pressure
Points   223

CHAPTER **15** Enterprise Capacity Planning for End-State Architecture   235

INDEX   253

ACKNOWLEDGMENTS

Nothing could be more inspiring than a chat with a friend or a colleague who not only ponders about the world that we live in, but also bestows upon others knowledge and wisdom. Special thanks to the individuals who inspired and offered great perspectives for the completion of this book: Isabella Tugman, Lisa Nathan, Monica Roman Gagnier, Edward Kelly, David Zaffery, John Beaufait, Carlos Melendez, Sandy Tugman, and Michael Julian.

ABOUT THE AUTHOR

Michael Bell is an enterprise solution provider with twenty-eight years of proven hands-on experience in the space of Business and Technical Architecture Modeling. He has consulted for a large number of institutions, such as J.P. Morgan, Chase, Prudential, Citibank, USB, American Express, AIG, and the U.S. government.

Michael is also the author of best-selling service-oriented modeling books promoting product time-to-market, consolidation, agility, reuse, and expenditure reduction. To support challenging business strategies, his expertise offers a variety of enterprise integration solutions for back-end and customer-facing systems, distributed and federated across large lines of business and enterprise domains.

CHAPTER 1

The Need for Incremental Software Architecture

Technical books rarely begin with conclusions. But the impetus for this book is so strong that it must be revealed at the onset. So, with no time to spare, here is the bottom line: IT and business organizations, in their current incarnations, must be *eliminated*. Replacing them with regional,[1] nimble, and smaller management and technical groups, called *Micro-Organizations* in this book, will be of immense benefit to the product and software development community.

Mere replacement is not enough, however. Merging a Micro-IT organization with its Micro-Business organization counterpart could diminish the constant battle for alignment efforts and improve firm-wide communication. Moreover, unifying smaller business and IT groups to provide rapid enterprise solutions could reduce the long-running frictions between the two, and create a more productive work environment.

This vision accentuates the need to break down the traditional *enterprise centralized management* into smaller *decentralized organizations* to boost efficiency and speed up decision-making. Consequently, regional, small-scale, and agile Micro-Organizations would seize governance and best practices responsibilities to deliver practical and superior systems.

As a result, joint business and IT teams would operate autonomously to deliver and integrate products on time and on budget. Rather than reporting to enterprise executives, teams would report to *regional management*, which understands the distinct culture and requirements of local business operations.[2]

Such a shift in organizational thinking would eliminate the difficulties of trying to conserve a centralized management structure that is slow to respond to critical business events. A lightweight Micro-Organization would then become proactive, reducing the staggering cost of enterprise policing and governance. *Enterprise-wide technology standardization*, therefore, would be the practice of the past. And *enterprise-wide architecture* best practices and standards would cease to exist.

This does not imply that enterprise-wide architecture groups would vanish, too. The charter of such a design organization would shift to a more tangible one. For that reason, architects should focus on providing certified architecture blueprints guaranteed to work in a production environment.

As you progress through the book, keep the Micro-Organizations idea in mind. And if time allows, imagine a workplace that accepts nothing less than devoting *all* its precious energy to producing high-quality and practical products.

For now, let us focus on chief thrust of this book: *presenting a new approach to enterprise software design, development, and integration—Incremental Software Architecture*.

The new method unveiled in the chapters that follow is suited for all enterprises, regardless of their structure and organization. Pursuing the incremental software architecture approach also may drive organizations to break down their convoluted structures into agile Micro-Organizations, accelerating time to market.

In the meantime, though, there is a compelling reason to understand what incremental software architecture is, and how it can be employed to ward off the deployment of failing systems to production environments. This new approach could also be pursued to save underperforming systems and improve enterprise integration of applications, middleware, and network infrastructure.

Now, we've got our work cut out for us. Let's roll up our sleeves and move on.

End-State Enterprise Architecture: A Risky Proposition

The design phase of enterprise applications and infrastructure integration calls for the delivery of an end-state architecture. Architects, typically senior designers, submit appropriate artifacts to communicate the future state of a production environment to the business, software development, and operations groups. Specifically, the delivery includes diagrams illustrating an ecosystem in which applications and middleware run on networks, exchanging messages to execute business transactions.

Again, *end-state architecture is all about future technological implementation, integration, and distribution of business services to consumers, empowered by enabling infrastructure, to ensure enterprise operation continuity and stability.*

Software architects who deliver an end-state architecture diagram typically claim that the design is solid and unbreakable. In many cases, however, such an artifact merely illustrates intangible and *unproven* deployment that later may fail to operate in production, despite the vast knowledge and experience of its creators.

Why is this architecture unproven? A theoretical enterprise end-state architecture diagram guarantees nothing. Would a depiction of a production environment meet business and technical requirements? Would the illustrated applications operate flawlessly in production? Would service level agreements (SLAs) be fulfilled?

No one really knows.

The consequences of such a theoretical and risky design could be devastating to the business organization that is unable to launch software products on time in harsh market conditions. The skyrocketing cost of the software development efforts that follow an unproven enterprise end-state architecture could be calamitous, and the loss of revenue is typically vast.

Do Not Invest in Unproven Enterprise End-State Architecture

What then would be the consequences of launching a large-scale, or even midsize, software development and integration project enterprise-wide without knowing if in fact the end-state architecture will work in production?

Traditionally, once teams are engaged in actual software development and delivery initiatives, budgets would have been already approved. Allocated funds deplete exponentially as time goes by. Development teams devour resources at the speed of light, and cost projections are proven false. Consequently, the actual software construction, deployment, and integration phases often commit organizations to overwhelming expenditure, with little chance to reverse the course of projects—resulting in irreparable loss of resources and time.

Business and technological management should not accept an *unproven* end-state architecture, of which no one can predict the pitfalls of ill-designed systems and their corresponding operating environments. Budgets should not be approved and allocated to implement theoretical or academic architecture blueprints.

Simply put, *do not support speculative architecture.*

To prevent such mistakes, a new enterprise design process is therefore required. One that is *proven* and *reliable.* One devised to strengthen the trust between software design practitioners and business organizations. The term "proven" means that the end-state architecture should *not* be a theoretical proposition. It must be a software design and development model based on *tangible and realistic* facts, *pretested, verified,* and *certified.* This approach should guide software developers and integrators to deliver smaller chunks of solid code for one purpose only—*verification of enterprise architecture assumptions.*

Consequently, the software construction phase, as we know it now, would transmute into a concrete form of *design proof,* circumventing financial calamity that is hard to recoup.

How can such a method be accomplished?

Focus on Incremental Software Architecture

A new enterprise approach for software product construction, deployment, and integration should be considered. Chartered to deliver proven and solid architecture, design practitioners should lead source code construction and delivery initiatives. They should be accountable for the quality of their design throughout the overall product creation and distribution life cycle.

Developers, on the other hand, should take the back seat, respond to the design pace, and follow successions of software architecture progression. Indeed, they should avoid organically grown environments that are not aligned with an emerging design strategy. Developers should also seek direction from design teams, rather than employing shaky technologies that may fail to perform in production.

Incremental architecture, then, should mark a shift in the phases of enterprise software design, development, and integration.

So What Is Incremental Architecture?

Imagine an end-state architecture diagram that illustrates a production environment, in which a number of systems depend on each other, integrated to enable business transactions. In this diagram, as depicted in Figure 1.1, you may also find a number of architecture components, such as the data access layer, business services layer, repositories, gateways, adapters, and software proxies. In addition, you may note an enterprise service bus (ESB)—a mediating middleware product—that enables message exchange between consumers and services.

Complex? Indeed.

4

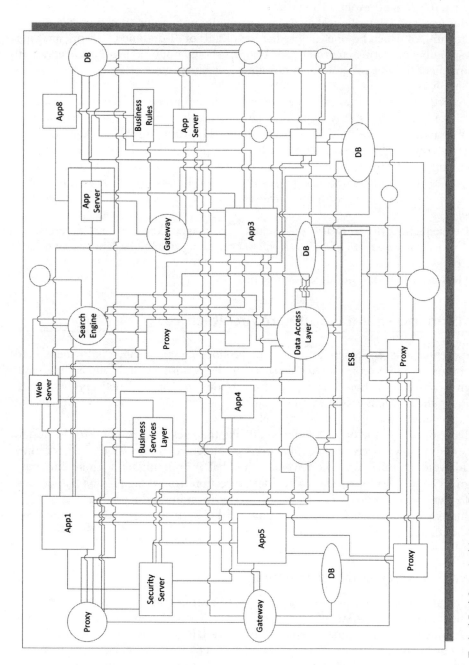

Figure 1.1   Typical End-State Architecture Diagram

Does such an end-state architecture diagram represent a feasible and a proven performing environment? Can anyone assure that such an illustration depicts an error-free software implementation deployed to production? Would the source code meet business requirements? Would performance bottlenecks be nonexistent?

Now, could the end-state architecture blueprint be proven and certified, avoiding a financial burden caused by systems design flaws? This question reveals the motivation for *verifying* the feasibility of a software design and integration throughout all stages of a product's development and deployment life cycle.

Then, how can software architects confirm that an end-state architecture is indeed practical, immaculate, and capable of flawlessly executing business transactions in a production environment that is already strained?

The Art of Architecture Discovery, Analysis, and Decomposition

To accomplish this mission, a meticulous architecture discovery and analysis should begin to study the proposed architecture. Systems, applications, and their supporting middleware and network infrastructure should be ascertained to understand the environment (refer to Chapters 4, 5, and 6 to read about the discovery and analysis of systems, applications, and their supporting production environment).

Next, the end-state software architecture should be sliced into smaller sections, just like cutting a cake into pieces. Subdividing the end-state architecture into smaller segments will enable software architects to drill down into the details of their design. This subdivision process is named *architecture decomposition*, during which an end-state architecture blueprint is *compartmentalized* into distinct areas of interest.

A physical section of an end-state architecture, for example, may include two applications and three databases. Another section may consist of a middleware product, such as an ESB. An additional section may contain a Web server and an application server and so on.

Architecture decomposition does not necessarily have to be based on physical partitions. End-state architecture sections may contain other areas of interest, perhaps contextual: business functions, lines of business, or even business ownership and/or sponsorship.

Decomposition could also be applied to a troubled architecture that has already been deployed to production—an existing implementation that harms the business and creates a great deal of organizational anxiety. In this case, a production environment could be sectioned into smaller segments to simplify the verification process. This effort characteristically helps to isolate underperforming segments of the architecture, narrow down existing issues, and discover root cause problems.

To learn more about architecture decomposition, refer to Chapters 7–11.

Architecture Verification

Next, in lieu of launching a full-fledged and costly enterprise application construction and integration effort, a section-by-section *architecture verification* process should take place. The process of verifying individual sections of an end-state architecture should be easier than attempting to implement and deliver an entire enterprise architecture blueprint. It is apparent now that this mission calls for confirming that each section would work properly in production.

So how can such an architecture verification process be accomplished and what does it entail? Led by design teams, small development groups should be commissioned to construct and deploy only sections of the end-state architecture—not the entire architecture blueprint. Again, the implementation—development, deployment, and integration—must tackle sections of the decomposed architecture. Thus, software construction should be a part of the end-state architecture verification process— pursuing gradual implementation, adjusting the development and integration progress to the *evolution of the design*, rather than leading the product life cycle.

As for that, *the traditional software construction phase in its current manifestation ceases to exist*. Now, *software construction means architecture verification*.

Enterprise architects should then be responsible for proving that vital sections of an end-state architecture meet business and technical requirements. For already deployed, unstable production environments that require repair, the verification process takes place when sections of the architecture are being tested for performance and capacity.

By now, it is obvious that the architecture verification means a gradual approach to proving that each part of the architecture would indeed work, or is working properly in production (if the verification process was performed on an existing failing architecture). Systematic verification will undoubtedly increase the confidence in an enterprise design. This method shifts the focus from development to design, driven by software architecture—not software development.

Not everything is rosy, though. Proving that each section in an architecture works as designed does not mean that the entire end-state architecture and its dependencies will function as they should, once integrated in production. The rule of thumb suggests, therefore, that an entire deployed environment must operate properly as a whole.

An additional verification stage is necessary then to ensure that the proposed end-state architecture is sound and the integration is solid. Enterprise architects, developers, and production engineers perform *architecture stress testing*. This supplemental effort would confirm that the architecture is indeed functioning appropriately under high-volume business transactions.

Finally, as a part of the verification endeavor, an enterprise capacity planning process is launched. Perusing this would ensure proper allocation of computing resources for current and future end-state architecture environment operations.

Chapters 12–15 elaborate on the methods of the ecosystem verification process.

Can Modeling and Simulation Substitute for Incremental Software Architecture?

Traditional approaches to describe software and its environment have been employed for years. One method is software modeling, used to depict a system or an application from different perspectives. Modeling typically illustrates the behavior of software, for example. Another view may identify the various components of an application. Other perspectives focus on physical, logical, and process aspects of a system.[3]

Software modeling is all about expressing a design by using an abstract language, a descriptive syntax and notation, visually depicting a future software implementation and its corresponding environment. A mere depiction of this architecture would divulge nothing about its ability to meet business requirements. Nor would such a diagram tell us anything about system response time and performance. The software modeling method, nevertheless, is a far cry from the incremental software architecture—an approach described in this book devised to verify if an enterprise architecture will indeed work in production.

Software simulation, however, may shed light upon the capabilities of a system and its environment to meet performance and stability requirements. The simulation of a production environment typically takes place in a virtual space, in which a production landscape is replicated for modeling the behavior of applications, middleware, and network infrastructure. By observing a simulated environment, one may identify a system's failures and ill-designed architecture components that miss the required performance mark. Since software simulation is not pursued in production, the modeling results are difficult to confirm. Nor can simulated models accurately forecast the behavior of a system and its related applications, middleware, and network infrastructure.

With software modeling and/or simulation, no one can accurately predict the solidity and readability of an end-state architecture. No one can ensure a system's stability. No one can pinpoint troubled sections of architecture. And no one can guarantee that a design meets non-functional requirements.

Platform for Change

There is nothing more frustrating to employees than lack of an enterprise platform for change. A platform for change is a powerful stage for those whose mission calls for organizational changes. A platform for change could be an open forum, perhaps gatherings or informal meetings, during which new ideas are voiced to promote technological endeavors or business objectives. A platform for change could also be a laboratory dedicated to technical experiments, during which open-source libraries and components are downloaded from the Internet for evaluation and proof of concepts.

Undoubtedly, there are myriad platforms that enable employees to foster a fresh enterprise direction or vision. The alterations to the way we do business could take many forms. Enterprise cultural changes, for instance, are arduous and slow to fulfill. Cultural aspects pertain to an alteration of a company's core values, communication practices,[4] and even staff attitudes. In contrast, adoption of technological implementations tends to be fast and vigorous. Technological developments occur constantly, influencing the way we run our production environments.

Microservices: A Product of Change

Changes imposed by upper management are named *top-down* initiatives. Executives typically perform reorganizations and issue best practices and policies to drive the direction of the business. These types of changes are slow, and as time passes, they may not be relevant any longer.

Similarly, enterprise architecture standards are not always issued in a timely manner. Governance departments whose charter is to draft best practices are not always synchronized with the various projects that typically take place simultaneously in the organization. On the other side of the aisle, software developers and integrators, commissioned to deliver source code on time and on budget, cannot afford to wait until enterprise decisions and standards are published.

Not many choices are left. In these cases, the change of architecture direction is propelled from the bottom. Specifically, with the absence of an established organizational platform for change, small development teams tend to ignore enterprise architecture best practices. Often named the *bottom-up evolution*, this movement uses open-source products and mixed and unstandardized technologies to build applications or smaller-scale services.

The outcome of such drive is indeed powerful—at the same time, though, unconventional. The upshot is refreshing since the chief attention is given to product development—not necessarily projects. The formation of such decentralized and self-governed teams allows the management of decentralized databases and the development of organically grown applications. The design method employed here is named *microservices.*[5] The products they deliver are independent, loosely coupled, and focus on smaller-scale problems. The overall emphasis is not on enterprise asset reuse. Here, reusability is applied to components that drive the construction of services—not on enterprise expenditure reduction or asset consolidation.

But even with the focus on small-scale and agile implementations, disregarding organizational standards and enterprise architecture direction, the contribution of the microservices architecture is vast. Turning away from the traditional *monolithic* system architecture is a leap forward in the right direction. This includes breaking off from tightly coupled implementation practices, rejecting a centralized governance approach for software development, and avoiding huge investments in large projects.

Incremental Software Architecture and Microservices Architecture

The incremental software architecture approach is a continuous section-based design, discovery and analysis, decomposition, and verification process. Akin to the microservices architecture, the risk of engaging in perilous and large-scale implementations or producing monolithic application formations is utterly reduced.

As explained in the previous sections, the driving motivation of the incremental software architecture is to conform to an enterprise software design—a high-level view that software developers not always are able to observe. Slicing an architecture blueprint into smaller segments and implementing them minimizes risks to the business as well.

As per the incremental software architecture approach, the gradual verification and certification of an enterprise end-state architecture enforces regional best practices and policies upon smaller development teams. Avoiding employment of unstandardized technologies and, at the same time, decentralizing the software development efforts are other benefits that are hard to ignore.

It is possible to envision, though, that the microservices architecture would be the design verification arm of the incremental software architecture approach. In other words, small development teams would focus only on constructing segments of the end-state architecture, an incremental approach leading to the overall certification of the overall enterprise design. This would be a combined effort to deliver high-quality software to production environments.

Incremental Software Architecture Process

This book elaborates on the incremental software architecture process and its chief tasks to accomplish in Parts 2, 3, and 4. Part 1 is a guide provided to characterize levels of system failures and assist business and IT professionals to identify and classify the causes of underperforming implementations.

There is nothing intricate about this method of design, implementation, and integration of organizational enterprise assets. There is nothing to fret about, because the approach calls for only three stages, through which an enterprise end-state architecture is discovered and analyzed, decomposed, and certified, as depicted in Figure 1.2:

1. *End-state architecture discovery and analysis.* This stage represents the methods employed to ascertain systems and their related applications in an end-state architecture proposition or in a production environment (Part 2).
2. *End-state architecture decomposition.* Structural, behavioral, and volatile attributes of end-state architecture drive the decomposition process, rendering two distinct perspectives: business and technology (Part 3).
3. *End-state architecture verification.* Proven end-state architecture is one that is certified by three authentication tasks: design substantiation, end-state architecture stress testing, and enterprise capacity planning (Part 4).

Finally, What Is a System?

It would be odd for a book about architecture not to have a definition for the term "system." Unfortunately, as nice as it would be, there is no common industry definition for such an entity. This term means many things to a myriad of organizations. It is so subjective that the various interpretations introduce only confusion to the business and IT communities.

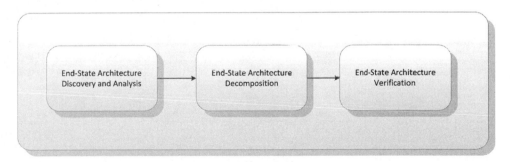

Figure 1.2   Incremental Software Architecture Process

So what is a system? In this book, a system is analogous to an operating technological *environment*. Moreover, a system is the largest entity in production. It encompasses enterprise assets such as applications, components, middleware products, and network infrastructure. When we say "system," we mean an autonomous run-time environment that offers business and technological solutions.

Furthermore, a production environment is typically made up of multiple systems. An end-state architecture, on the other hand, may contain one or multiple systems.

Notes

1. Regional management and technical groups are geographically disbursed business domains, known as lines of business, that specialize in providing services to communities of consumers: Patrick Heinecke, *Success Factors of Regional Strategies for Multinational Corporations: Appropriate Degrees of Management Autonomy and Product Adaptation*, 2011, Springer Science & Business Media, p. 5.
2. Eric Flamholtz, Yvonne Randle, *Corporate Culture: The Ultimate Strategic Asset*, 2011, Stanford University Press, p. 8.
3. The various perspectives of system modeling are elaborated on in Philippe Kruchten's 4+1 well-known research paper, published in 1995.
4. Edgar H. Schein, *Organizational Culture and Leadership*, 2010, John Wiley & Sons, p. 7.
5. Lucas Krause, *Microservices: Patterns and Applications: Designing Fine-Grained Services by Applying Patterns*, 2015, Lucas Krause, p. 44.

PART ONE

Why Do Enterprise Systems Fail?

When planning, designing, implementing, and integrating an enterprise system, the stakes are high. An enterprise project typically involves many stakeholders who bring talents and a variety of expertise to the table. But a large number of collaborating partners does not inevitably lead to system success. Indeed, in certain circumstances, the more people on board, the more likely the implementation will fail. But is the reverse true? Do fewer people on a project guarantee the satisfaction of system performance?

No one really knows.

Still, one of the most eyebrow-raising questions is how it is possible that a large number of professionals put their heads together, spend umpteen hours and countless resources to provide a solution, and ultimately produce a system that falls short of expectations. How does it happen? And who is really responsible for the astonishing expenditure that an organization must bear?

George Bernard Shaw once said, "The minority is sometimes right; the majority always wrong." To balance this, read what Mark Twain claimed: "Whenever you find yourself on the side of the majority, it is time to pause and reflect." Finally, this from Leo Tolstoy: "Wrong does not cease to be wrong because the majority share in it."

There is plenty of blame to go around when an enterprise system fails to perform. And there are many reasons why an imperative application may not meet business requirements. In some cases, corporate anxiety surges to uncontrolled levels. Mudslinging and finger-pointing are perhaps the most common reactions to a deadbeat system that an organization is trying to revive from a detrimental shutdown. The efforts to repair a failing implementation are costly. Allocated human resources and precious time only add to the already overwhelming expenditure.

It is typical for an enterprise production environment to host hundreds of servers, applications, components, middleware, and network infrastructure products.

Integration initiatives call for linking these organizational assets to form complex asset dependencies on large networks. Finding the root causes of an underperforming system in such a multifaceted operating landscape doubles the challenge.

It is not hard to understand why strenuous conditions in a production environment could affect the system's performance. The integration scheme of a high-volume information flow is not the only cause of failure. Software development, architecture, and integration mistakes could also contribute immensely to a broken implementation. The full picture, however, may divulge additional system failure causes that some organizations fail to admit. Surprisingly, these may be cultural, strategic, and management issues that often influence the faulty process of system implementation.

The underlying reasons for deploying a floundering system to production are indeed staggering.

The chapters that follow identify the anatomy of a failing system and introduce the chief reasons for such erroneous implementations. Use this guidance to classify system failures and study the questions that should be asked to identify each category.

CHAPTER 2

What Is a Failing Enterprise System? Is It Management's Fault?

The term "failing" is not only about a sluggish performance. Nor is it only about an implementation defect that prevents a system from providing services to subscribed consumers. Simply put, *a system that does not meet business or technical requirements is a failing one.* From an enterprise perspective, *a product that does not offer solutions to potential problems is doomed to fizzle.*

There are good enough reasons for management to define a system as an ineffective or failing entity. But how should this be determined? Cutting the losses is not a bad thing to do if executives believe that a product is defective and unable to deliver services. Such a valuation, however, should not only be based upon the symptoms of failure. The assessment should encompass a number of perspectives, some of which may offer indications as to why an implementation flopped. These multiview findings would provide a strong justification for halting operations and support of a product in production.

The art of system failure analysis is indeed intricate and consuming. As discussed, a wide range of reasons may contribute to a disappointing system performance or improper functionality. A full *product life cycle* then would provide multiple perspectives to help understanding the contributing factors of system mishap. By correcting the faults in a product life cycle process, future system failures could be avoided.

Now, consider some life cycle stages, during which potential misjudgments or errors may occur. In the course of the product conceptual stage, for example, ideas drive the motivation for launching a software development, delivery, and integration project. However, ideas may not always offer proper solutions if the problem domain is not well defined. Clues for delivering an impractical system could also be detected during the business requirements phase. Nebulous business requirements typically drive unclear technical requirements. Moreover, sloppy system testing may be the reason for skipping source code defects. Disregarding capacity-planning recommendations is another reason for a system to underperform in production.

It is time to revise the definition of a failing system: *Devised to mitigate threatening enterprise problems, an enterprise product that does not meet business or technical requirements is doomed to fizzle. Removing it from a production environment should be motivated by faults found in its full life cycle development and integration activities.*

Can We Learn from Other Failures?

Before moving on to sections characterizing different kinds of system failures, let's take a glimpse at some documented system failures that shook the business and IT communities across the industry. These are not case studies; the presented cases merely provide selective insights into the process, implementation, and integration of software projects that flopped during the product development life cycle. Failing initiatives like these imposed financial burdens on the organizations involved. In one case, even taxpayers bore the enormous cost of failure.

Some analysts claim that nearly 50 percent of all software development and integration projects worldwide fail. The rate of success is indeed low. In some cases, those who approve and pay the bills are not found accountable for the irresponsible and hasty manner they allocate budgets. Furthermore, studies show that no enterprise is immune against system failures. This could occur in any industry, such as financial, government, insurance, credit card, auto and transportation, defense, security, and many more.

The sections that follow suggest that the reasons for the system failures seem complex and at times, the root cause analysis is vague. It is still unclear, however, why organizations bite off more than they can chew. Why do executives agree to launch projects that by any human standard or capability are extremely challenging or impossible to control? Are mega projects destined to fail?

One Billion Dollars Spent on a Dud System

In November 2012, an article in the *Air Force Times* magazine,[1] titled "How the Air Force Blew $1B on a Dud System," the Air Force's controller admitted publicly that "the service spent seven years and $1 billion on a logistics management system that had 'negligible' capability."

This article suggested that the decision to halt the implementation of the system was not primarily because of technical glitches. Neither were the source code defects the reason for executives to scale back the replacement of 240 legacy systems to only 12.

The Air Force would have had to invest $1 billion more to save only a quarter of the initially planned system's features. "It just became a financial decision," claimed the Air Force's director of system integration.

So, what were the chief project challenges and mistakes, according to this article, that eventually led to canceling the project other than the rising expenditure?

- Lack of a master schedule
- A change in acquisition strategy
- Infrastructure issues
- Relinquishing project management control to the prime contractor
- Prime contractor incapable of adapting commercial software to fulfill the distinct activities that the system was supposed to accomplish
- Technical defects that delayed the project
- System that was slow to exchange information with Air Force installations
- Testing initiatives taking place despite the design flaws that had been detected in the software product
- Air Force's incapability of keeping the project alive after dismissing the prime contractor

Finally, when the representative for the Air Force was asked if anyone had been demoted or fired over the massive failure to build the system, the answer was, "We didn't feel it was necessary to do that."

One ought to ask a few questions after glancing at the presumed root causes of system failure:

- Had the Air Force analyzed and certified the end-state architecture of the project to ensure system delivery success?
- What were the leading assumptions that the logistic management system would indeed work?
- On what conceptual and vision grounds was such a gigantic project approved?
- Was the vendor's software product evaluated and justified prior to using it?
- Was the prime contractor skilled enough to deliver the system?
- Were the project goals realistic?

The Bigger They Come, the Harder They Fail[2]

In late August 2004, Ford Motor Co. discontinued a five-year-old Web purchasing effort[3], named Everest, an investment as high as $400 million. Not only were the budgets slashed, 350 IT personnel also were affected.

So what was this initiative about? The project was launched to cash in on the e-commerce exploding market, utilizing Web technologies to serve a large number of suppliers. The driving vision was to consolidate about 30 archaic procurement and purchasing systems into a single one, reducing organizational expenditure, and decreasing operational redundancy. In addition, an environmental-friendly goal was an impetus: fostering paperless reporting and transactions.

There were good intentions and shrewd business thinking behind the grand project.[4] The principles of reuse, efficiency, and time-to-market were the driving justifications for the investment. To accomplish this, Ford collaborated with a software manufacturer, with whom they produced a poor design and a failing integration environment. Neither did this architecture meet suppliers' requirements and sustain the high demands of the production ecosystem.

According to various analysts,[5] a number of design and implementation hurdles contributed to the failure of the system:

- Cumbersome user interface that forced suppliers to navigate through multiple pages to attain vital information
- Incomplete system functionality, such as pricing and volumes
- Failing enterprise-wide integration efforts
- Poor planning and lack of technological strategy

There are crucial questions to be asked in the light of such disappointment:

- What were the concepts and business requirements that led to launching the project realistic?
- Was any verification process in place to confirm that such a gargantuan initiative would succeed?
- Was the task force skilled and trained enough to execute the business mission?
- Was it a management failure?

A Blackout to Remember

In 2003, one of the biggest power blackouts in history affected about 55 million people in the U.S. Northeast and Ontario, Canada. An investigation of the calamity following the dire events suggested that the power network had been under immense stress. As a result, a heavy electrical load heated up the power lines, some of which expanded and sagged lower, bringing down trees and further increasing the pressure on the power network grid.

It all started after the shutdown of a power plant along the southern shore of Lake Erie, Ohio, because of high demand for electricity. This alone, experts claimed, should have not caused a blackout of epic proportions. The events leading to the plant shutdown could have been avoided by responding appropriately to normalize the increasing consumption rates.

But no one in the control center was aware of the emerging catastrophic occurrence because the alarm system had failed—it was simply frozen. A further examination of the source code revealed that a software defect prevented the system from sending alerts. Consequently, business seemed to be running as usual, while a cascading failure expanded onto neighboring circuits, which may also have been running at or near their capacity. This in turn forced the shutdown of more than 100 power plants. As is already known, millions lost power, businesses were disrupted, and chaos prevailed.

So, it was a "bug," they said. A small software fault that no one could have predicted until it really happened. Big things emanate from small ones. And when it comes to software, the devil is in the details; small bugs can turn into huge ones. In this case, the defect was found deep within thousands of lines of code.

It is mind-boggling how an undetected source code glitch in a system could affect so many lives and vital sources of existence. Without delving too much into the details, consider this: Transportation, communications, water supply, power generation, factories, finance, and much more were affected.

One may ask numerous questions to understand how a few lines of programming code could not be detected prior to launching the vital alert system. Similar concerns must be raised to avoid a repeat of such system failure:

- If the alert system had been rigorously tested prior to the blackout, then what were the testing results? Did they indicate anything out of the ordinary?
- Was it a known programming glitch?
- What kinds of system testing were applied, if any?
- Had system capacity planning and analysis taken place prior to deployment to production?
- One of the investigation's conclusions identified a condition of the system's parallel threads to grab precious computer resources. Were computer resources enough to meet the technical requirements?

Characterization of System Failures

The most difficult puzzle to resolve is when there are multiple causes for a failing system. No one would be able to correct easily, if at all, a system with a combined set of operational issues. For example, issues caused by management, plus source code defects, plus inefficient integration would be challenging or impossible to detect. Putting the malpractice blame on a particular team would be counterproductive as reality often indicates otherwise. The root cause analysis frequently renders surprising findings.

Despite the complexity of this matter, an analysis is required to determine the practicality of fixing broken systems and/or their environments. If the cost of mending a malfunctioning system outweighs the benefits, organizations, rightfully so, tend to scrape the implementation. The analysis effort, however, is not wasted. As indicated in the previous section, lessons learned could be as valuable as repairing a vital product.

A root cause analysis, therefore, is justified. This effort calls for characterization of malfunctioning systems, and most important, categorization of their failures. To be able to classify what system issues are involved, one ought to understand the type of failures an organization might face during a product development life cycle.

The next sections in this chapter and Chapter 3 identify the chief classes of failures and elaborate on their severity levels. Figure 2.1 illustrates a classification model for system failures to be used by organizations to categorize failing systems.

- Management- and business-level failures
- Technological system-level failures
  - Enterprise-level architecture failures
  - Software development-level failures
  - Testing-level failures
  - Operation-level failures

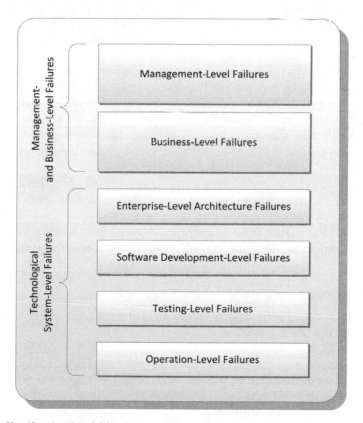

Figure 2.1   Classification Model for System Failures

Management-Level Failures

Erroneous management decisions, policies, and strategies often derail imperative software development projects, causing substantial loss to the business. As a result, the negative impact on enterprise earnings and loss of jobs could shatter an organization that struggles to withstand harsh market competition.

Evidently, management-level failure is all about lack of leadership and inability to make bold and at times unpopular decisions that can save a firm from collapse or disarray. Management failure is also about wrong, careless, or sloppy judgments and choices resulting in poor atmosphere and conditions that lead to system failures.

When a system fails to perform or satisfy business requirements, the tendency is to blame the fiasco on software developers. Another favorite group to denunciate is the software testing organization, suspecting it neglected to detect system-critical issues. These accusations may be pointed at almost any practitioner, stakeholder, or computing environment. There are endless people to blame and infinite environment conditions to criticize. Even root cause analysis, a practice designed to dissect and examine the facts on the ground, often ignores the leading reasons for a system failure.

Management Failures

Executives' strategies, vision, and performance seem out of range when an inquiry is conducted to identify the actual reasons for a malfunctioning system. For some reason, the inspection tends to delve into technical aspects of a system, disregarding management's decisions, business direction, or technical strategies. Executives seem to be out of reach while the blame is pointed toward the lower levels of the food chain in the organization. In rare instances, however, investigations point to management for its share in a colossal systems collapse.

Clearly, not all system failures are due to management execution. The term "execution" points to the manner in which executives run their organizations. When an enterprise embraces ineffective business model and strategies, it could affect business performance and revenues. Furthermore, enterprise systems are impractical, and the solutions they provide are inadequate when management's vision and mission are blurry. Lack of business, technology, and project direction produces dire consequences.

When it comes to delivery of software products, not only business executives but also technology managers carry heavy responsibilities. IT executives' accountabilities include development, deployment, integration, and operations in production. Acquiring technologies, such as middleware and network infrastructure assets, requires experience management who understand business requirements, architecture, and operations.

Ask These Questions to Identify Management-Level Failures

To identify management-level failure, ask the fundamental questions that follow when a system fails to operate as designed:

- Were executives skilled enough to manage the enterprise-level system project?
- Did management define clearly the strategy and the vision for the system?
- Had management defined the problem domain before approving the development and integration of the system?

- Did management carve a practical project plan that included achievable milestones and realistic goals?
- Did management provide clear system requirements?
- Were the proposed enterprise-level solutions practical?
- Did management accommodate enough resources and establish adequate system development and integration environments?
- Did management acquire and adopt proper technologies to build and integrate the system in production?
- Did management hire skilled professionals to construct and integrate the system?
- Did management establish a clear and easy-to-implement system development life cycle process?
- Did management contract experienced and skillful vendors to assist in building, integrating, and maintaining the system in production?
- Was the scope of the project clear enough?
- Were the allocated budgets realistic?
- Were the important stakeholders involved? This may include end users, business partners, sponsors, and others.

Business-Level Failures

In most enterprises, the business organization is running the show. It not only pays the bills, but also provides justification and allocates budgets for impending projects. Business management must lead. Business leadership is about understanding the business, competition, customers, and market. It is also about providing solutions to address organizational problems. Moreover, without business requirements, no product development project should be sponsored and launched.

Segmentation Analysis

Even before the business comes up with ideas and concepts to provide a solution and sponsor systems, it must understand what type of products it should develop to meet consumers' requirements. But how would a business know what products to market and sell? How would a business identify consumer preferences? What would be the most effective approach to discover whether the market would embrace a certain line of products? And what would be the return on investment after launching software development and integration initiatives? Knowing how the business incurs revenue and what the strategy is for generating steady income in the future are also responsibilities of business executives.

The business must conduct extensive research that will offer clear answers to address these concerns. To understand the environment in which a business operates and recognize the competition, business organizations engage in segmentation studies. This multifaceted effort eventually points out what type of products the business should be funding. There are a few types of segmentation analysis; the most common ones are listed here:

Market segmentation This analysis identifies to which industry a business can best contribute. Matching the business with its proper market space fosters creation of products to compete more efficiently against its competitors.

Consumer segmentation   This study discovers what kind of products consumers like, need, or want. But the focus here is on consumers' preferences and their consumption habits. Understanding this would typically drive the development of powerful systems that meet consumer demands.

Product segmentation   This research helps organizations to discover the most revenue-incurring products. Matching products with the right consumers segments typically results in the creation of potent and profitable systems.

Managing Business Risks

The business has its work cut out for it, doesn't it? Carrying such heavy responsibilities could immensely affect the survival of an enterprise. How? Wrong decisions, unclear business direction, lack of business strategy and vision, nebulous business requirements, or any other mistake of this nature could result in a financial catastrophe.

Risk management is one of the most crucial practices a business should employ to protect and alert the business from failing. Risk should also be assessed before launching grand product development projects and/or investing in enterprise core systems. *Business impact analysis*[6] is required to evaluate potential pitfalls of business investments and ongoing operations. Executives should be aware of a business risk benchmark, and consider it when planning to approve and assign budgets for system construction, deployment, and integration. A simple risk scale may look like this:

- A system failure is very likely to occur.
- There could be some chance of system failures.
- There could be a small chance of system failures.
- There is very little chance of system failures.
- It is safe to invest in a system.

If the risk in system investment is defined as high, funds should not be allocated to launch system development projects. Tolerable perils, however, should be considered when the risk is very low or does not exist. Obviously, such a scenario is optimal and would not be likely to occur with many projects that are being sponsored.

Examination of IT Solutions

When risk assessment is performed, the business management should also understand what technological propositions could help mitigate business problems. Common questions that a business organization should ask before sponsoring a system development project should be:

- Are the IT software architecture solutions meeting business requirements?
- Is the system design safe and practical?
- Does the technology organization understand the business domain problems?
- Is the IT organization capable of delivering the system?
- Will the acquired technologies, such as middleware and network infrastructure, support the system requirements in production?

Ask These Questions to Identify Business-Level Failures

Clearly, there is a direct correlation between business-level failures and system failures. Faltering executive leadership is detrimental to business initiatives and the foundation of products. When analyzing a system failure, ask a few fundamental questions to determine if the cause is rooted in a business-level failure:

- Did business management provide clear business requirements?
- Did the business requirements offer practical solutions?
- Did the business offer adequate justification for investing in the system?
- Did the business model support the construction of the system?
- Did business executive perform risk impact analysis before investing in the system?
- Did business management understand the proposed technological approaches to mitigate business problems?

If a failing system has already been deployed to production, ask the questions below:

- Does the system offer solutions to the business problems?
- Does the system offer proper services to the industry?
- Does the system meet consumers' demands?
- Does the system offer a powerful user interface to satisfy consumers?
- Can business partners benefit from the system's services?
- Were the funds allocated properly?
- Were business executives involved in the system development life cycle?

Notes

1. http://archive.airforcetimes.com/article/20121126/NEWS/211260304/How-the-Air-Force-blew-1B-on-a-dud-system
2. http://news.cnet.com/Ford-scraps-Oracle-based-procurement-system/2100-1012_3-5315058.html
3. http://adtmag.com/articles/2004/11/01/oops-ford-and-oracle-megasoftware-project-crumbles.aspx
4. http://www.computerworld.com/article/2566114/enterprise-applications/ford-kills--everest--procurement-software-system.html
5. http://www.nytimes.com/2005/01/22/opinion/22carr.html?_r=0
6. https://www.business.qld.gov.au/business/running/risk-management/risk-management-plan-business-impact-analysis

CHAPTER 3
Technological System-Level Failures

We continue here with the technological reasons for system failures. This chapter covers a significant portion of the product development life cycle. It centers on the system design, implementation, testing, and operations. Once again, these failure levels emphasize the need for discovering and analyzing malfunctioning systems throughout the product development life cycle. And once more, the root cause analysis may ascertain that a system shutdown has been triggered by more than one level of failure. Indeed, it is a complex puzzle to resolve.

The technical reasons for a broken system may be found in the design process. This may be caused by unskilled staff. Wrong architecture strategy and mistaken employment of design patterns are other aspects that could defiantly miss the performance and quality mark of an implementation. When it comes to finding out why a system flops, the software development process is not excused from inspection, either. Lack of software construction talents or inadequate development tools and hardware could also affect the quality of a system. Ignoring potential software defects during the testing phase could be a crucial factor in a system failure. Finally, poor system maintenance in production could be another reason for a system operation fiasco.

Enterprise-Level Architecture Failures

It is recognized that design errors may be found in small implementations, such as in a software routine, library, component, service, or application; but this section, in contrast, focuses on enterprise-level architecture failures. In other words, enterprise-scale solutions are larger in magnitude.

At this level, the search for design mistakes may include a system comprised of various applications, running on middleware, and empowered by production network infrastructure. Moreover, not only should the behavior of a single system be inspected. System of systems[1] is another pattern to consider. This implies that multiple system dependencies and/or challenging configurations may be the cause of failures.

Types of Enterprise-Level Design Failures

What kind of design mistakes could be observed in this system failure category? Infinite architectural blunders may be spotted in a complex deployment and integration environment. The challenge is even greater when multiple systems depend on each other, forming a distributed environment that is hard to analyze. This intricate deployment would introduce a challenging task to production engineers whose role is to identify troubling implementations and integration issues. With the naked eye, it would be almost impossible to discover which parts of the architecture underperform.

Analysis efforts then should determine if the design mistakes emanated from improper utilization of *architecture patterns*. System *integration* is another aspect to investigate: Would the overall scheme sustain an end-state enterprise architecture? In addition, incorrect *distribution of software assets* across an organization, or improper *federation of systems* across enterprises should also be examined to determine if the deployment is practical and bulletproof.

Again, enterprise architecture patterns, system integration, software asset distribution, and system federation are the *fundamental categories* in which architecture-level mistakes could be found. Here are examples that point to errors in design:

> *Lack of interoperability*. Two or more systems are unable to exchange messages.
> *Workload overflow*. Architecture centralization pattern forms network traffic bottlenecks.
> *Performance degradation*. Improper distribution of software assets increases system response time.
> *Overexpended system federation*. Two or more organizations experience delays in exchange of product information.
> *Low scalability*. Inadequate system scalability could not sustain unanticipated message volume.
> *Low reuse*. Implementation redundancy increases resource utilization.
> *Tight coupling*. Developers and integrators unable to apply rapid changes to a monolithic system.
> And many more ...

Spotting Design Failure Symptoms

Advanced monitoring techniques should be employed to search for the symptoms of design faults. The software market is saturated with products and utilities that can perform continuous scanning and analysis to detect problems occurring at run time in production. However, these monitoring platforms will not always reveal the actual architecture problems. But they can assist inspectors in locating the weak design points. Consider examples of production utilities used to analyze a deployment environment:

> **Application discovery**   With this type of utility, a production engineer scans a production environment to discover deployed business applications and offered services. Advanced production management tools like this are also capable of visually depicting the physical locations of applications.
> **Topology building and discovery**   This utility category illustrates the arrangement of message paths, connecting lines, and nodes on a network. Servers and applications that operate in production are discovered in the network structure.
> **Application dependency discovery**   Such a class of tools maps the dependencies between systems and their related applications, middleware, and network infrastructure.
> **Software cataloging**   Managers, analysts, designers, and production engineers use these types of tools to store information about systems and their affiliated applications, services, and components.

Configuration management   This utility category helps production engineers to store configuration information in a repository.

Business transaction discovery   This is another class of discovery tools capable of depicting business transactions and their routes on a network.

Change management   A range of tools that store information about changes applied to a production environment. This may include upgrades to software versions, integration modifications, and configuration alterations.

Network performance and availability   To identify network bandwidth and capacity, these tools provide a wide range of network stress analysis information.

To read more about application discovery, topology mapping, and application dependency, refer to Chapters 4–6.

Design Failure Example: Improper Use of an Architecture Pattern

Almost every organization has experienced slow system response time. This common performance issue may stem from a variety of reasons, some of which may be connected to programming defects. Others may be system integration and configuration errors. Here, however, we focus on a design flaw. Such an architecture mistake can halt business operations and cause substantial financial damage. The example that follows demonstrates how improper use of the hub-and-spokes architecture pattern can affect system performance.

Depicted in Figure 3.1, the hub-and-spokes architecture pattern resembles a hub and extending spokes supporting a rim of a bike wheel. The hub in the center, named Book Orders Service, is a central software application that enables readers to order books online. Not only do readers communicate directly with the hub, suppliers do, too, utilizing it to reserve books.

The hub-and-spokes architecture was initially devised to eliminate the challenges introduced by the point-to-point design pattern. In the latter style, applications and systems communicate directly with each other. This communication method increases the number of message routes on a network and raises architecture complexity. In contrast, with the hub-and-spokes pattern, the hub exchanges messages with subscribing consumers. Such a central processing unit could simplify the design and even reduce implementation redundancy by offering a single and reusable set of business functionality.

But there is also a drawback. An increased number of consumers, linked to Book Orders Service (the hub), could apply an enormous pressure on the book ordering process by sending and receiving high volumes of data. In essence, the hub, a single point of failure, could become a performance bottleneck, slowing down the system's operations. Over time, consumers would experience a substantial degradation in services.

A design mistake like this could even have a cascading effect on large parts of a production system. In many cases, however, merely testing the performance of the hub alone would not reveal the magnitude of the design problem. This is because the testing did not include the whole environment. In other words, the examined environment should have also included the readers and suppliers ordering books. Repositories and any other system components of the book ordering implementation should have been included in the test plan too.

Unfortunately, design faults such as this are often discovered after a system has been tested, integrated, and deployed to production. And what is even worse,

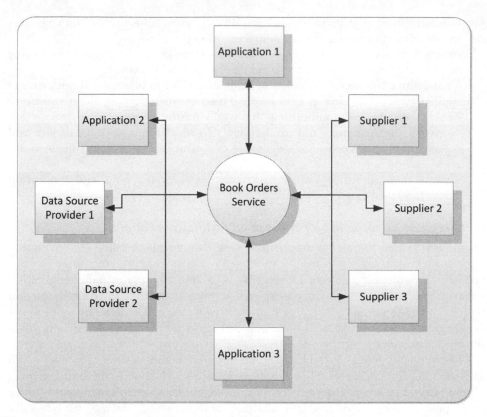

Figure 3.1   Typical Hub-and-Spokes Architecture Style

performance issues arising from the misuse of the hub-and-spokes architecture may be noticeable only when system activities increase due to a surge in business transactions. Indeed, too late.

Another Design Failure Example: Improper Architecture Expansion Mechanisms

A production environment tends to grow when a business expands. The spike in business transactions is typically due to the increasing number of consumers who are willing to pay for enterprise products. Subsequently, more systems, applications, middleware, and infrastructure must be added to accommodate the rise in business demand.

This upswing business condition must be strategized. Along with the planning effort, enterprise architecture must provide adequate technological solutions to enable the business to flourish in a rapid pace. Architecture expansion, therefore, is now required. It is a daunting challenge to every manager whose success hinges on recruiting more staff and budgets. If budgets were limited, among other options would be to *reuse* existing systems and supporting production platforms. This would require experienced enterprise architects who must put their heads together to work with less, and produce more and better.

This brings us to the discussion about architecture expansion. Extending an enterprise architecture would require modifications to network configurations, middleware installations, repository structures, and much more. For example, a growing production environment would probably adopt an enterprise service bus (ESB) to increase the reuse of message queuing, message routing, data transformation, and other offered ESB features.

An expanding architecture could also make use of gateways to enable interoperability of distinct operating environments. For instance, a gateway could bridge protocol gaps between two incompatible platforms. Similarly, a gateway could enable communication between applications constructed by different languages.

ESBs and gateways are only a few of the enabling technologies being used to expand an architecture. In addition, a production environment, for example, may employ proxies to shield repositories from direct access. These brokers are typically named data access layers.

Increasing installations of middleware intermediaries should be exercised with caution. Indeed, the architecture could be expanded by adding mediating software products; however, too many brokers would extend the routes of messages on a network. Information, therefore, would have to travel farther to reach end points (such as consumers and services.) The consequences are clear: sluggish message exchange and increase of architecture complexity to unmaintainable levels. Figure 3.2 illustrates an example of a production environment with excessive intermediary installations.

Design errors like this are exceedingly common. Organizations constantly struggle to overcome flawed architecture expansions by throwing more hardware and supporting infrastructure at the emerging performance problems. Not only do such attempts fail, they also add extra architecture layers to already troubled production environments.

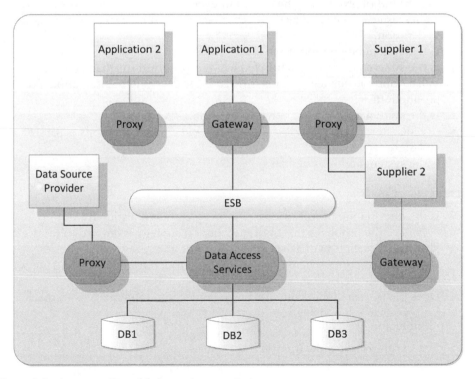

Figure 3.2   Improper Use of Software Intermediaries

Ask These Questions to Identify Enterprise Design-Level Failure

Undoubtedly, design-level failures are hard to detect. Analysis of an end-state architecture with the naked eye will not always unveil design errors. Experienced architects do tend to understand the implications of a bad design. But with today's rush to deliver a system and deploy it to production, such mistakes are often overlooked.

There could be myriad permutations for erroneous architecture decisions. Design-level errors are countless. This section, therefore, covers the chief error-prone conditions that should be investigated and queried. Again, ask the questions that follow to identify errors in an enterprise design:

Architecture patterns

- Is the system architecture driven by a clear design strategy? For example, does the design offer adequate solutions to expand the architecture? Or is the intention of the design to constrict a production environment?
- What type of architectural patterns does the end-state architecture depict?
- Does the architectural pattern promote the system design strategy?
- Does the utilized architecture pattern cause performance degradation?
- Does the utilized architecture pattern foster software asset reuse?
- Does the utilized architecture pattern encourage software asset consolidation and expenditure reduction?

System deployment and integration

- What is the system integration strategy? Is it clear enough?
- What kind of problem is the system integration devised to resolve? Interoperability issues? Security issues? System migration issues? Data migration issues? Federation?
- Is the system integration practical?
- Is the system integration supported by unjustified intermediaries?
- What kind of challenges and threats does the system integration pose to production?
- Is the system scaled enough to avoid workload overflow?
- Are disaster recovery (DR) mechanisms and implementations a part of the end-state architecture?
- Is the system highly available?

Software asset distribution

- Is the distribution of software asset strategy clear and justified?
- What are the problems that asset distribution strategy is devised to resolve?
- How the distribution of assets offers solutions?
- Is the distribution scheme supported by proper middleware and network infrastructure technologies?
- Does the system architecture use proper enterprise integration patterns[2]?

System federation

- Is the architecture federation strategy understandable?
- What problems is the system federation design proposing to resolve?

- Is the architecture federation strategy justified?
- Can partnering organizations exchange information?
- Does the system design meet interoperability challenges? Is data interoperable? Are protocols interoperable? Are security models interoperable?
- Does the system architecture promote business interoperability?
- Is system federation scaled enough to sustain large consuming partners?

Software Development-Level Failure

The devil is in the details. Evil things might happen if the devil wins. This is precisely what occurred during the calamitous blackout in 2003 (refer to the A Blackout to Remember section in Chapter 2.). It was a power shortage affecting about 55 million people in the U.S. Northeast and Ontario, Canada.

It all started from a glitch in the software system, designed to alert during electrical power failures. But a bug in the source code does not tell the entire story. There are numerous reasons why software development turns into an organizational nightmare, causing abandonment of systems and damaging the business. Errors in programming, however, are common.[3] Organizations employ various testing methods to find mistakes occurring during development and later repair them.

A glitch in a crucial system that results in a major calamity divulges more than just an occasional mistake. There must be an explanation as to why an organization delivers a system with such an implementation error. Is the software development process broken? Is the management responsible? Are unsuitable development conditions and facilities preventing the release of high-quality systems? Are the developers skilled enough? Are technical requirements clear?

What Are Software Development Level-Failures?

The broken process, unqualified or untrained development teams, lack of proper development facilities, and shortage of budgets are the chief causes for development-level failures. It is not hard to understand why these reasons may lead to an irreversible system catastrophe. Moreover, a broken development process and its outcomes could be affected by other project-related mistakes. These may be associated with poor project planning, unrealistic business expectations, unclear business requirements, improper software development platforms, insufficient budgets, and more.

Some would even argue that lack of communication and unacceptable social interaction between team members might affect the outcome of a software development effort. Unfortunately, this is related to an organizational culture that is hard to change straightaway. If an enterprise culture, however, impedes product development, not only does this imperil software construction initiatives, it could even drive an organization out of business.

Table 3.1 identifies the root causes of development-level failures. The columns beneath elaborate on each reason.

Ask These Questions to Identify Development-Level Failure

Ask the questions that follow to find out if a software development-failure caused a system failure.

Table 3.1   Root Causes of Development-Level Failures

Process	Tools, Facilities, and Environment	People	Budget
Planning	Integrated development environment (IDE) and versioning control software	Culture and codes of conduct	Work environment
Project management	Software management tool	Expertise	Employment
Requirements analysis	Testing and configuration software	Communication and information sharing	Training
Development and unit testing	Software modeling software	Training and education	Tools, platforms, and facilities
Release management	Code generators and compilers	On-site technical support	Hardware

Requirements:

- Did the development team understand the business requirements?
- Did the development team understand the system architecture?
- Were technical requirements clear and practical?
- Were business and technical requirements reviews conducted to understand the product and project?

Planning:

- Was a development plan in place?
- Was a realistic release management in place before handing the system to production?
- Was the development life cycle process clear to the development team?

Budget:

- Was the allocated budget realistic to accomplish software development tasks?
- Did the budget allow the hiring of highly skilled developers?
- Did the budget include staff training and education?
- Was the budget sufficient for software development tools, facilities, and platforms?
- Did the budget include funds for servers and infrastructure?

Software construction:

- Was a modeling software platform used to depict programming modules and components?
- Did the development team utilize proper IDEs?
- Has the development team used the proper code generators and compilers?
- Did the development team employ appropriate source code unit testing and configuration tools?
- Has the source code undergone unit testing?

Training and skills:

- Was the development team skilled enough to build the system?
- Was the development team trained to accomplish development tasks?
- Did the software team communicate effectively and share vital information about the system?

Testing-Level Failures

There is a direct correlation between testing-level failures and failing implementations. In fact, testing practices are so fundamental to ensuring system operations continuity that no organization can afford to disregard them. Many would even argue that most systems would fail because of lack of testing. Undeniably, this assertion has been established during decades of software development life cycles.

But testing mistakes always occur because nothing is perfect in the business of computing, and such is true with the testing process. It does not mean that a system will be free of defects or clear of design errors just because an organization employs testing practices. Almost every system that is shipped to production, even after testing initiatives, carries abnormalities. With time, software glitches could be remedied, integration errors could be fixed, and architecture mistakes could be recognized.

Testing-level failures are all about the lack of capabilities to detect system issues. It is about disregarding system defects. It is about not detecting system failures. It is about ignoring system idiosyncrasies. It is about misunderstanding functional and non-functional requirements. It is about misconstruing architecture, deployment, and integration strategies. It is about not complying with system design and integration requirements. Most critical, though, it is about allowing a system to be deployed to production immaturely.

Why Do Testing-Level Failures Occur?

Recall that rushing a system to production before completing thorough testing should be avoided. But what does thorough testing mean? The software development and integration life cycle calls for multifaceted testing methods to minimize the probability of production failures. As implied, these tests are not performed only at the end of the software development phase. They take place throughout the development, deployment, and integration process. Organizations typically do not employ all available testing approaches, for some are redundant, and others do not apply to particular environments. The decision of which testing method to employ is characteristically conveyed in a *test plan*—a strategy for implementing tests.

Most testing-level failures occur when a testing team skips an essential type of testing. The industry recommends five fundamental types, each of which is typically automated and supported by testing tools, utilities, and platforms. Consider a brief overview of these classes:

Unit testing Tests that are being performed by developers on source code during the software programming efforts to verify the functional integrity of independent software components.

Integration testing This method is performed after unit testing and focuses on the interfaces that link software modules to each other. Many organizations, though, ignore the opportunity here to test the integrity of messages traded between systems and their related applications, and middleware components.

System testing   Functional and nonfunctional testing of an entire system, which may be comprised of various applications, repositories, data access layers, proxies, middleware components, and more.

System load testing   This type of testing is affiliated with capacity planning assessment and modeling to help production engineers and project managers to size and budget a system. Capacity planning is about the utilization of resources that allow a system to operate flawlessly without being challenged by lack of computer resources, such as network bandwidth, CPU capability, IO performance, and response time.

Acceptance testing   This type of testing refers to end-user acceptance testing, during which users verify that the system functionality meets business requirements.

Ask These Questions to Identify Testing-Level Failure

During the analysis of a system failure, a number of questions should be asked to determine if testing could have prevented the dysfunctional implementation. As discussed, the testing process alone would not contribute to a system failure. Testing-level failure is related to lack of testing or mistakes during the testing process.

Consider the questions that follow to discern if a system has been tested properly and what would have been the implications had the testing process been omitted.

- Did the project life cycle include a test plan?
- Did the test plan convey a testing strategy?
- Did the test plan consist of practical tests?
- What were the mandatory tests in the test plan?
- Has the system been tested at all?
- Did the system pass all the required tests?
- Did the testing organization understand the functional and nonfunctional requirements?
- Did the testing organization understand the problem domain?
- Did the testing organization understand the solutions that the system offers?
- Did the testing organization understand the system architecture?
- Did the testing organization have adequate environments, facilities, tools, and platforms to pursue the system testing?
- What kind of testing scripts were developed for the testing efforts?
- Did the system pass the load testing?
- Were capacity planning tests devised to tackle system performance issues?
- Was a service-level agreement (SLA) in place?
- Did the system comply with the SLA?
- Were the test results documented and published to the involved development and integration teams?
- What were the chief issues of concerns for the system?
- Were any defects allowed to persist?
- Was the system certified?
- Was the end user satisfied with testing results?

Operation-Level Failures

Operation-level failures occur in a production environment. There are an infinite number of reasons for a system to fail in production. But the most critical disaster that damages an enterprise is the inability to ensure *business continuity*. When a vital business system malfunctions, services are not provided to consumers and products are not being sold. Business continuity, then, requires overwhelming resources, maintenance, and monitoring. This makes production one of the most challenging environments to keep up.

The final state of every system is in production, an environment in which "live" services must perform flawlessly. This endpoint is also the place where the process of release management[4] ends. Now, development and testing are behind, and maintenance begins. But the term "maintenance" does not convey the full magnitude of efforts it takes to support a product. In production, there are sundry moving targets and activities, each of which could potentially break down a system if operations are not carried with utmost care.

Unlike in development, a production landscape is typically multifaceted, complex, and populated with myriad systems that must collaborate to provide services. Furthermore, when deploying a system to production, the work of configuration and integration starts. This is the time when the system may undergo external and/or internal changes to accommodate the transition. This is the place where mistakes characteristically occur, during which system behavior may be modified to fit in production. And this is where mishandling system requirements can lead to integration disasters.

Now, let us have a look at chief operations to understand where things can go wrong during deployment, configuration, integration, and maintenance of a system in production.

System deployment   This is the actual delivery of a system to production. Deployment follows a step-by-step release plan devised after development and testing.

System configuration   A system must be configured to fit in its new environment. Configuration is the art of enabling a system to operate within the provided production parameters.

System integration   This process is all about linking a system to its peer systems, repositories, and other architecture layers. System design blueprints and integration instructions are the guiding principles to integration success.

System maintenance   Wide arrays of efforts are related to this practice. These usually include system reconfigurations, redeployments, networking, backups, and many more.

System monitoring   Tools and platforms that offer various perspectives into a production environment are also designed to perform system monitoring. Monitoring includes security guarding, alerting of message load abnormalities, and reporting on interruption of services.

Supporting software and infrastructure acquisitions   A production environment should be upgraded with superb technologies to preserve business continuity. Adopting infrastructure and middleware products is an immense mission.

User provisioning This is management of user credentials and access control to various systems in production. It is also known as user administration: administering users' capabilities to access repositories, information, reports, e-mail, networks, and more.

Ask These Questions to Identify Operation-Level Failures

The causes of system failure because of operations mistakes in production are attributed frequently to environment alterations, changes to system configurations, and integration errors. Not as frequently, however, other events may inflict severe damage to business revenue. These vulnerabilities may include severe security breaches, infrastructure disasters, harm to data centers,[5] and even long-term weather impacts.

Ask the following questions to determine if a system failed because of operation-level failures:

- Was a release management document provided to guide proper system deployment?
- Was the release management document feasible?
- Did the release management document include a recovery plan to revert system deployment?
- Was an integration plan provided to assist production engineers in linking software and network infrastructure assets?
- Was the integration plan practical?
- Did the integration plan include a recovery strategy from a failed integration?
- Did the production engineers understand the system's business and technical requirements?
- Did the production engineers understand the system architecture?
- Was a configuration plan in place?
- Was the system shut down after maintenance activities had taken place? This may include system redeployments, reconfigurations, backups, and network upkeep.
- Did system monitoring interfere with ongoing system operations?
- Did a security breach halt the system?
- Was high transaction volume a cause for slow system response time?
- Was improper adoption of new technologies the cause for system failure?
- Were the middleware and network infrastructure acquisitions properly supporting the system?
- Were any provisioning activities causing a system failure?

Notes

1. Mo Jamshidi, *Systems of Systems Engineering: Principles and Applications*, 2008, CRC Press, p. 28
2. Gregor Hohpe, Bobby Woolf, *Enterprise Integration Patterns: Designing, Building, and Deploying Messaging Solutions*, 2012, Addison-Wesley, p. 603
3. B. S. Dhillon, *Reliability in Computer System Design*, 1987, Intellect Books, p. 71
4. http://wiki.servicenow.com/index.php?title=ITIL_Release_Management#gsc.tab=0
5. Hwaiyu Geng, *Data Center Handbook*, 2014, John Wiley & Sons, p. 57

PART TWO

End-State Architecture Discovery and Analysis

When pursuing the discovery and analysis of an enterprise architecture, there are a few vital steps to accomplish. The chief aim of such an exercise is to study and understand the strategy of the proposed architecture, and fully grasp the *design* and *technological means* it employs to propose enterprise *solutions*.

For that reason, the process of end-state discovery and analysis must answer fundamental questions pertaining to the essential keywords: *problems*, *requirements*, and *solutions*:

- What enterprise business and/or technological *problems* are an end-state architecture devised to resolve?
- What are the business and technical *requirements* for the end-state architecture?
- What are the enterprise *technological solutions* that an end-state architecture proposes?
- What architecture assets (such as systems and their related applications, components, and middleware) does the end-state architecture encompass to offer enterprise *solutions*?
- How are the end-state architecture building blocks devised to solve organizational problems?

The end-state architecture discovery and analysis process should yield critical decisions that could immensely affect business operations and the capability to offer products and services to consumers. Various conclusions can be drawn from such a process. Some of these would support those who are adamant about abandoning the design proposition and canceling the impending project. Others, on the other hand, would tend to drill down further into the architecture and learn more about its potential. Obviously, the best outcome would be to allow the continuation of the incremental software architecture until completion: namely, moving on with the architecture decomposition process (Chapters 7–11) and concluding with the architecture verification efforts (Chapters 12–15).

Remember, an end-state architecture discovery and analysis process that ends without a clear decision about the future of the design proposition is an ineffective effort. This is necessary because business capabilities hinge upon the development and integration of new systems and their corresponding environments. Even the decision whether to discontinue a project might be beneficial to the business. This could save spending on impractical implementations.

Architecture Discovery and Analysis Scenarios

The discovery and analysis of an enterprise architecture pertains to two different scenarios of implementation. The first is known as the *"to be" architecture*, referring to the *future* deployment and integration of software assets. In simple words, this design has not been implemented yet. The discovery and analysis process, therefore, applies to a nonexistent environment. In this case, enterprise software architects who seek to validate their design deliver an end-state architecture blueprint to the involved stakeholders and the development community.

The process of architecture discovery and analysis of the "to be" architecture then starts with meticulous studies of the design proposition. This typically entails understanding the architecture strategy, motivation, and proposed implementation. Once the design has been inspected, the examiners, typically business and IT personnel, weigh in to determine if the proposition is practical and if budgets should be assigned to continue with the incremental architecture process.

The second scenario refers to the *"as is" architecture*. Here, the end-state architecture discovery and analysis process is focused on an existing production environment. There are myriad reasons why a current deployed implementation should be subject to investigation. In most cases, organizations dedicate resources to inspect the root cause analysis of an underperforming system. Integration failures and other environment configuration-related errors could also be the motivation for such an inspection endeavor.

Attend to Architecture Discovery and Analysis Prerequisites

When an architecture diagram is presented, the preliminary mission is to understand it. In most instances, these illustrations are complex. The overall design does not reveal the motivation behind creating it. Moreover, it is often perplexing what the perspective of such a diagram is. More specifically, a "10,000 feet above ground view" would divulge fewer design details. Naturally, the more we zoom into the design, the more architecture components are unearthed.

The end-state architecture discovery and analysis process, therefore, comes in handy. Drilling into the design to understand its comprising elements would be a logical task to start with. But wait, before even pursuing this, one must understand the motivation and justification behind such an architecture proposition. To attain this vital knowledge, the end-state architecture discovery and analysis process must begin with three fundamental tasks:

1. Study the *problems* that the end-state architecture proposes to solve. Are these imperative business issues? Technological challenges? Others?
2. If the problem domain is understood and the motivation is clear, then study the business and technical *requirements*. Are they practical? Clear?
3. Additional business supporting documents could shed more light on the motivation for embarking on a system development, deployment, and integration project:

   Business model This paper depicts the chief organizational services and products, corresponding industry, customer base, finance overview, and business goals.

   Business strategy This document describes the business vision and mission, elaborating on how the organization is prepared to fulfill the strategy.

   Business risks This includes identification of business threats, competitors' information, and risk mitigation tactics.

   Market, product, and consumer segmentation This paper identifies business industry opportunities, feasibility of products and services, and consumers' preferences.

   Business product description This document specifies features and capabilities of current and future business products.

   Business process models These charts illustrate business activities and tasks performed to achieve the business strategy and goals.

CHAPTER 4

System Fabric Discovery and Analysis

We start here with the end-state architecture discovery and analysis process by learning about the future or existing operating ecosystem and its deployed software and hardware assets. There is no better language than *fabric* to describe an *environment in which a system operates*. Resembling a woven piece of cloth, the fabric of a production landscape contains system elements, such as software and hardware entities (known as nodes on a network) linked by message paths to enable business transactions. These message exchange capabilities also facilitate the collaboration of production systems to provide solutions to achieve business goals.

One would argue that fabric means network *topology*. There is some truth to this claim, since the term "topology" in itself identifies the arrangement of elements, such as nodes and links in the space of a computer network. In other words, the structure of a network depicts the locations of nodes and identifies the way data flows from one node to another.

Recall, this fabric analysis and discovery task is about *logical arrangement* of architecture elements on a network and the manner they relate and communicate. This process is not about ascertaining network-enabling hardware, such as cables, routers,[1] switches, gateways, bridges, hubs, or repeaters.[2] Indeed, these underpinning technologies are deployed to route and control message exchange on a network. Routing configurations is not the chief subject, either. These topics could be studied independently, by reading about information routing mechanisms offered in Internet and networking configuration–related books.

In this chapter, then, we are not only looking at the system's business functionality. Here, the system's elements, identified in this book as *nodes* on a network, such as applications, software components, middleware, or network infrastructure, play important roles to promote the business. Therefore, the focus here is on three chief *system fabric discovery* aspects:

- Contribution of system elements to provide *business solutions*
- *Arrangement* of the system elements on a network
- *Message paths* and *information flow* patterns linking system elements

Discover and Analyze System Fabric Patterns

Think big. Think enterprise, think space, think environment, think distances, think connectivity, and think integration of software and hardware assets in production. This is all about the system fabric. This is about the direction of message flow.

It is about the patterns created by the flow of information depicted in an overall system design. It is also about how message streams connect enterprise software and hardware products.

The bottom line: These discovery and analysis tasks call for understanding the impact of the end-state architecture elements' dependencies on each other. Studying the various patterns of the message routes and learning about potential message workload pressure on architecture layers or components is another essential analysis task. In addition, identifying troubling performance or potential bottlenecks is an incentive for conducting these meticulous discovery and analysis sessions.

Now, we are about to study the various types of *message paths* and the *formations* they create along with their *originating, intercepting,* or *endpoint nodes*. In this book, we refer to these shapes on a network as *system fabric patterns*. One of the most significant aspects of this exercise would then be to understand the nature of data flows and assess their feasibility. Therefore, ask these fundamental questions to evaluate the enterprise architecture at hand:

- Are message transmission routes in the end-state architecture practical?
- Is the arrangement of system nodes (software and hardware) on a network logical?
- Would the integration of system nodes be feasible?
- Would the inspected message paths yield performance issues?
- Is the design complex due to the convoluted message paths?
- Is the architecture too intricate to maintain?

If there are any concerns about the answers to these questions, the process of architecture discovery and analysis should be halted until they are addressed.

Community Fabric Pattern

We choose to start with the simplest fabric pattern illustrating a *community* of system assets depicted by linked nodes. Once again, each node may represent a production system asset, such as an application, component, or middleware product. Figure 4.1 demonstrates such a scenario, in which the message paths are the lines connecting the nodes, depicted as circles. Indeed, it is plain and one of the most common message path patterns we find in production environments.

The reason for such an asset arrangement on a network is typically rooted in unplanned and organically grown system deployment. In other words, generations of systems and their related applications, or other entities were added to production without an integration strategy. Each addition to the fabric created messy webs of communications. Thus, the disarranged assets appear randomly connected. Such an unorganized fabric pattern could affect business performance and challenge the messaging network infrastructure in production. The increase of inadvertent information routes also yields redundant system configuration and integration efforts. Ultimately, the business suffers execution delays that are hard to address. An overall redesign effort then must be launched to repair such a cluttered architecture.

In terms of a computer network topology, such an arbitrary integration is named *mesh*. There are two types of mesh formations: One is tightly connected, where each node is linked to its peer. The other depicts a more relaxed pattern, in which message paths do not relate to all nodes, as illustrated in Figure 4.1.

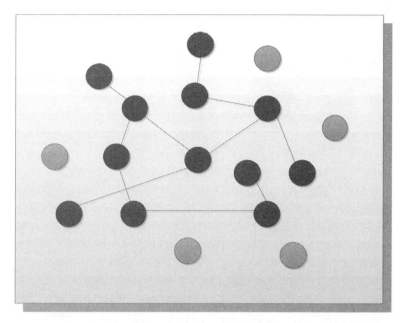

Figure 4.1   Community Fabric Pattern Example

Note that the unlinked nodes (in lighter gray) are referred to as orphans. These unconnected points are still a part of the community and consequently belong to the system's fabric. There could be a number of reasons for including the unlinked nodes in such an illustration. The chief one could be that their affiliation to the environment is merely contextual. The term "contextual" indicates that nodes could be related to their system fabric by their functionality or the solution they provide to resolve problems. Logical connections are depicted in the illustration. However, contextual relationships are not apparent. For example, if a fabric were to include accounting system nodes, such as Accounts Payable and Accounts Receivable applications, a System Backup utility node could be a part of such a community without exchanging messages with the accounting-related nodes. Namely, the System Backup utility node is considered orphan.

At last, a great deal of consideration should be given to the distance between nodes, lengths of message paths, and node locations in a system fabric. These environmental properties could eventually affect system performance. For example, a message path that connects two nodes residing in two separate networks would appear longer than a message path that links two nodes in a single network. Think about a West Coast and East Coast node affiliation scenario in contrast with two nodes connected by a path on the East Coast only. Logically, a message that travels in a longer path would reach the destination later than one in a shorter path.

Community Center Fabric Pattern

As illustrated in Figure 4.2, the community center fabric pattern links surrounding nodes to a central node, which is metaphorically named the community center. In the real world, each node may represent a production asset, such as a service,

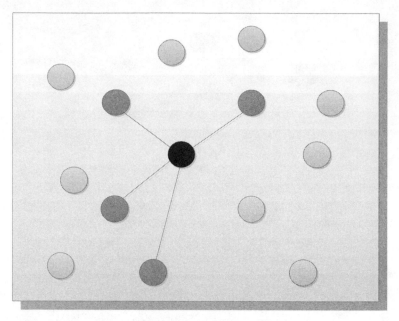

Figure 4.2   Community Center Fabric Pattern Example

an application, an off-the-shelf middleware product, and even a physical server. There must be a minimum of three nodes connected to the community center. This arrangement of assets suggests that messages flow only from the neighboring nodes to the central node. That is, no messages are exchanged directly between the surrounding nodes.

This message path formation resembles the known star network topology. From an application point of view, however, it differs. Such a pattern arrangement could consolidate redundancy of business processes. How is this possible? If the community center node, for example, were a Customer Profile application, it would more likely offer reusable functionality, such as customer lookup, and customer information. Therefore, the surrounding nodes, such as applications or components, would be able to utilize the same Customer Profile components.

Does it mean that the community center fabric pattern would yield a more efficient system than the community fabric pattern discussed in the previous section? In some ways, the answer is "yes." A message path scheme or an integration that enables information to flow back and forth from a mediating central node reduces message routes in an overall system design. Compare it with the community fabric pattern, which could potentially include more routes for the same amount of nodes.

Figure 4.3 exemplifies such a comparison. Note that Exhibit A is a community pattern with 10 routes connecting all five nodes. Linking the same amount of nodes, Exhibit B depicts a community center pattern with only five routes.

Finally, for the same reasons as with the community fabric pattern (refer to the previous section), orphan nodes that are not linked in the community center fabric pattern are placed in a system fabric because of their contextual affiliation. Some orphan nodes may represent software utilities or auxiliary stand-alone applications without the need to be linked to the central node.

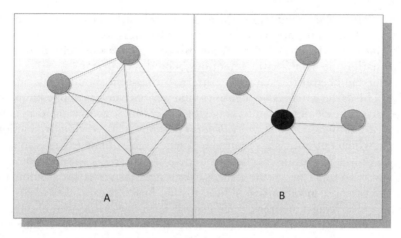

Figure 4.3   Community and Community Center Fabric Patterns

Message Transport Fabric Pattern

If the analyzed architecture contains a message flow pattern that looks like the linking routes shown in Figure 4.4, the direction of the design unveils a unique distribution of system assets. This illustration bears a resemblance to a citizen community that utilizes public transportation to get around from one place to another. Similarly, nodes in a system must subscribe to this service and agree to comply with its requirements. This enterprise middleware capability relies on *bus technologies*[3] that enable bidirectional exchange of data between nodes.

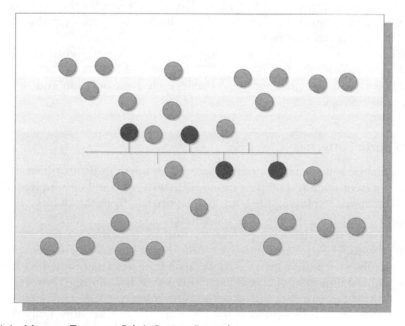

Figure 4.4   Message Transport Fabric Pattern Example

When analyzing an architecture, the mission is to justify the usage of such a pattern and understand the implications of the design. The message transport fabric pattern obviously elucidates the business and technical strategic reasons behind forming such a route formation. So what are the intentions behind such design?

To understand better this data flow pattern, the analysis should focus on an enterprise view. This large perspective identifies vital players, such as applications and network infrastructure elements that leverage the bus technology to expand an enterprise architecture. The phrase *architecture expansion* pertains to a growing production environment, in which not only is it required to queue high-volume information, but also to employ a powerful routing mechanism to deliver data to distant end-point nodes.

The ability to trade electronic records over longer distances with remote business partners and peer organizations amplifies growing business capability needs. In commerce terms, this requirement is named *business federation*. Moreover, eliminating the necessity for direct links with related partners, the message transport fabric pattern strengthens business collaboration through indirect communication.

Allowing any third-party organization to join this message exchange path is another business advantage that should not be disregarded. There would not be any limit to the number of partners a business could establish relationships with, as it is apparent in Figure 4.4. Bus technologies support such a capability by permitting quick integration with remote systems and peer organizations. In other words, there is always room to grow; the message transport fabric pattern allows it.

Another vital aspect with a growing architecture is *interoperability*. There are many types of interoperability aspects. But here, the message transport fabric pattern emphasizes the business capability to trade information with different organizations that are driven by diverse business models. For example, an insurance firm could exchange messages with a trading organization despite their strategic differences and visions. Business interoperability is another leap forward for the enterprise, a unique sign of enterprise maturity. This also means that regardless of the diverse technologies that organizations possess, they are still able to understand each other by employing universal protocols and interfaces.

The contribution of the message transport fabric pattern to *business interoperability* and development of common languages to overcome business dialects is indeed a grand achievement. Organizations could reduce business isolation and at the same time increase revenue.

Family Fabric Pattern

The family fabric pattern, illustrated in Figure 4.5, enables top-down information routing from a parent node to its offspring nodes. Messages could also be routed in the opposite direction, employing the bottom-up approach, from the children to the parent. In addition, data could flow between siblings.

The drive for this pattern is hierarchical information sharing where the flow of data is contained within a close relationship, typically in smaller implementations. This path pattern resembles a tree, of which the trunk expands into branches and the latter forms twigs. Again, the information could flow top-down or bottom-up. However, there is no route formed to share data with other tree structures.

This isolation of information is necessary for data protection. Only the nodes belonging to the tree have access to data that is shielded from outsider nodes on a

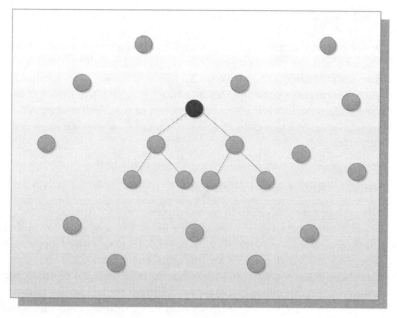

Figure 4.5   Family Fabric Pattern Example

network. The isolation effect enables integrators to segment a system fabric into contextual sectors, such as business lines, product types, or even levels of revenues incurring by applications. For example, a car manufacturer can employ the family fabric pattern to group car brands. Or a company that sells clothing online could fragment the production environment into different types of outfits.

But utilizing the family fabric pattern merely for grouping nodes, such as applications, would not be justified. Only the hierarchical formation of the message flow style should drive the motivation for such a message routing implementation. To explain the benefit of forming a hierarchical relationship, imagine a parent node named Accounting Application, which routes messages down the tree to its offspring Accounts Payable Application and Accounts Receivable Application. The value of this method would be that both offspring would perform accounting-related work on behalf of the parent. Messages could even be propagated in parallel to the children nodes to save processing time. Such division of business processing responsibilities could speed up system performance and avoid implementation delays.

Business isolation and performance are valuable propositions to an enterprise. However, the perils of implementing the pattern could be costly. A system fabric that contains the family fabric pattern would require substantial maintenance efforts to keep the node hierarchy intact. In addition, if any of the nodes fails to perform, the entire tree formation could collapse. This is called a "single point of failure." Despite the capability of production engineers to scale the tree nodes on separate servers , this implementation would still be vulnerable to operation-level run-time failures.

Remember, scattering nodes over large production environments without strong architecture justification could yield degradation in performance and increase design complexity. This means that no design effort should employ the family fabric pattern to distribute software and/or hardware over long network distances. Nodes belonging to the tree, though, should be confined to local implementations in a sub-network, avoiding the distribution across regional boundaries, organizations, or continents.

Finally, what about tree size in terms of levels? It all depends on the required depth and the business requirements that drive such a tree structure. Consider this: The more tree levels such a formation encompasses, the more complex the message flow design will be. But the minimum levels must exceed a count of two. Otherwise, such structure would fall under the category of either the community fabric pattern or the community center fabric pattern.

Circular Message Route Fabric Pattern

The circular message route fabric pattern resembles a ring formation of humans holding hands to demonstrate relationship or convey unity. Clearly, such a rounded pattern made up of linked nodes, as illustrated in Figure 4.6, forms a closed circle structure.

This depiction reveals that there are no apparent open ends. There are also no dominant members in such a pattern—no node in the structure controls the overall flow of messages or the direction. The responsibility of each node is then to transmit the data to its peer in the chain. This track of information is predictable and steady. Since messages are routed from each member to another, most production implementations do not employ a central server to control the message exchange. In other words, the data is transmitted by software, such as services or applications or middleware.

It is easy to understand why an organization would use the circular message route fabric pattern to meet business requirements. A *circular business transaction* justifies such design. To understand this concept, consider, for example, a shopping online

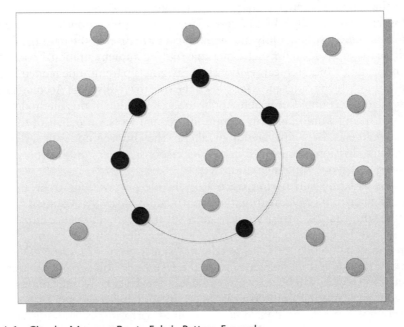

Figure 4.6   Circular Message Route Fabric Pattern Example

activity that always requires a customer to repeat orders of a number of items. That is, there are always similar steps to accomplish for each ordered product. Made up of services, Figure 4.7 demonstrates the circular business transaction, which justifies such a message loop implementation.

1. The customer searches for a product.
2. The online application lists a number of similar products.
3. The customer selects a product from the list of suggestions.
4. The product page appears with all the options to select from.
5. The customer selects the quantity and proceeds to the checkout page.
6. The checkout page appears, asking the customer to review the order.
7. The customer approves the order by clicking on the Order button.
8. The "Thank You" page appears, and then the customer can search for another product and start a new round of ordering.

As depicted in Figure 4.7, a circular message path never ends. It commences from a starting node and continues along the circular chain of services until it reaches the same originating node. Such a circular message path links the ring of nodes to satisfy certain business requirements. Perpetual transaction cycles are common to businesses keen on simplifying their business model. Consumers, who dislike complex

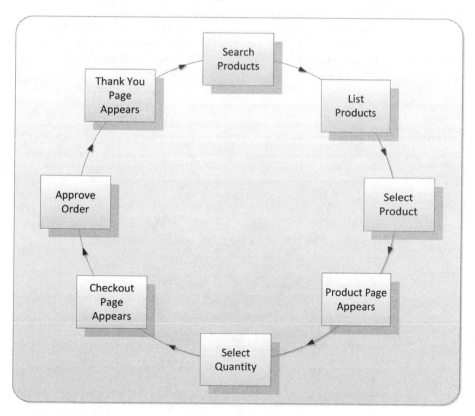

Figure 4.7   Circular Business Transaction

business transactions, are comfortable with this commerce pattern. Furthermore, from a business perspective, employees who deliver the goods or provide services easily understand how circular activities can help them to achieve business goals. For that reason, agile business organizations support process repetitions to shorten the staff's learning duration.

One of the most troubling aspects of the circular message route fabric pattern is the lack of technical redundancy to avoid a system failure. The term "redundancy" suggests that if one of the nodes fails, the message flow would be interrupted, and thus business transactions would not be completed. Consequently, this pattern introduces a potential risk for business interruption, since each node in the ring is considered a single point of failure.

Chained Message Route Fabric Pattern

The circular message route fabric pattern is similar to the chained message route fabric pattern. In both approaches, the nodes are linked with a single message route. However, the former completes a circle while the latter forms a straight line. Figure 4.8 illustrates this concept. Note that each node member is chained to its two adjacent peer nodes, forming a linear shape. In this design, the information flows in one direction, propagating the data in sequence and reaching one node at a time.

One would justifiably argue that the chained message route fabric pattern is somewhat inefficient. This assertion would be correct if a system fabric contains such integration over a large network distance. To explain this, imagine three applications, each of which is physically located far apart from each other. More specifically, the first is deployed to a production environment in New York; the second operates in Chicago;

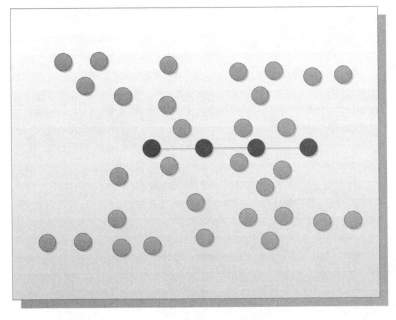

Figure 4.8   Chained Message Route Fabric Pattern Example

and the last in Los Angeles. Indeed, the intervening spaces between the three are large. This design scheme should be considered risky since the long-range distribution of these applications does not justify the employment of the chained message route fabric path pattern. There are many reasons to consider such an architecture approach as dicey:

- Messages flow only in one direction, transmitted from one node to another. This style is more appropriate for message broadcasting,[4] where the volume of information exchange is low and there is no need for a request-response type of interaction between applications.
- The chained message Route fabric pattern is best suited for small implementations, operating in sub-networks rather than across networks to avoid slow repose time.
- Each node in the chain is considered a single point of failure. If a node in the chain fails, the message routing would halt.

One of the most compelling reasons to employ the chained message route fabric pattern is the requirement for *linear business transactions*. The term "linear" means that a business process has a visible and predictable end. That is to say, a transaction starts from the originating message node and ends with the last node in the chain. In contrast, as discussed in the Circular Message Route Fabric Pattern section, a circular business transaction does not necessarily stop after a single message transmission loop. The business process repeats only after the user ends it.

A system fabric that includes a linear business implementation employs the chained message route fabric pattern to meet specific business requirements. As mentioned, a business process that uses this pattern necessitates a deterministic end to a transaction, which does not require frequent repetitions. Let us have a look at Figure 4.9 to understand better this point:

1. An applicant requests a car insurance premium quote online.
2. The system displays an application form online.
3. The applicant fills in the application and submits it.
4. The system saves the application.
5. An insurance underwriter performs risk assessment to determine risk factors and premium rates.
6. If the application is accepted, the company issues an acceptance letter.
7. Finally, the company issues an insurance policy.

Clearly, an applicant would not be able to repeat this process after the insurance firm had approved the application. The process then ends when the policy is

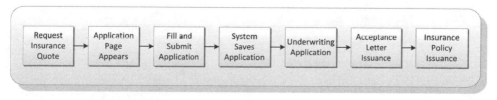

Figure 4.9   Linear Business Transaction Example

issued. This linear business process, hence, is well suited for the chained message route fabric pattern.

Is the chained route message fabric pattern expandable? Could the message path be extended beyond infinity? Could more nodes be added to the implementation? Theoretically, there should not be any limitations to extending the chain of nodes. However, a design decision to keep the chain of nodes short must be driven by system performance concerns. The lengthier the message path, the more likely it is that the business transaction will last longer. An architecture, though, should not be expanded by the node-chaining method just because there are no limitations on the number of chained applications. For that reason, a design should not leverage the chained message route fabric pattern to accomplish system interoperability and federation.

Bridge and Crossroad Fabric Patterns

Bridges and crossroad nodes are never considered destinations. These intermediate brokers connect two or more nodes. They are only midpoints that are designed to offer paths to other midway or end-point nodes. They are not central hubs that provide repeatable services like the community center fabric pattern. Nor in particular are they devised to offer business logic processes. In this book, they are named intermediary nodes for their vital role of message interception and facilitating distribution of software and hardware assets in production.

Figure 4.10 illustrates the bridge and crossroad fabric patterns. Note on section A the structure of a simple bridge that provides mediation and passage services for two communicating nodes. At first glance, such design may seem strange. Why would two nodes in a community utilize a connecting node for trading information? Would this fabric arrangement impede system performance? Is the extended message path practical? Why just not link the nodes directly without the need for a broker node?

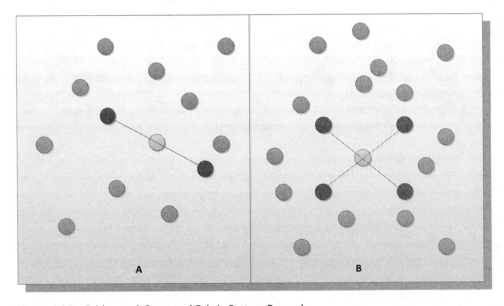

Figure 4.10   Bridge and Crossroad Fabric Pattern Example

These questions are relevant and must be investigated prior to approving an architecture. With the great advance in technology, especially with distributed computing developments, designers have learned that intermediary nodes can loosen up tightly coupled systems. One of the most effective methods to form a loosely coupled environment is to insert mediating nodes between services and consumers. There are many approaches to attain such an effect. One is to deploy a *data access layer* between applications and their corresponding repositories. This layer is typically an intermediary middleware that not only shields repositories from direct access by consumers, but also isolates vital enterprise storage facilities from unauthorized parties.

The bridge fabric pattern is then a communication broker that links business services to consumers. Along with the isolation and protection effects that such a mediator offers, the computer industry is also employing bridging technologies to facilitate security measurements. Other usages are affiliated with linking communities to each other, known as gateways, or even employing brokers to augment message data. Message augmentation means that information is added to a traveling message midway, for example, adding addresses to customer profiles to offload such responsibility from service providers and consumers.

A crossroad node, depicted on section B of Figure 4.10, provides similar mediation services. Along with its related message path, this node, however, forms a pattern for connecting multiple nodes. In fact, every orphan node in the fabric community could potentially use the mediating crossroad to communicate to other nodes. The traffic through the crossroad node, though, is expected to reach higher volumes than the bridge pattern.

Both the bridge and crossroad patterns should be considered as local implementations to facilitate the distribution of assets in a production environment. An enterprise design should not be employing these patterns for message transmission across networks, regions, or continents. These fabric arrangements are mostly suited for message interception and data augmentation. Instead, use the message transport fabric pattern (elaborated on in the Message Transport Fabric Pattern section) as an enterprise intermediary facility to enable business transactions in larger production landscapes.

From a business perspective, the bridge and the crossroad fabric patterns could be employed to connect various business segments. For example, if a production environment is comprised of multiple lines of business, such as car insurance, life insurance, and home insurance, interconnecting nodes such as bridge and crossroad can be useful lightweight gateway facilities. They can provide protocol conversion, data transformation, and security protection services.

Compound Fabric Patterns

Continuous deployment and integration efforts carve intricate shapes in the system fabric by increasing network nodes and message routes. As a result, communities of enterprise software and hardware assets create complicated grids that are hard to analyze and manage. This raises architecture complexity, making it difficult to modify and decouple. Attempting to simplify such a multifaceted production environment is time-consuming, potentially delaying product launch, and ultimately affecting enterprise earnings.

It is important to remember that a complex, hard-to-maintain production environment has not been evolving this way just because of the accumulation of network infrastructure and systems. Indeed, evidence of unjustified spending and waste of resources may be found on the ground. But the motivation for expanding an architecture is rooted in growing business demand and requirements. After all, the business organization is the party who sponsors and approves technological endeavors, delegating the production management and maintenance duties to IT.

Isolating and analyzing complex enterprise architectures like this can be accomplished despite the complexity. The approach is to discover the multiple fabric patterns of which a production environment consists. Once ascertained, the process of analysis comes next to understand the impact of the patterns on the proposed architecture. This would contribute immensely to the design assessment we ought to provide.

Figure 4.11 represents a design that consists of two fabric patterns: community and message transport. The latter crosses a community of nodes, some of which are linked to each other. This pattern partnership is required in an architecture because neither pattern alone could provide their combined capabilities. In other words, the message transport fabric pattern is devised to route messages to nodes in a community. The community pattern, on the other hand, offers point-to-point connectivity services to community members.

Architecture analysis is not a predictable science. There are many points of view to consider. No two analysts come up with similar conclusions. When inspecting a distributed production environment, one analyst may discover different fabric patterns than the other. End-state architecture discovery and analysis is a subjective process.

Another example illustrating a compound fabric pattern is presented in Figure 4.12. As apparent, the circular message route fabric pattern along with the bridge and the crossroad fabric patterns are combined to provide some sort of solutions. In this depiction, message routes link nodes belonging to both patterns.

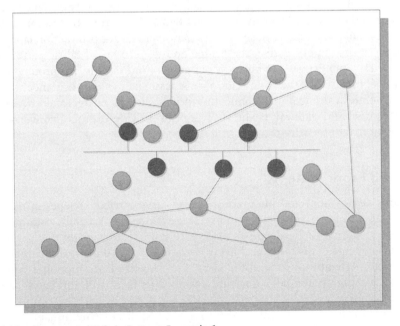

Figure 4.11   Compound Fabric Pattern Example 1

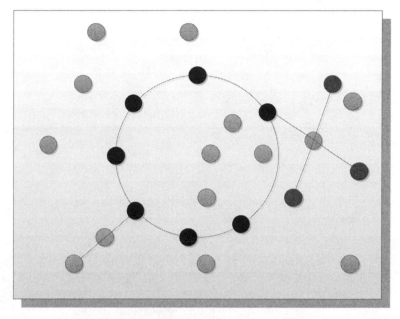

Figure 4.12   Compound Fabric Pattern Example 2

After such a discovery process, an analysis process should take place to study and determine whether such a fabric design is justified. A number of questions, then, should be presented to the architects to alleviate design concerns:

- What business and/or technological problems does the employment of the compound fabric patterns propose to resolve?
- Why are these particular fabric patterns being used?
- Do the bridge and crossroad fabric pattern capabilities augment the circular message route fabric pattern? Or, does the circular message route fabric pattern augment the bridge and crossroad fabric patterns' capabilities?
- Why are the bridge and crossroad node intermediaries employed? What business and/or technical capabilities do these patterns offer?

Notes

1. Bassam Halabi, Sam Halabi, Danny McPherson, *Internet Routing Architectures*, 2000, Cisco Press, p. 93
2. Deepankar Medhi, *Network Routing: Algorithms, Protocols, and Architectures*, 2010, Morgan Kaufmann, pp. 19-23
3. David A Chappell, *Enterprise Service Bus: Theory in Practice*, 2004, O'Reilly Media, Inc.", Jun 25, 2004, p. 7
4. https://en.wikipedia.org/wiki/User_Datagram_Protocol

CHAPTER 5
Application Discovery

There is good news coming from the application discovery space. Innovative tools and platforms are capable of discovering business implementations deployed to production. To address organizational problems, these business capabilities are delivered by systems. The vehicles that enable such delivery within a system are *applications*, which are the nucleus of business services offered to consumers. Application discovery tools then offer a diversity of production mapping capabilities to drill down into systems, identify applications, and even zoom farther down into an application's components and processes.

The term "application discovery" is about reconstructing and understanding business services. It is also about ascertaining business process patterns in production. During the application discovery process, we are searching for the business solutions and the approach pursued to meet their requirements. Remember, the emphasis is on the business imperatives and the way they are designed to deliver services. The incremental software architecture method calls for such a discovery activity to assess if indeed business goals can be achieved with the proposed end-state architecture.

Finally, before moving on, consider the mission of the application discovery:

- Identify what business solutions the ascertained business applications are devised to address.
- Study the various business services offered by the discovered applications.
- Identify the proposed design approach to deliver the solutions
- Assess if the business goals can be achieved with the proposed end-state architecture.

Application Discovery Instances

The process of application discovery should be applied to two different instances, one of which, the proposed enterprise architecture, is merely on paper. That is, the design has not been implemented and is often referred to as a conceptual design. Business requirements and business services should be reflected in these conceptual end-state architecture artifacts. Such diagrams typically depict business applications and their relationship with their peers or middleware and network infrastructure.

The process of application discovery may also take place when the end-state architecture already has been developed, deployed, and integrated in a production environment. The purpose of pursuing this is to inspect failing application and their components that do not meet business expectations. In this case, there are a myriad of tools capable of mapping a production environment, discovering applications, and drilling down into the services they provide.

Continuous Application Discovery

There is nothing evolving more in a computing environment than a vibrant production landscape. There, ongoing deployments, configuration, and integration work are being performed on an hourly basis. These incessant efforts to monitor, maintain, and analyze production also necessitate *continuous discovery* of applications. Understandably, constant application discovery occurs only after the architecture implementation already has been deployed to production.

Therefore, an existing underperforming or failing application should be continuously re-examined because of the ever-changing production ecosystem. True, this task could be tedious at times, but the actual work of sighting is vital to insuring flawless application operations. To fulfill this continuous task, various tools enable automated discovery. In other words, nowadays a production environment can be scanned, discovered, and mapped unremittingly.

Continuous application discovery would require one more thing called *delta analysis:* unveiling what type of changes an application has undergone since its last inspection.

What Can Be Revealed with Application Discovery Tools?

The computer industry is saturated with a wide range of application discovery and mapping tools. They offer rich content and graphical displays for studying and configuring a production environment. Tools like these enable analysts to not only discover deployed software and hardware assets, but also to collect performance and capacity planning data. Along with this impressive list of capabilities, certain tools provide return on investment (ROI) information, and even power utilization of devices in a production environment.

The application discovery mission, though, does not necessarily require such a wealth of information. But an application does not operate in vacuum. It requires proper middleware and network infrastructure to run on. Monitoring and alert mechanisms are also necessary to guarantee error-free operations. Furthermore, an application may be linked to peer applications, and e-mail and printing systems. The list of *dependencies* is even longer. Consequently, the process of application discovery is not only about applications themselves. It is about the environment in which they operate. It is about the integrated software and hardware organizational assets deployed to offer collaborative business solutions.

The *application* discovery capabilities, discussed in this chapter, could also be used to analyze *system* fabric patterns, as elaborated on in Chapter 4. This dual purpose is a powerful instrument that analysts can employ during different phases of the incremental software architecture process. Remember, however, that here the focus is on application discovery along with the supporting technologies such as middleware and network infrastructure. Application mapping, on the other hand, is largely discussed in Chapter 6.

The sections that follow, therefore, identify the chief discovery efforts devised to understand what is the contribution of an application in the context of an end-state architecture. Assuring that an application is indeed capable of accomplishing its business goals is another vital aspect that the discovery process ought to verify. To accomplish these tasks, the process calls for a number of activities:

- Classifying application architecture
- Examining application performance and consumption of computer resources
- Ascertaining if the application is ready to operate in production
- Identifying asset management tools and platforms for control of the applications' life cycles

Application Identity Discovery

When either inspecting an architecture proposition or examining an ill-designed application already deployed to production, the process of identity discovery must take place. Identity in this context means that an application's business functionality and technical aspects must be recognized and understood.

The business perspective, on one hand, is about understanding what type of services the application offers, the solutions it provides, and the related business goals. For example, a human resources application may provide a wide range of services dedicated to the management of employee recruitment, such as admission process, benefit initiation, and health insurance enrollment. The business identity of an application, then, is affiliated with its offerings to consumers.

Moreover, the technical aspects are related to the application type. The term "type" refers to the kind of technologies an application is based on. In addition, an analyst must be able to classify an application by the environment in which it operates and the manner it communicates with its peers, middleware, and network infrastructure. Consider the list of types that shed light on an application technical identity:

Web application   This class is affiliated with browser-based implementation employing Web technologies running on central servers.

Thick client   Known as a "desktop application" in the client-server architecture space, with complete set of user interface, business, and communication functionality not utilizing back-end servers.

Service   Considered as an application's component, a service offers a narrow range of business offerings to subscribed consumers.

Mobile   This application operates on handheld devices, such as smartphones and tablet computers. The implementation is usually downloaded to mobile devices from back-end infrastructures or cloud computing environments.

Rich Internet Application (RIA)   This type possesses the characteristics of the thick client desktop application. The RIA relies on Web and browser technologies and plug-in components. As an autonomous entity, it is empowered by installed frameworks that provide most of its functionality, such as user interface, protocols, and communication capabilities.

Finally, if the application is an off-the-shelf product, the publisher typically identifies and classifies it. This may include the industry that the software is best suited for, recommended consumer base, and product trademarks and copyrights.

Not only limited to a software manufacturer, an in-house made application should be delivered along with its installation, configuration, and integration manuals. This may include an in-depth product description and functionality, user interfaces, and technical and architecture specifications.

Discovering an application identity could facilitate its classification and cataloging efforts (read about application cataloging methods in Chapter 6).

Application Architecture Discovery

At this stage, during the incremental software architecture discovery process, we ought to center on discerning parts of the design to justify their contribution to business goals. The most important task then would be to identify the application *architecture objectives*[1] and examine how they meet business goals.

Elements of Application Architecture Discovery

There are numerous aspects of an application architecture that can be discovered in an integrated environment. One, for example, could be to understand how the design exposes services to consumers. The mechanisms that are being employed to connect to the outside world are vital to an application's existence and its overall performance. These means of communication may include adapters and interfaces that enable message exchange with external entities. Components that handle communication protocols and data formatting should also be a part of the application architecture discovery process. Again, an application's collaboration with its message exchange parties to promote business purposes is an important view that ought to be subject for inspection.

Not only could the communication of an application with its external environment affect its existence and performance. The internal architecture, too, is an important ingredient that must be taken in consideration. The application design is what enables its behavior and operations. To understand how an application functions, we ought to break down its structure and decompose its modules. Once the various elements have been revealed, the internal architecture would be subject to feasibility inspection and evaluation.

The process of taking an application apart should not be mistaken for reverse engineering. In contrast, these architecture discovery activities are pursued to identify an application internal inventory and study the viability of its business processes. The capability of an application to promote business strategies and offer meaningful services to consumers is what makes this discovery process so compelling.

Unfortunately, not all applications in production are designed the same way. From an additional architecture point of view, some fall under the monolithic implementation category. This implies that an application is tightly coupled and large in magnitude to the extent that operation engineers are challenged by its intricate design. Loosely coupled applications may be found, too. These are lightweight business implementations that offer a narrower range of capabilities, yet are interconnected with other applications or components.

Presenting Application Architecture

Indeed, there are many ways to depict an application architecture for the purpose of examining its contents. A popular presentation method is to create a reference architecture diagram, showing the various logical layers that make up an application. The archetypal parts of an application design are depicted in Figure 5.1:

Consumers   Users or consuming entities, such as applications or even middleware products

Presentation   Components that provide user interface and page navigation capabilities

Business   Segment comprised of services that provide business functionality

Data   Section that includes data access mechanisms and data sources

Crosscutting   Section that identifies common application components reused by the presentation, business, and data sections

But this model is a very rudimentary depiction of an application architecture. The internal structure could be more involved. A multifaceted design may also include crosscutting components, such as security, configuration elements, communication entities, supporting libraries, message exchange and routing capabilities, and data persistence mechanisms. Figure 5.2 conveys an intricate application design with additional layers.

Consider the breakdown of the application reference architecture example depicted in Figure 5.2:

Users   Typically customers or consumers who are using application user interfaces to obtain services

Consuming systems   Other automated processes subscribing to application offerings

Presentation layer   Included are user interface mechanisms and page rendering technologies

Interfaces   May be adapters enabling external systems to communicate with the application resources and services

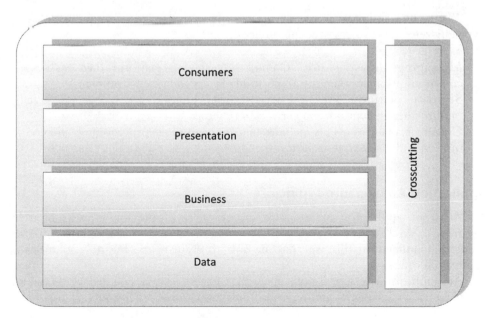

Figure 5.1   A Model for Application Reference Architecture

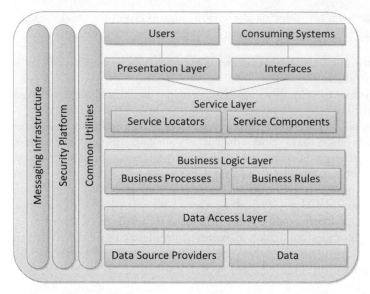

Figure 5.2   Application Reference Architecture Example

Service layer   Layer comprised of service locators and components that provide a narrow scope of services or interfaces to the business logic layer

Business logic layer   Business processes and business rules

Data access layer   A proxy that provides access to information stored in databases or data source providers

Data source providers   Any business or technical entity that offers content for the application's presentation layer and its related repositories

Data   Contains persisted information for the application

The list that follows contains the application's common services used by its layers (typically referred to as crosscutting services):

Messaging infrastructure   Common messaging platform that enables the communication between the application's layers and its environment

Security platform   All necessary security utilities, access control, tracing, monitoring, encryption, and certificate facilities

Common utilities   This includes management tools, provisioning, and configuration and installation facilities

Application Architecture Typing

The task of application architecture discovery also calls for typing an architecture. An architecture category is affiliated with an application's capabilities. Study and understand this aspect to be able to evaluate the business solutions an application offers.

An application design, for instance, that fosters loosely coupled best practices would be easy to maintain and expand. Implementation elasticity such as this would enable a business organization to launch a product on time and on budget to compete in harsh market conditions. Consider examples of application architecture styles that may be revealed during the process of application discovery and analysis:

N-tier This architecture fosters decoupling chief application components into reusable and manageable parts, named tiers. The most common style is the three-tier separation, composed of presentation, business logic, and data.

Service-oriented architecture (SOA) This architecture style follows many principles of implementation, such as loose coupling, reusability, statelessness, granularity, and autonomy. Related SOA technologies enable these best practices and drive application composition and processes.

Client-server The style of distributed computing comes across when there is clear separation between the consuming and providing parties. Respectively, servers and clients trade messages to execute business transactions. This interaction occurs on a network, and in many instances, the client and the server parts operate on a single server.

Model-view-controller (MVC) An application adopts an architectural style like this to help simplify its design. In this case, the MVC pattern delegates specific roles to the three application components. First, the model consists of business logic, data, and processes. Second, the view piece is responsible for the presentation and user interface functionality aspects of an application. Last, the controller executes commands on behalf of the former two.

Refer to Chapters 7–11 to learn more about architecture styles and the methods employed to decompose a design. These chapters discuss approaches to prepare for the process of architecture verification and certification.

Discovery of Application Performance and Resource Utilization

Application consumption pertains to a wide range of affiliated performance measurements. In general terms, these tasks are a part of a larger testing scale. The incremental software architecture process calls for validating a design proposition of an application by analyzing its capability to exchange information in certain performance rates. *Application capacity planning*, therefore, is the practice mostly recommended to address such measurements. Once again, the use of capacity planning tools are essential to the discovery of performance and consumption requirements.

Remember, here, capacity-planning activities take place to assess if computing resources are adequate for proper application performance. On a larger scale, Chapter 15 discusses a different type: enterprise end-state architecture capacity planning, namely planning resource utilization for an environment.

When it comes to measuring the capability of an application to meet service level agreements (SLAs), performance and response time are the most critical parameters that should be investigated and tested. Here again, there are two scenarios for determining if indeed an application can sustain high-volume message load. The first is when an application has been implemented and integrated in production. In this case, capacity-planning tools are employed to gather related data and test message load capability.

In the second scenario, an application is only in its conceptual state, merely a proposition that ought to be evaluated for its feasibility. Here, the practice of *capacity predictive modeling* comes in handy. Forecasting the behavior and assessing the resources needed for flawless performance are essential tasks that must be accomplished when the design is merely on paper.

Application Capacity Planning Goals

Applications that have undergone the capacity planning process typically demonstrate stability and exceptional capabilities to sustain future growth in message loads. How is this possible? Capacity planning encompasses a number of activities devised to determine if an application or a system is capable of meeting key nonfunctional requirements. The tests performed during this process are *not* affiliated with validation of business functionality and the type of services an application provides. In other words, nonfunctional requirements are not about the business aspect of such scrutiny. When it comes to application capacity planning, consider the fundamental goals of the practice:

- Approve application architecture nonfunctional compliance.
- Certify application *performance*.
- Assure that an application is *operationally ready* for production activities.
- *Forecast* future application behavior and performance.
- Provide application's *resource sizing* recommendations for current and future operations, such as memory and CPU utilization.

Application Capacity Planning Process

These capacity planning goals boil down to the most fundamental aspect of application existence: *funding*. This not only pays for ongoing application operations in production, such as engineering maintenance costs. Application backups, monitoring, and performance tuning are only part of the effort to ensure business continuity. Application resource sizing, as may be recommended by capacity planning initiatives, is an additional expenditure that must be budgeted, too. Financing the increase in capabilities of hardware, middleware, and network infrastructure to keep an application alive could be substantial. Without capacity planning, however, the consequences may be even more disastrous. Not including funds for an application's future growth could measurably slow down its performance, and as a result, harm business objectives.

Consider the chief activities performed during application capacity planning:

Architecture analysis and validation   This activity calls for decomposing an application architecture into various components to determine which one should be tested for capacity and performance. The analysis should also include the study of an application environment and its capability to operate within infrastructure parameters.

Nonfunctional requirements (NFR) study   A review of application nonfunctional requirements to set proper testing thresholds and performance benchmarks

Performance testing   Considering the inspected NFR, performance testing is conducted for each vital architecture component. The tests should also include application response time for increasing intervals of consumers.

High-availability (HA) testing   The process of HA testing is conducted to confirm that an application survives outages and is capable of providing business services without interruption.

Capacity utilization testing   Application resources, such as CPU, memory, disk I/O, network utilization, and even server power consumption are tested for resource sizing and improvements.

Forecast application performance   At this stage, future consumption and utilization of resources are being projected. Capacity planning models for the various application resources indicate future application sizing requirements.

Reporting   A comprehensive capacity planning report that includes the results of all performed tests should be presented to the development and integration teams.

Network Infrastructure Discovery: Is an Application Production Ready?

This discovery activity should determine if application operational needs could be met by the supporting middleware and network infrastructure in production. Operational needs refer to application design requirements, such as sufficient network bandwidth, proper messaging frameworks, and appropriate security measurements. Merely finding out what the network infrastructure elements are may be somehow counterproductive. The process of discovery then should determine if an application is *production ready*.

This practice is widely exercised by many organizations to insure that an application can survive in a real-time environment—a different ecosystem than pre-production. Another motivation for the application readiness examination is to prevent the deployment of an ill-designed implementation. However, in case of an existing application that is already in operation, this discovery should determine if it has been installed and integrated prematurely.

Pre-Production Application Readiness Testing

Pre-production is merely a space on the network dedicated to testing applications before deployment to production. Many organizations find out that testing an application for readiness in a pre-production environment is challenging and the results are unreliable.

There are other methods to consider, most of which are not viable. Two are worth mentioning, though. One would be replication of a real production world—in other words, reinstalling, reconfiguring, and reintegrating most software and hardware assets that reside in production in a different environment. This would be costly and require substantial effort to accomplish. The other is simulating a production ecosystem in a virtual space by using a simulation product that can mirror a production environment along with its software and hardware assets. This approach would be easier to pursue.

However, mimicking the actual production workloads and parallel events would be almost impossible.

Application Readiness Queries

Ask the following questions to determine if an application is production-ready:

- What network devices are required to maintain application operations? These are typically networking hardware, such as routers, switches, hubs, bridges, protocol convertors, and wireless controllers.
- Are any virtual servers required?
- What are the infrastructure peripherals that an application necessitates? Printers? Scanning devices? Mobile appliances?
- Are there any software licenses required to support infrastructure services? When do the licenses expire? Would license expiration interrupt business activities?
- Are there any patches to be applied to network infrastructure entities to ensure application business continuity? What is the cycle of installing patches in production to maintain regular application operations?
- What are the production environment operating systems? Are they updated?

Asset Management Discovery

In the context of the application discovery, asset management includes vital processes to ensure software stability and service continuity. Every so often, asset management is construed as a process pursued merely in production. However, the rule of thumb suggests that the management process should not be confined only to operating landscapes. An application, then, should be controlled, configured, and observed throughout the progression of its entire life cycle. This timespan includes development, deployment, and integration stages.

In this section, we stress the continuous and critical need for *asset management* because of the vibrant nature of a production environment, in which applications, middleware, and network infrastructure evolve. This implies that an application, among other assets in production, necessitates constant monitoring and modifications to avoid interruption of operations and ensure safe business operations.

Asset Management Practices

Once more, umpteen asset management tools exist on the market to assist with the documentation and monitoring of application in production. The incremental software architecture discovery and analysis process calls for verifying if indeed applications that take part in an end-state architecture are properly managed and controlled.

The application discovery, then, calls for the examination of the various *asset management practices*. This is to ensure that there is an established support and intervention means to address application failures. An organization, therefore, ought to embrace high-standard rescue and ongoing support procedures to maintain and manage an application, no matter in which product life cycle it is. Without such indemnities, no funding should be allocated for an implementation until asset management practices are sound, effective, and proven.

The sections that follow elaborate on a few asset management activities that must be in place to strengthen application processes and guarantee robust performance.

Configuration Management

One of the most recognized practices is the software configuration management[2] (SCM). The charter of this undertaking is simply to track, monitor, and control changes in software. However, as simple as it may sound, SCM tasks include expanded activities, such as version and configuration control, and even defect tracking.

To be able to accomplish these activities, SCM mandates the founding of a software baseline—in our case, *application baseline*. That is, to monitor and manage changes, an application should be versioned. If unsolvable problems arise, each advanced version could be compared and/or reversed to its previous state—its baseline.

Consider a number of activities pursued during the SCM process:

Build management   This activity is about selecting the proper tools and controlling the source code build process.
Environment management   This process is devised to manage software and hardware of development, pre-production, and production environments. Software licensing and hardware memory and space verifications are only a few tasks related to this activity.
Defect management   This activity identifies and records software defects.
Configuration control   This effort is established to track and review application changes for the purpose of source code certification or modification rejection.
Configuration auditing   This ensures that changes applied to an implementation are in line with best practices, policies, and business and technical requirements.

Other Application Management Practices

Another application management practice that could affect an implementation quality is the application life cycle management (ALM).[3] This controlling mechanism ensures that the construction and the maintenance of an application are handled in accordance with organizational standards. ALM involves a variety of management responsibilities. These include the gathering and compilation of business requirements, software design and development, software quality assurance and certification, software deployment and integration control, and more. In a broader sense, many organizations recognize these management and maintenance activities as the software development life cycle (SDLC).

Finally, the process of controlling software releases, named release management [RM], is also vital to the application discovery process. This practice requires meticulous planning to execute the installation and integration of an application in a complex production environment. Production engineers, software architects, and developers collaborate to accomplish a successful release initiative. The involved practitioners must not only possess business requirements knowledge, but also be familiar with the application design. In addition, when releasing an application to production, the team must also understand the ecosystem in which an application would be deployed. This should include network devices and appliances, network topology, and middleware.

Notes

1. http://pubs.opengroup.org/architecture/togaf8-doc/arch/chap05.html
2. Stephen P. Berczuk, Brad Appleton, *Software Configuration Management Patterns: Effective Teamwork, Practical Integration*, 2003, Addison-Wesley Professional, p. 7
3. http://www.davidchappell.com/WhatIsALM--Chappell.pdf

CHAPTER 6

Application Mapping

I t is inconceivable that some organizations would not leverage existing technologies to discover and analyze their production environments, especially when the architecture is vast and complex. There is no defense against ignoring such vital activity. Not being able to view an integrated ecosystem graphically is a symptom of organizational blindness that typically leads to grand-scale system and application failures.

What is this all about? The capability to discover how applications are integrated is an immense advantage over lack of vision. The ability to trace message flows and spot routes of business transactions in an intricate production environment reduces maintenance and configuration expenditure.

Ever-changing production environments introduce enormous challenges to asset management and business continuity. The ability to follow such trends, monitor how an environment is evolving, and observe the rapid pace of technological progression bestows an overwhelming advantage over the competition.

In the context of the discovery and analysis process, when an end-state architecture is in its conceptual stage, proposed on paper, the process calls for identifying the dependencies of an application on its peers and supporting environment. In this case, mapping application with tools would be an impossible task to accomplish, since the implementation would not exist. However, the work of mapping such a conceptual proposition could still take place to understand how an application will be integrated in a production environment.

Application Logical and Physical Topology Mapping

This brings us to one of the most fundamental aspects of application discovery: *application topology mapping*. To understand how an application is linked to its message exchange parties, simply produce a *topology map diagram*. But the term "linking" does not only point to the advantages of such a graphical depiction; it means the logical relationship an application forms with its surrounding environment. The term "logical" denotes business association, partnership, or collaborative efforts to accomplish business goals. A link also indicates physical network configuration, such as cable and router settings.

An application topology map, as depicted in Figure 6.1, brings all the logical and physical perspectives together. This powerful feature tells the story of a production environment without the need for extensive documentation. The ability to look at an integrated application environment, understand the formed partnerships, and view the association of business services to their supporting middleware, hardware, and network infrastructure is beneficial to the application discovery and analysis process.

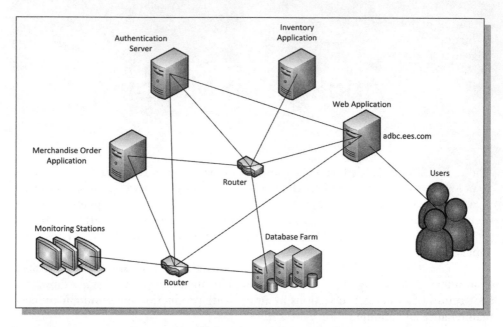

Figure 6.1   Logical and Physical Application Topology Map

With this approach, analysts are able to determine if the design meets business and technical requirements and if the implementation is feasible.

Obviously, the process of application topology discovery is most efficient when using automated mapping tools in production. Even if there are no major reported issues, this activity should be pursued. The process is named *continuous application topology discovery*. Since a production environment keeps changing, subsequent mapping would depict a corresponding alteration in the topology.

Topology discovery is not only about using actual mapping tools and platforms. What if the proposed architecture is delivered in a diagram? What if there is no implementation? What if the design is merely conceptual? In this case, the application topology discovery and analysis process should be conducted by inspecting end-state architecture artifacts. These may include diagrams and a variety of charts depicting the logical and physical links of an application's environment.

Application Tier Distribution Topology Mapping

Another contribution of the application topology mapping is the capability to discover the physical distribution of an application in production. As discussed earlier in Chapter 5, not all application tiers may be located on a single server. Application components may be dispersed across an entire production environment.

The practice of packaging most application's components and deploying them on the same host would not necessarily ease production maintenance or reduce upkeep cost. Design principles, such as loose coupling, may call for separating complex N-tier application architecture elements and distributing them to different segments of a production environment. This may include the dispersal of security components and application management services, such as provisioning and configuration. Moreover, in other cases, not all applications' business logic services are deployed in the business tier. Reuse, components sharing, and scalability may be the reasons for splitting up an application's physical implementation.

Figure 6.2 illustrates the various tiers a Web application consists of. A diagram like this could divulge where the architecture components are located. As apparent, users typically operate remotely. Data repositories are distributed to an organizational data warehouse. Other tiers, such as the data access implementation, are also located apart from the business tier.

Business Performance Discovery in Topology Mapping

One of the most compelling reasons to pursue the application topology mapping is to discover the *key performance indicators* (KPIs)[1] of offered business services. This analysis can be accomplished by selecting the proper topology mapping tool. The application KPI could reveal a number of business perspectives that should not be ignored. While mapping application relationships, analysts should also take time to observe the actual contribution of an application to business imperatives. The task of discovering the business KPI of an application should center on a number of goals:

- Increase return on investment and revenue.
- Foster expenditure reduction of business operations.
- Improve customer satisfaction.

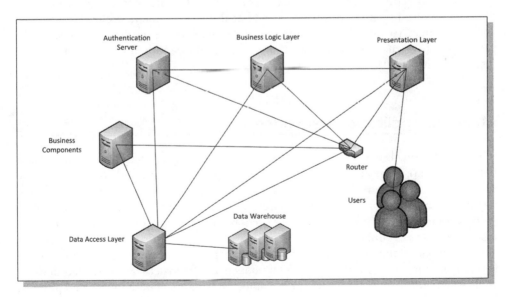

Figure 6.2   Logical Application Tier Distribution

The KPI for an application service level agreement (SLA) would be a good place to start. Note a number of SLA measurements to observe:

- Application unavailability occurrences or production outages over the past six month or a year
- Slow application performance that may have resulted in customer dissatisfaction
- Additional operational cost allocated for repairing an application's response time

KPI for quality of application services is another aspect to examine during the topology mapping analysis:

- Does the application functionality meet business requirements? Would the customer be satisfied?
- Would inadequate services prompt customer complaints?
- Can the application handle a large number of consumers?
- Would application defects turn away customers?
- What would be the cost for enhancing the quality of services (QoS)?
- Would the application downtime for improving the QoS frustrate customers?

Evaluating business processes, service efficiency, and compliance with business strategy and mission are other KPI aspects that may be of interest to organizations. These measurements are vital to assessing the execution of business goals. Such discoveries typically lead to identifying gaps in business performance. As a result, these findings galvanize organizational initiatives to improve customer satisfaction.

In addition, to keep track of the state of a business, the enterprise should study the benefit of employing the balance scorecard.[2] This performance measurement platform, offered by numerous tools, would enable management, architects, analysts, and developers to evaluate the effectiveness of a deployed application. The application topology mapping initiative, therefore, should include business performance discovery activities.

Mapping Application Dependency

The application discovery and analysis activity calls for studying the dependencies between an application and its operating environment. This task is vital to every architecture assessment. What is it all about? An application forms *logical and physical* dependencies in production to enable information exchange and business transactions. A logical dependency merely ascertains a contextual relationship, perhaps a business association or even links with consumers.

The physical topology does not necessarily depict such a conceptual bond. A physical dependency, in contrast, is shaped by network infrastructure and related devices, such as network connections formed by cables and routers. These logical and physical business associations and message paths could be easily spotted in a topology-map diagram, as illustrated in Figures 6.1 and 6.2. Indeed, topology mapping is a prerequisite to discovering application dependencies.

Application Dependency Discovery and Analysis Motivation

Why would anyone be interested in viewing application dependencies during the application discovery and analysis process? Why is such activity so intrinsic to application performance and maintenance? Why is the term "business continuity" so much about the way we design applications?

The answer to these questions is rooted in lessons learned from ill-designed application cases throughout decades of product development. Not long ago, *monolithic applications* used to dominate the computing landscape. Simply put, the term "monolithic" stands for huge implementations that offer a large amount of business processes. They are autonomous and deployed in central production locations. These applications are tightly coupled, single-tiered, undistributed, or federated. Furthermore, the monolithic application internal components depend so heavily on each other that the cost of separating them outweighs the benefits.

Similarly, two or more applications that are extremely dependent on each other could increase modification and maintenance costs and ultimately affect performance. With the expansion of today's production environments, architecture strategies call for distribution and federation of software. This is to avoid tightly coupled implementations, increase reuse, and simplify enterprise integration. Therefore, we ought to analyze the impact of application dependencies on *architecture elasticity*. The questions that follow explain the term "software elasticity":

- Is the application design flexible enough to enable changes for business growth?
- Can a business compete with highly dependent applications in a production environment?
- Is then the proposed architecture practical?

Mitigating Interoperability Concerns

The increase of application dependencies introduces another strategic architecture concern: failure to achieve effective computing interoperability. That is, the design is not flexible enough to accommodate efficient communication between two or more distinct computing environments. This may include different language platforms, or even diverse hosting hardware and operating systems. To understand better the problem, remember that there could be enormous undertaking and affiliated costs to break down tightly coupled applications. If the separation of application components carries such a high price tag, organizations instead should consider employing interfaces and adapters for externalizing internal application business processes. But this in itself is another taxing endeavor.

Types of Application Dependencies

Unlike the monolithic implementation, where all parts of the architecture are typically bundled in a single physical location, distributed and federated enterprise architecture calls for accommodating physical communication over greater production distances. The challenge then would be to strike the right balance between overwhelming and fewer dependencies. Setting a measurable scale between a tight coupling and loose coupling design is what drives the dependency classification effort.

As discussed earlier, physical associations are driven by tangible configuration and actual integration structures. The term "physical" also implies that the routes between applications and the supporting network infrastructure and middleware entities are created to enable information exchange. Moreover, forming physical relationships in production is a costly integration endeavor. To assess the benefits and feasibility of the links, an application forms in production, classify the various associations and understand their contribution to application integration.

Discovering application dependencies is a vital activity that is not only about internal reliance of components on each other, but also connecting external entities, such as applications, middleware, and network infrastructure elements. Classifying application dependencies, internal or external, could uncover the motivation for creating physical associations in production. In due course, these relationships could be reconsidered to reduce asset dependencies. Therefore, this section explores common dependencies found in a distributed computing landscape and discusses the advantages and drawbacks of each association.

The sections that follow, therefore, elaborate on four types of application dependencies:

1. *Application private dependency*. An application exchanges messages with a single software entity, such as a peer application, component, or middleware product.
2. *Application public dependency*. An application exchanges messages with multiple message exchange peers or partners.
3. *External application dependency*. An application trades messages with the environment, in which other applications and/or software components collaborate on executing transactions.
4. *Internal application dependency*. Internal components of an application exchange messages.

Application Private Dependency

Privately formed application dependency only takes place between an application and an information trading partner. The term "partner" may pertain to a peer application, a database, a middleware product, a remote system, or even a cloud. Recall, this exclusive relationship forms only one message route between an application and another entity to fulfill a business transaction.

Furthermore, communication between an application and its related peer could be driven by two types of information trading patterns: two-way message exchange style and one-way message exchange style. These are explained in the sections that follow.

Two-Way Message Exchange Style: A Private Conversation

The *two-way message exchange* occurs when an application and its single information-trading consumer exchange messages. This implies that the message sender entity is always expecting a response. As apparent in Figure 6.3, the two-way communication takes place between application 1 and the DB. Request-response is the technical term for such data exchange method. This information trading activity is named "conversation."

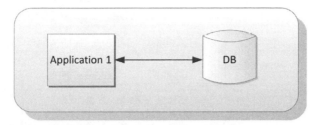

Figure 6.3   Application Private Dependency: Two-Way Message Exchange Style

As implied, this dialogue takes place between a message requester and responder. The technology behind this approach supports synchronous and asynchronous communication. The former implies that the sender must wait until the response returns. This pause of operation is known as *blocking*. With the latter, the sender continues with its duties until the response arrives. Timeout conditions could be set in both cases if a message is delayed.

One-Way Message Exchange Style: Private Communication

As mentioned, the *one-way message exchange style*, on the other hand, is another type of application private dependency (illustrated in Figure 6.4). This information transmission occurs when one party, either an application or a related consumer, sends a message without any reply expectations. Accordingly, in this illustration application 1 sends a private message to application 2. This approach is devised for business notifications—not business conversations. One side employs this approach to send periodical updates of any sort: for example, sending a bank account status or informing of a mortgage account outstanding. In these one-way examples, a message request-response implementation is not necessary.

Application Public Dependency

In most instances, an application depends on more than one party to accomplish a business transaction. This relationship is named one-to-many. Although the private conversation, discussed in the previous section, is an easy method to exchange information, a more intricate relationship involves multiple message trading partners, namely public dependency. This widely implemented scenario entails that for completing a business activity, an application must exchange messages with multiple peers.

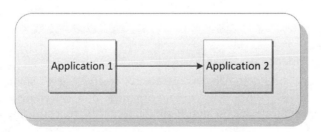

Figure 6.4   Application Private Dependency: One-Way Private Message Exchange Style

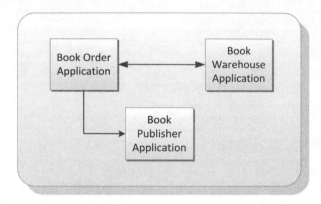

Figure 6.5   Application Public Dependency

To understand better the application public dependency, review the simple example in Figure 6.5. Once a user completes an order online, the Book Order Application communicates with the Book Warehouse Application to verify if the book is in stock. If the book were not available, a request notification with a one-way alert message would be sent to the Book Publisher Application, asking for a replenishment.

Application Public Dependencies with Two-Way and One-Way Message Exchange Styles

Not only can application private dependencies utilize the two-way and one-way message exchange styles. Application public dependencies may also employ the two-way or one-way message trading patterns to accomplish a business transaction.

The decision of whether to use either the two-way or one-way message exchange style (or both) depends on design preferences. Since an application public dependency scheme is typically complex, of which multiple entities must trade information to accomplish a transaction, the two-way and one-way patterns may be utilized.

External Application Dependency

External dependencies, *either private or public*, pertain to relationships that an application forms with outside message-consuming parties. These associations also are about the integration of an application in a production ecosystem. The term "external" means that the analysis effort is not about the interrelationship of application-containing components. The sections that follow introduce common external application dependency examples.

Application Dependency on Data

An application may be highly dependent on external resources such as data source providers, data access component, or an organization's warehouse. The growing dependencies of applications on data storage facilities, repositories, and archiving platforms may have been raising organizations' concerns to new levels. The mounting demand for information is so staggering that enterprise architecture must come up with innovative solutions to reduce tightly coupled dependencies.

But no matter what the new solutions are, the traditional application dependency on data is still a burning enterprise issue. Solutions such as replicating data storages, and later synchronizing the information in an enterprise master repository, only increase application dependency on data.

Other efforts to decouple application from data introduce data proxies, such as data access layers, to isolate information from direct and tightly coupled access. Lastly, caching data is an additional method devised to separate an application from the main repository and speed up the CRUD (create, read, update, and delete) operations. This in itself is another approach for duplicating information that yields greater dependency on data.

Application Dependency on Proxies

Another example of application dependency on external software implementations is the overwhelming utilization of proxies. This approach fosters loose coupling design, by which an application communicates indirectly with its messages exchange parties. The increase of software intermediaries in production indeed enables the expansion of enterprise architecture. In different words, proxies are the means of distributing and federating software.

There is nothing wrong with the utilization of intermediaries to execute business transactions. Their contribution to application integration is vast. Software brokers, like an ESB or gateway for example, intercept messages for different purposes, such as security enhancements, credential passing, data augmentation, protocol conversions, data formatting, message routing, and more. Brokers offload these functionalities from applications and expose them to other enterprise applications for reuse.

With the growing scope of production environments, the role of software inter-mediaries has expanded considerably. Enterprise architecture practices have adopted the concept of message interception, enhancement, augmentation, and routing. This approach, however, increases application dependencies on proxies. As a result, messages must travel longer distances, interrupted by brokers, to reach destinations. Meanwhile, the long transport takes a toll on application performance and response time. An architecture discovery and analysis, therefore, should assess if the intercept-ing brokers introduce message delivery and performance challenges. Brokers may be the reason for slow application execution.

Application Dependency on Middleware and Network Infrastructure

This brings us to another topic that should be considered during the application discovery and analysis: *middleware and infrastructure dependency*. The vital operational support of an application in production by middleware and network infrastructure is undisputed. There is no application that can run without proper routing mechanisms, robust and scaled hardware, and network devices such as routers. The configuration efforts to integrate an application in production are immense and infinite. Constant integration initiatives take place because of new additions and enhancements to a production landscape.

These adoption and deployment tasks only increase external application dependencies on production. An application migration to another computing environment, therefore, has become a nightmare for production engineers. The struggle is to recreate an integrated environment for the relocated application. That is to say, the dependencies that an application has created with time are hard to replicate.

Internal Application Dependency

A self-contained application, such as a monolithic implementation, for example, does not tend to establish many external dependencies since its internal implementation is tightly coupled. Self-sufficiency, therefore, is a necessity because of an application's limited capabilities to collaborate with external message exchange partners. Namely, a tightly coupled application is made up of almost all components it needs to survive without relying extensively on external distributed applications. These internal and isolated functionalities may include message routing mechanisms, protocol conversion, security, user interface implementations and presentation mechanisms, data queuing and formatting, and more.

Accordingly, tightly coupled applications are not only hard to maintain, their reusability factor is typically low. To expose their business logic to outside service requesters, *functionality externalization* is therefore required. Externalization means adding interfaces or adapters that extend application capabilities, enabling outside consumers to utilize contained business processes. This undertaking typically takes place with legacy applications that are hard to decouple or decompose.

A tightly coupled application relies heavily on internal functions that are hard to separate because of the close-fitting dependency they form. The most common example of such design is the thick client or the rich Internet application (RIA). Each consists of a wide range of bundled internal capabilities and resides on a single host. These may include application business logic, user interface elements, protocol handling, and even routing capabilities. An abundance of similar examples could be found in almost every production environment.

One of the most common application design errors is the insertion of business logic into user interface implementation, in this case, a mix of business with user interface processes running from the presentation layer. An example is a loan calculator built in the loan application page. Or to fill in a customer profile page, user interface functions make calls to a repository. Obviously, such design does not comply with reusability best practices and should be rejected on the merits of tight coupling principles.

Reduction of unnecessary internal dependencies could be achieved by constructing reusable components and avoiding usage of inline functions. Therefore, an architecture proposition should support component-based implementation over library-based usage. A component-based design could be externalized and exposed to the outside world.

Application Dependency Patterns

To identify application dependencies, it is advised to rely on the various system fabric patterns discussed in Chapter 4. Although these patterns identify the arrangement of nodes and message paths in a system, they can also be used to discover and understand application dependencies. Fabric patterns can also depict the integration scheme under which an application exchanges messages in production. For reading convenience, the list of fabric patterns is provided here. For this purpose, we renamed them *application dependency patterns*:

Community dependency pattern   This is a point-to-point entity integration style, often named mesh pattern. An application that executes business transactions employs this style to connect to other applications, middleware products, and network infrastructure elements.

Community center dependency pattern   This arrangement, which resembles the network star topology, typically places an application in the center, where it exchanges information with the surrounding message exchange parties.

Message transport dependency pattern   In this scheme, an application is linked to a transport broker, such as an ESB, to trade messages with other entities on the network. Distribution and federation of applications could be achieved by employing this pattern.

Family dependency pattern   Application and related production entities are arranged in a hierarchical formation. Here, messages flow downstream from the parent application node to the offspring nodes, or upstream from the children nodes. Sibling nodes are able to communicate with each other, too.

Circular dependency pattern   A message path is formed with the arrangement of applications and its information trading parties in a circular structure. Circular business transaction is achieved with this style.

Chained dependency pattern   A linear business transaction is formed when employing this dependency pattern. Here, applications are chained to each other along with middleware, users, and network infrastructure elements.

Bridge and crossroad dependency pattern   This dependency patterns depicts the use of a broker to communicate to other applications or other entities on the network.

Compound dependency pattern   Compound patterns may consist of some or all mentioned patterns in this list.

Application and Supporting Environment Cataloging

The focus so far has been on application discovery and analysis. Application information has been gathered, and, in addition, we were able to compile facts and material about the supporting production environment. The task of cataloging, classifying, and indexing organizational assets, therefore, is now the mission. It is time to begin documenting the applications, middleware products, and network infrastructure elements.

This endeavor should not be pursued manually. There are countless asset management products on the market that offer cataloging and registration capabilities. These tools also keep track of production software and hardware versioning. Change and release control are among other additional features offered.

An effective asset management product should offer fundamental capabilities as described in the list that follows. Note that the itemized features not only provide technical information about software or hardware assets, but also make available related business facts:

Ownership   Identification of software or hardware owners and also sponsor information

License   Information that pertains to asset licensing terms, cost, and expiration

Configuration management   Current and historical configuration parameters applied to product installation, integration, and maintenance

Inventory management   Tracking in stack or on-site available licensed software components or hardware products

Maintenance   Information indicating life cycle maintenance activities for a product, such as installations, reconfiguration, migration, and applying patches

Contract   Contracts and vendor information stored to trace product upkeep agreements

Procurement   Initial cost of a product and its related components, manufacturer detail, and so on

Expenditure   Accumulative and periodic costs related to product maintenance in production

Return on investment (ROI) management   Typically measured in percentage, the incurred product revenue in relation to the initial and ongoing investment

Status   Identification of a product state in production, such as active, inactive, discontinued, removed, or relocated

Application Cataloging

When it comes to cataloging an application, the first thing to be done is to ascertain its identity. At least three identification keys would be required. First is a description of the overall application functionality and the solutions it provides to resolve business problems. Second, ownership and sponsorship information is another vital piece of information that can shed light on the application's purpose and strategy. Third, design and technical specifications are other artifacts that can elaborate on how the technological solution is devised to resolve business problems.

The contribution of the application cataloging is vital to development teams, production engineers, and executives. To achieve asset reuse, the application catalog can provide a wealth of information about an application or a system that is comprised of multiple applications. To decrease business process redundancy, architects should foster reuse of legacy implementations to leverage existing functionality.

Production engineers can also benefit from application catalogues. The entries in such a repository can provide valuable information for application deployment, configuration, and integration.

Consider the list of common fields in an application catalog for the establishment of application identity:

Ownership and sponsorship   This field is associated with the organization or executives who own an application. A sponsor may be a different entity.

Publisher   If an application is created by a software manufacturer, the publisher's information is provided.

Development team   These are application project managers, team members, and maintenance individuals.

Business purpose   This includes the business problem domain and concern statements.

Business requirements   These include an outline of business requirements and descriptions of business solutions.

Services   This field itemizes the solutions that a specific set of services offer.

Line of business   This is the affiliation of an application to a line of business or occupation.

Business group   This is the business division or departments an application is affiliated with.

Application architecture class   This field indicates the type of architecture or design pattern the application is based on, such as N-tier, client server, and more.

Application tiers   These include a list of application components and tiers, their location on a network, and solutions they provide.

Service consumers   These involve an identification of the application's consuming parties, such as online customers, business partners, and consuming applications or systems.

Development platforms   These include languages, integrated development environment (IDE), source code building tools, and libraries.

Cost of ownership   This is the cost to maintain, repair, and enhance an application in production.

Application Data Cataloging

Application dependency on data is fundamental to information sharing, persistence, and message exchange. Data cataloging, though, is one of the most significant activities that should be pursued during the application discovery and analysis. This activity entails the location and documentation of application-related repositories for their capacity, formats, data model, and more.

Cataloging data sources, such as data providers, data warehouses, or data proxies, is essential to understanding the dependencies of an application on external information. Data maintenance, such as provisioning, applying security, and modifying data models, is an additional reason to catalog data sources.

The cataloging activity should also include knowledge about application data produced internally. Monolithic applications, for example, tend to create, persist, and manage their private data. This internal information can be shared with the outside world by utilizing adapters or interfaces.

Consider the following list that includes fields of interest when pursuing the data cataloging activity:

Data sources   Types of data sources an application utilizes and their locations on the network

Data warehouse   Information about organizational data storage facilities, their locations, and access permissions

Data repositories   Information that pertains to database locations and other storage facilities that an application can access directly

Data access layers   Facts gathered about brokers or intermediaries that provide data access services and data manipulation capabilities, such as CRUD

Data capacity   Storage limit for a data source and the allowable usage capacity over time (typically yearly permissible capacity)

Data exchange format   Data layout and taxonomies used for message exchange and manipulation, such as ACORD, HL7, and XBRL

Data model   Diagrams or illustrations depicting the elements of the provided data and their relationships

Data type   Itemization of the various media a data source provides, such as text, video, and images

Cataloging Supporting Middleware and Network Infrastructure

Middleware and network infrastructure products support application operations in production. Cataloging production assets, then, would be an immense contribution to the asset and inventory management. More than anywhere else, the ever-changing production ecosystem must employ mechanisms to itemize and track network devices, platform components, servers, and a wide variety of middleware products. The number of organizational assets that take part in a production landscape could be overwhelming.

Organizations that conduct orderly fashion cataloging use the open systems interconnection of the International Standards Organization (ISO)[3] model to collect information about organizational assets. This framework describes how devices operate on a network and how hardware and software enable the communication between computers. The ISO model consists of seven stacked layers. The network infrastructure and middleware cataloging initiative, however, refers only to first four layers:

1. *Physical*—the electrical and physical networking devices that carry the data across a network
2. *Data link*—the mechanisms used to transmit data in a network, including topologies and transmission protocols
3. *Network*—switching and routing network mechanisms
4. *Transport*—the hosts and the methods they use to transport the data from end to end

The two lists that follow depict fields that capture infrastructure and middleware information. First, the infrastructure cataloging information:

Manufacturer   Information about the hardware manufacturer

Model   Hardware model or sub-model, including the manufacturing time stamp

Serial number   Hardware serial number

Device type   Identifies the role of a network device, such as routing, switching, bridging

Contract details   Contract affiliated with the rent and/or maintenance of a network device or host

Business organization   The business entity that is utilizing the infrastructure

Cost of ownership   The cost of maintaining, repairing, and enhancing infrastructure assets in production, including also the ongoing energy and air-conditioning expenditure, replacements, and upgrades

Operating system   The operating system a host uses

Capacity   CPU, memory, and disk capacity information for a particular host
   For middleware products, consider the list that follows:

Middleware category   Identifies the role of a middleware product, such as an ESB, gateway, or proxy

Publisher   Manufacturer details and date of creation

Version   Middleware version

Contact   Contract affiliated with the maintenance of a middleware product

Interfaces   Identification of middleware communication protocols and adopters

Capabilities   The functionality related to a middleware product, such as message routing, data formatting and transformation, security enforcement

Consuming applications   A list of the applications consuming a middleware product

Notes

1. Bernard Marr, *Key Performance Indicators (KPI)*, 2013, Pearson UK, p. 27
2. http://balancedscorecard.org/Resources/About-the-Balanced-Scorecard
3. http://www.iso.org/iso/home.html

PART THREE

End-State Architecture Decomposition

The art of architecture decomposition[1] has been discussed extensively in research literature during the past few decades. This research delves into the methods and explores different motives for architecture decomposition. Some focus on breaking down applications; others raise the perspective to subdivision of systems on an enterprise level. The leading cause for pursuing segmentation of an architecture, according to some studies, is chiefly rooted in improving design and increasing software component reuse. This typically calls for dissecting software implementations into smaller units. Such subdivision is performed to foster distribution of software entities, such as tiers and layers, to achieve high cohesion. Striving for high cohesion means separating software components to achieve loosely coupled design. This typically reduces architecture complexity and enables easier maintenance of software assets.

In this book, however, the justification for decomposing an end-state architecture is entrenched in promoting the practice of incremental software architecture. True, design improvement and increasing software reuse are still noble goals to achieve. Helping enterprise architects to produce a potent enterprise grand-scale design is another imperative goal that should not be ignored.

In addition to these end-state architecture decomposition benefits, the promise here is utterly clear: Before committing budgets and resources and launching software development initiatives, a grand-scale design must be certified. To accomplish this, an end-state architecture should be subdivided into smaller pieces to confirm that each of these design segments would operate flawlessly in production. This verification activity would prevent business and IT management from engaging in speculative and unproven design propositions. Note that end-state architecture decomposition methods are discussed in this part of the book (Chapters 7–11) and the verification process is largely discussed in Chapters 12–15.

Consistent with the incremental software architecture practice, end-state architecture decomposition is all about breaking down an *environment*. The term "environment" is crucial to this engagement. An environment is an ecosystem in which multiple design components collaborate to offer solutions. This is not about sectioning one application, one server, one system, or one middleware product. This is about slicing an environment that contains aggregated associations, possibly of myriad production environment assets.

Therefore, in the chapters that follow, a real-time environment is associated with certain behaviors that would be necessary to decompose. A production landscape also possesses vast knowledge to accomplish intricate business goals that ought to be broken down into smaller cells of intelligence. In addition, a production landscape is formed by recognized or undefined structures that must be segmented. Finally, an end-state architecture deployed to production that is driven by contextual aspects, such as business requirements or domains, should be divided into smaller units that are easy to understand.

The discussion of ecomposition practices in the chapters that follow focuses on three fundamental aspects:

1. End-state architecture structural decomposition
2. Dissecting an end-state architecture environment into behavioral sections
3. Breaking down an end-state architecture into volatile segments

Note

1. Grady Booch, *Object-oriented Analysis and Design*, 1994. Benjamin/Cummings. pp. 16–20.

CHAPTER 7

End-State Architecture Structural Decomposition through Classification

When an end-state enterprise architecture is proposed and put on the table for feasibility assessment, the task of understanding what it is all about begins. If the architecture is complex, perhaps most stakeholders will have difficulty comprehending what the proposed solutions of the architecture are. In most cases, the inability to decipher the design puzzle leads to deployment delays that cannot be compensated for. This is commonly attributed to a lack of a methodological process to break down a distributed environment and understand how business goals are being attained.

Another struggle to overcome is the nature of *architecture heterogeneity*. In different words, this term indicates that an end-state architecture is not simple. In fact, nothing is simple or straightforward when it comes to decrypting the language of enterprise architecture. Design heterogeneity means that an end-state architecture proposition may be composed of many patterns and styles, some of which have been devised many years ago. Other formations are being studied as we speak. And many more have not been discovered yet.

So the language of an enterprise design comes with a complex vocabulary that perhaps no one before has ever encountered. The conclusion may be disappointing to those who expect to find a clear and generic category of an end-state architecture. But more discouraging is the fact that an architecture of such magnitude cannot be classified only by applying the traditional means of identification and analysis such as design patterns or styles.

Instead, to understand what an end-state architecture stands for, and how it is devised to promote the business, the art of classification ought to focus first on the *architecture parts rather than the whole*. It would be wise to categorize sections of the design, perhaps mustering the energy to understand first what the smaller units contribute, then draw a bigger picture, a *unified identity*, for the end-state architecture.

Remember, using this method of end-state architecture classification and decomposition could also assist enterprise architects not only to improve their architecture, but also produce an effective enterprise grand-scale design.

The list that follows reviews the fundamental reasons for classifying an end-state architecture:

- Decompose the grand-scale enterprise design into structural segments.
- Understand how business goals are being achieved.
- Discover architecture technical objectives.
- Learn the language and vocabulary of enterprise architecture.
- Analyze parts of the architecture to study their business duties and technical capabilities.
- Draw a unified identity for the overall end-state architecture.
- Ultimately, enterprise architects could use this classification and decomposition approach to build a powerful enterprise architecture.

Before delving into the architecture decomposition sections, the next section emphasizes the focus on enterprise architecture by contrasting it with application architecture.

Identifying Architecture Perspectives

Call it micromanagement or anything else—there is nothing more disheartening than to watch executives making decisions about architecture details that should be left to the discretion of design and implementation teams. In lieu of being bogged down by day-to-day operations, leadership ought to lead, inspire, guide, strategize, and envision organizational direction. The bottom line is clear: Management's precious time should be dedicated to tackling the big picture—the strategic aspects of business and technological endeavors. There is no time left for running the show if it is consumed by addressing trivial architecture problems.

Part of the problem lies in pure misunderstanding of what architecture really is. Another issue is related to the confusion between architecture perspectives. Imagine an airplane hovering 40,000 feet above ground. Unless one was viewing the earth below through a telescope, details such as the eye color of a person strolling in the park or a license plate number on a whizzing car would be hard to detect. The more the airplane descends, the more details are uncovered. This simple analogy explains the difference between high-level and low-level architectures.

It is simple, yet the concept of architecture perspectives is unclear to some executives who cannot make the distinction between *application-level* and *enterprise-level* design. Unless there is a strategic discussion and decisions to make about an enterprise-level architecture, there is no justification for upper management to waste time on technical issues that could easily be addressed by developers. Efficient executives, though, understand the difference between strategy and tactics, high-level and low-level, generalization and specification, abstraction and concrete. They comprehend the important value of decision-making pertaining to solving organizational problems. They also avoid getting involved with inconsequential issues that could be undertaken by lower management.

This brings us to the realization that *application-level and enterprise-level architectures are two different views of design.* Between the two perspectives, perhaps there are mid-level architectures. But for this discussion, the drawn contract emphasizes the need to focus on what matters to enterprise architecture. In this chapter, enterprise-level design is what drives the architecture classification topic. Therefore, before moving on to the architecture structural decomposition method, let us have a look at the two in detail and understand what each level is all about.

Application-Level Architecture

Application developers understand that for constructing an application, skills and knowledge about a variety of disciplines and technologies are required. This expertise, however, is focused on a very specific necessity: implementing business goals. No matter what an application is about or what it promotes, it still requires a person who understands the business motivation for launching a software development project and the solution an application offers. Indeed, application architects and application developers understand this monumental task very well.

Scope of Application Architecture

With all that said, the scope of application building is still narrower than most enterprise architecture initiatives such as enterprise software integration or data warehouse architecture. Application architecture therefore should focus on specific business processes and activities. The emphasis also should be on a more confined range of technologies. The list that follows identifies the areas about which application architecture is typically concerned:

- Users and consuming entities
- User interface
- Business functionality and requirements
- Application tiers: presentation, business, data
- Reusable components
- Crosscutting application components
- Libraries
- Data transformation
- Application security
- Application protocols
- Message content
- Message security
- Language and script platforms
- Message marshaling and un-marshaling
- Application interfaces and adopters

Application Architecture Types

To understand better the scope application-level architecture, we must be familiar with design patterns and architecture types. There is nothing academic about application design patterns, for they convey an application fingerprint and expose an identity. A number of application architecture types are mentioned in Chapter 5 in the Application Architecture Typing section. This is discussed to explain why an identity of application architecture is also about the application structure, internal components, tiers, and behavior.

For example, the N-tier application architecture type divulges the chief reason for selecting such design. As apparent, application tiers are about separating business and/or technological concerns. That is, each tier is assigned a district responsibility for which an application must address. Breaking down an application into distinct processing units would increase reuse and enable expandability of its capabilities. The recognized signature of an application architecture, therefore, explains the scope of the provided services and reveals the perspective level of implementation.

The model view controller (MVC) application architecture is another pattern of execution. Here, not only is the separation of concerns principle addressed, but also the internal process of command delegation and component responsibilities are tackled. This is fundamental to every application with the charter of executing business processes efficiently. For that reason, the MVC resembles a state machine that manages the transition of activities. Indeed, this architecture type sheds light on the scope of the design.

Enterprise-Level Architecture

The enterprise-level architecture is what we are largely discussing in this book. This perspective level encompasses a wide range of business and technological concerns, related mostly to strategies on a grand scale. This is truly a larger scope of integration, software and hardware distribution, and message capabilities, all devised to promote the business. This means that the enterprise-architecture scope is not about controlling the manner by which specific applications are implemented.

Scope of Enterprise Architecture

This drives us to the conclusion that enterprise-level architecture is merely an overarching proposition concerned with conceptual and logical level design and generalization of enterprise solutions. In view of that, enterprise architects should be able to abstract technological solutions and generalize private instances so the products an organization sponsors are reusable and meet consumers' demands. The list that follows identifies only a few common enterprise architecture-level concerns, conveying the range of concerns addressed by enterprise operations:

- Messaging infrastructure
- Network infrastructure
- Integration
- Configuration management
- Release management
- Enterprise product integration
- Middleware installation, configuration, and maintenance
- Middleware and network infrastructure requisitions
- Contract management
- Licensing management
- Distribution of assets
- Federation of assets
- Single sign-on
- Proxies and gateways

Enterprise Architecture Types

Enterprise architecture practices, obviously, do not come without patterns and implementation styles. Since the inception of computing, patterns have played major roles in design visualization. In other words, a design pattern tells the story of implementation, deployment, and integration. On an enterprise scale, this is all about distribution of organizational software and hardware across an enterprise or even beyond. This may include the federation of assets spanning organizations, regions, and even continents.

Myriad enterprise architecture patterns can be found in computer literature. The industry has learned that architecture patterns are effective in resolving technological problems. An architecture pattern is generalized enough and can be applied to reoccurring design challenges. That is, patterns abstract problems to a degree that they can be employed for repeatable issues.

Unfortunately, enterprise architecture patterns are not pre-configured solutions in a box, delivered to propose directions to all design challenges. Enterprise architecture patterns are a far cry from instant and perfect propositions, especially on the enterprise level. On an application-level architecture, this may be the case since the solution scope is confined to a narrower range of concerns. But enterprise architecture faces monumental issues that continuously evolve. An enterprise environment never stops changing since network topologies morph into different forms. Integration and collaboration between enterprise assets constantly develop. And software and hardware configurations differ from one deployment instance to another.

The evolution of a production environment has made some enterprise architecture patterns ineffective to a certain degree; also, the diversity and magnitude of business implementations and the numerous technologies employed make it hard to type an enterprise architecture. Employing patterns that in most cases tackle issues of a narrow scope would be counterproductive. This topic is discussed in greater detail in the sections that follow.

For now, let us look at a number of industry-recognized enterprise architecture types and understand their contribution to the enterprise-level architecture perspective:

SOA   The service-oriented architecture is a pattern promoting message communication between service providers and consumers over a network by employing software components and enabling technologies. In the broader context of enterprise-level architecture, SOA fosters asset distribution and federations to achieve business and technological interoperability.

Bus   This architecture type depicts the means to promote enterprise messaging strategy by providing routing, data transformation, data augmentation, security, queuing, business rules engine, orchestration mechanisms, and more. The bus architecture is commonly employed during SOA projects.

Federated   Organizations employ this type of an enterprise architecture to enable transmission of information across business domains and partners to address business and technological interoperability. By employing this type, an enterprise achieves architecture expansion.

Distributed   As opposed to the tightly coupled monolithic implementation, the distributed architecture fosters loose coupling, by which enterprise software and hardware assets are separated to achieve reuse and agility. Architecture expansion is also attained by distributing organizational assets.

Broker   Enterprise broker-based architecture typically uses proxies or intermediaries that intercept messages to isolate parts of an architecture, enforce security, augment information, or enforce design loose coupling, and more.

Gateway   This design type enables interoperability between distinct operating environments by offering protocol transformation, message format alignment, or security model transformation, and more.

Hub-and-Spokes   Resembling a bike wheel, this architecture type arranges enterprise software and hardware entities around a central processing unit, called a hub. Enabling information exchange, message routes then connect the entities to the central hub. This architecture type is also known as the star formation.

Point-to-Point   An architecture based on this design type enables individual enterprise assets to communicate directly to each other, forming an unplanned grid of relationships. This arrangement on a network increases dependencies between systems, applications, middleware, and network infrastructure.

Application Architecture and Enterprise Architecture Scopes of Concerns

To visualize the difference between the scope of application architecture and enterprise architecture, view the example in Figure 7.1. There are two perspective layers to consider. The first is apparent on the bottom. Depicted is the application architecture scope of concerns: user interface, libraries, business logic, components, application data, application development tools, application integration tools, and application provisioning tools. The enterprise-level architecture perspective includes a number of

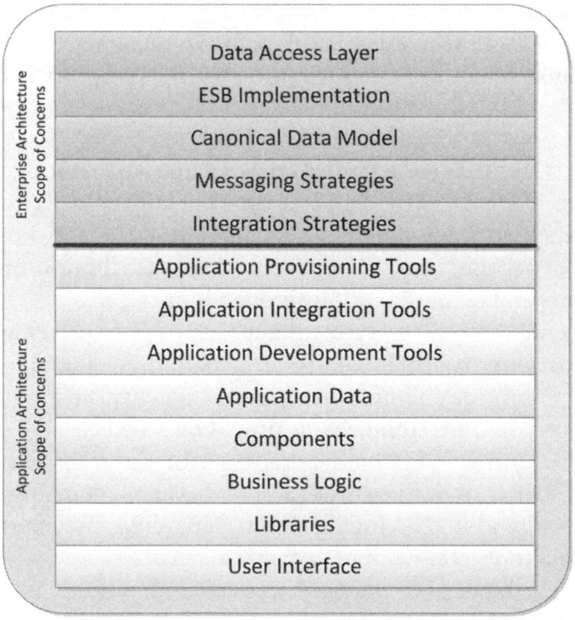

Figure 7.1   Application Architecture and Enterprise Architecture Scopes of Concerns

concerns that are addressed by executives and enterprise architects: integration and messaging strategies, enterprise canonical data model, ESB implementation, and data access layer.

Keystone Architecture Structure Classification and Decomposition Diagram

From now on, until the rest of this chapter, we are about to employ classification activities to enable the structural decomposition of an end-state architecture. So let us start with a simple method to dissect an enterprise end-state architecture environment. A systematic approach by which a proposed, or an implemented, end-state architecture can be analyzed for categorization and decomposition is presented here.

To simplify the end-state classification and decomposition process, let us start with a rudimentary diagram, named here *keystone architecture structure classification and decomposition*. But before we begin, remember that architecture is a subjective discipline. The claim is, "you end up having ten opinions when ten architects huddle around a table." This is truly remarkable, since we ponder sometimes how much of a science is enterprise architecture. Is it only about personal preferences and opinions?

Having diverse views and perspectives about an architecture is not a bad thing. In fact, the more opinions are thrown around, the better the outcome of the analysis. One thing must be considered, though: A unified stand about an architecture assessment could save the business from calamity. Therefore, the preliminary steps of architecture categorization typically yield a variety of views, each of which should be analyzed with a great sense of responsibility to maximize the quality of the inspection process.

The sections that follow explain how the keystone architecture structure classification and decomposition diagram skeleton is constructed. The skeleton is merely a frame in which decomposed segments of the end-state architecture will be placed for categorization and analysis. Consider the steps to prepare the diagram:

Identify scales of architecture concerns   The concerns of an architecture are presented by the two axes of the diagram (see Figure 7.2): *architecture decoupling* scale (x axis) and *architecture distribution* scale (y axis). To be able to categorize and decompose an architecture these measurements can shed light on the implementation motivation and how the design fulfills business goals.

Establish architecture environment panels   The keystone diagram also requires means for decomposing an end-state architecture and categorizing its components. . Therefore, architecture panels should be embedded in the diagram to define the boundaries of end-state architecture segments (see Figure 7.3). As apparent, the four panels named mesh, federated, centralized, and monolithic will contain segments of the decomposed end-state architecture and obviously help classifying parts of this enterprise grand-scale design.

The sections that follow explain in detail these keystone architecture structure classification and decomposition diagram elements.

Identify Scales of Architecture Concerns

The keystone method for architecture classification and decomposition calls for identifying two chief architecture concerns to be depicted in a diagram. These pivot design apprehensions are the center of the initial categorization. When it comes to enterprise architecture concerns, two parameters always come to mind: the *magnitude of design distribution* and *design decoupling levels*. No worries. All will be clear in a moment.

Again, to be able to categorize and decompose an architecture, consider the two parameters that will help us assess a design. These concerns are depicted in Figure 7.2. For preparing the categorization diagram, position the concerns as seen in the illustration: The architecture decoupling scale is the horizontal axis (known as x axis) and the architecture distribution scale is the vertical axis (y axis).

Architecture decoupling scale (x)   This measurement indicates the degree to which a design is decoupled on a scale from 1 to 10. A tightly coupled design (lower numbers on the scale) indicates that its elements, such as components, applications, middleware products, and even network infrastructure are highly dependent on each other. Higher numbers on the scale mean a loosely coupled design, in which enterprise assets are not as dependent on each other.

Architecture distribution scale (y)   The vertical measurement quantifies the distribution value of a design (from 1 to 10). Lower numbers indicate the design is less distributed, containing assets such as monolithic applications. Higher values, however, pertain to greater distribution of organizational assets, such as in a federated architecture scenario.

Add Architecture Environment Panels to the Keystone Architecture Structure Classification and Decomposition Diagram

So far, we have established two design concerns for the end-state architecture: decoupling and distribution. Both are typical areas of interest and challenge for an architecture environment. Combining the design decoupling and distribution scales in a classification and decomposition diagram will allow later categorization of any end-state architecture portion. As discussed earlier, the entire architecture is not subject to classification as of yet, since now we are focused on decomposing an end-state architecture.

We are not ready yet for the classification and decomposition process. The next step calls for defining the types of architectures this diagram supports. As illustrated in Figure 7.3, we are required to position four architecture panels in the keystone architecture structure classification and decomposition diagram:

- Monolithic architecture panel
- Mesh architecture panel
- Centralized architecture panel
- Federated architecture panel

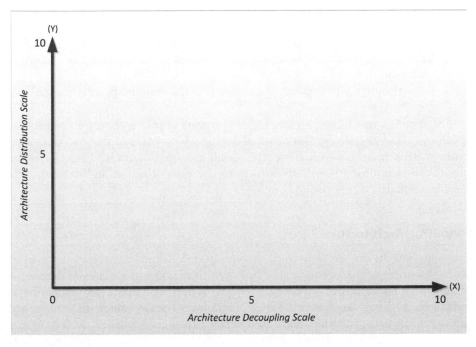

Figure 7.2   Scales of Architecture Concerns

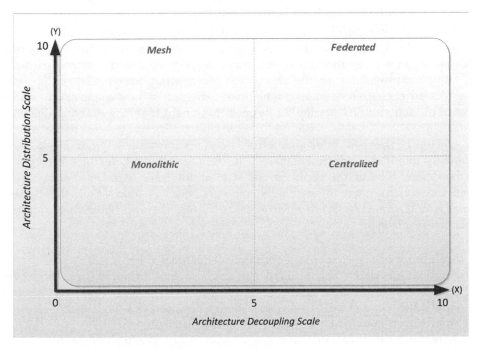

Figure 7.3   Architecture Environment Panels in Keystone Diagram

Now, these chief questions come to mind:

1. What architecture category does each panel represent?
2. What are the technical mechanisms employed to deliver business solutions in each panel?
3. How should the placement of the panels in the diagram be determined?

The sections that follow answer these questions in preparation for the end-state classification and decomposition process, during which parts of the end-state architecture will be matched with the corresponding diagram panels. Thus, let us first study the vital contribution of the panels to the categorization and decomposition upcoming initiative.

Monolithic Architecture Panel

As is apparent in Figure 7.3, the monolithic architecture panel is placed in the lower-left corner of the keystone structure architecture classification and decomposition diagram. This location is where the design decoupling and the design distribution axes intersect. They cross each other at their lowest scale values. In other words, the monolithic architecture panel would encompass design entities, such as systems and/or their related applications, middleware, and network infrastructure classified as tightly coupled and non-distributed.

Monolithic Architecture Technical Environment

In essence, the monolithic architecture panel defines an environment boundary for end-state architecture entities that matches the profile of monolithic implementations. This means that an application in this panel, for example, would subscribe to the old-fashioned monolithic profile of software construction. Specifically, this application's design is characterized as autonomous, extremely tightly coupled, containing most of the functionality needed for its operations, hard to separate, and challenging to maintain.

Obviously, the monolithic architecture panel is named this way not only because it contains monolithic implementations. The term monolithic here, foremost, applies to the design type of the analyzed end-state architecture segment. Furthermore, when categorizing an end-state architecture segment as monolithic, the classification is determined by a few environmental factors that are observed during the architecture analysis:

Scalability of deployment   Poor implementation scaling
Application tiers   Single-tiered applications: user, business logic, and data bundled in a single code base
Application codebase   Lack of modularity, deployed to a single host
Application components   Components not distributed
Application integration   Coupled application data and functionality
Overall integration   Limited integration, minimal distribution of assets, lack of intermediaries, some degree of interfaces, all resources attached to a single host

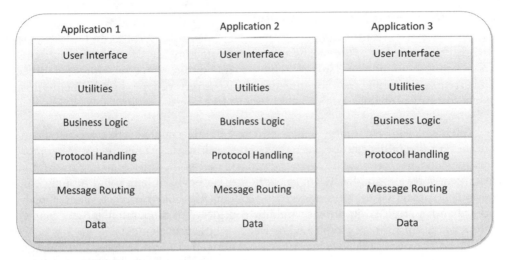

Figure 7.4   Monolithic Architecture Environment

A monolithic architecture environment would look like the one depicted in Figure 7.4. Note the single-tiered applications, limited asset distribution, and tightly coupled implementations.

The Business Perspective of a Monolithic Environment

From a business perspective, the monolithic architecture environment introduces a number of disadvantages that most organizations attempt to cope with. The chief issue is lack of business nimbleness: On one hand, modifications to such an environment are so challenging that the efforts to mend the design outweigh the benefits. On the other hand, revamping the systems and applications involved is an undertaking that few executives would consider because of strained budgets and time-to-market constraints. The only method to manage a monolithic architecture, as per some organizations, is to throw more hardware and other middleware resources to compensate for the lack of business agility. This approach rarely yields positive outcomes as the expense rises exponentially.

There are, however, successful initiatives to bypass the constraints imposed by monolithic environments. Instead of replacing such a challenging architecture, some solutions focus on interfaces and adapters to externalize the business functionality of monolithic implementations and distribute them across the organization. This solution is the lesser of two evils, since the core monolithic environment is merely wrapped around with interfaces.

Mesh Architecture Panel

As apparent in Figure 7.3, the mesh architecture panel is placed in the upper-left corner of the keystone architecture structure classification and decomposition diagram. This location indicates that a mesh architecture is identified as tightly coupled or somewhat loosely coupled, and moderately or extremely distributed. This assertion is based on the coupling and distribution scales of the classification diagram.

Mesh Architecture Technical Environment

An end-state architecture section that is placed in this panel subscribes to the mesh design characteristics. This means that the architecture elements, such as systems, applications, and network infrastructure, communicate directly with each other. This style is also known as the point-to-point architecture type, by which enterprise assets form relationships implemented by message routes, without the employment of brokers.

Such a design environment is considered tightly coupled when a considerable number of dependencies between end-state architecture assets exist. The more relationships are formed, the more tightly coupled is the environment. In extreme instances, software and hardware assets in a mesh environment could be fully connected; in other words, all architecture elements are linked to each other. On the other hand, a mesh environment would be considered as moderately loosely coupled if fewer relationships are established between architecture elements.

From the distribution perspective, as mentioned, a mesh architectural environment could be classified as moderately to extremely distributed because of its location in the keystone architecture structure classification and decomposition diagram. That is, elements of architecture positioned in close proximity to each other, perhaps in a sub-network, may exchange messages across short production environment distances, namely, moderately distributed. A mesh architecture, however, could span across organizations, production landscapes, and even regions or continents. This architecture would be categorized as extremely distributed.

Figure 7.5 illustrates a mesh architecture type. It brings to mind the concept of the community fabric pattern, discussed in Chapter 4. Indeed, schematically they bear a

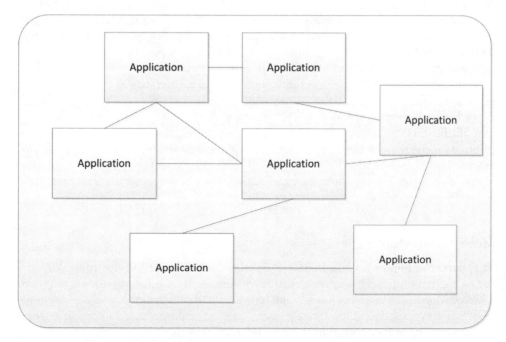

Figure 7.5   Mesh Architecture Style

resemblance to each other. But here, the perspective is even wider since the discussion revolves around classifying an architecture (not just a fabric pattern) and the solution it proposes to meet business goals.

The Business Perspective of Mesh Architecture

This brings us to the business perspective of our discussion. How does the mesh architecture category facilitate the delivery of business imperatives? What are the advantages of such an environment? These are only a few questions that should be answered when categorizing a section of an end-state architecture and delving into the business aspects of the design.

There is no good news on this level, either. The chief reason is that the mesh architecture environment is not considered structured. In many instances there is no strong driving strategy behind such organically grown integration. Software and hardware assets seem randomly connected because there is no long-term integration and enterprise-messaging plan. The web of message routes tends to grow with every new deployment. Maintenance, monitoring, and configuration efforts become more challenging. As a result, *new business initiatives must muddle through the complex architecture*, an effort consumed by an intricate production environment.

Centralized Architecture Panel

As depicted in Figure 7.3, the centralized architecture panel is located in the lower-right section of the categorization diagram. Any end-state architecture segment placed in this diagram panel would be classified as moderately to extremely loosely coupled, and non-distributed to fairly distributed. The decoupling and distribution scaling of the diagram makes this determination.

This architecture formation is common in production environments. It is widely employed to integrate systems, applications, middleware, and network entities. This pattern resembles the star network topology, and from a system fabric perspective, it is known as the community center fabric pattern (discussed in in Chapter 4). Moreover, in software architecture terms, this design type is recognized as hub-and-spokes. Despite the multiple labels, the concept is clear. A central processing unit, whichever architecture component it might be, serves as a hub and provides services to its subscribing consumers. In this scenario, there is very little direct interaction between the consumers themselves. They still can talk to each other, but only through the hub position in the center.

Centralized Architecture Technical Environment

It is easy to understand why such a centralized architecture is so compelling in certain production environments. First, comparing it to the mesh architecture, the configuration and integration efforts are not as challenging. The centralized architecture arrangement on a network would require fewer message routes. To understand better this point, recall a related comparison between the community and the community center fabric patterns (refer to the Community Center Fabric Pattern section in Chapter 4). Similarly, here five applications arranged in a fully connected mesh architecture formation would yield ten message routes. To enable communication between consumers with the centralized architecture, only five message exchange paths would be required.

Second, by definition, the hub offers reusable services, offloading message routing responsibilities, and in certain cases, business logic implementation duties from its subscribing consumers. This idea obviously promotes reuse and functionality consolidation. Other advantages are affiliated with the simplicity of the design. The centralized architecture seems more stylized than the mesh. Perhaps the star-like integration shape gives the impression that architecture elements are more organized by centering on a concern. In this case, the hub represents a focal point, an area of interest that serves motivated consumers. This architecture approach is illustrated in Figure 7.6.

The chief challenge with any centralized architecture is the dependencies that service consumers form on hubs. In other words, if the hub, the central design element that connects all service subscribers, fails, the entire centralized structure shuts down as well. This is known as a single-point-of-failure effect. True, adequate scalability could prevent the discontinuation of the operation. However, the cost of maintaining and monitoring a large centralized architecture could be overwhelming. This may include vertical or horizontal scaling or even adding failover and high-availability (HA) environments.[1]

Another issue that must be taken into consideration when designing a centralized formation is related to workload management. The term "workload" indicates the volume of messages that might flow back and forth from the central hub. The hub may buckle under the burden of high volume of information exchanges. This pressure point could introduce major challenges to system and application performance and ultimately affect response time. Such delays in service delivery typically affect customer satisfaction and harm business goals.

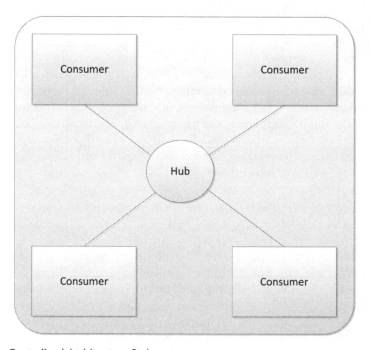

Figure 7.6   Centralized Architecture Style

Centralized Architecture Business Considerations

Despite the simplicity of the centralized architecture and its potential to form a loosely coupled operating environment, in some architecture assessment cases there may not be any particular business justification for such a design. Some would even argue that all the business organization needs is a solid and agile implementation and integration. Those who claim it doesn't matter how a particular architecture fulfills its business goals take this argument to the extreme.

But understanding what the centralized architecture offers could shed light on how the design intends to accomplish business goals. Again, this architecture type and the capabilities and risks it introduces should be assessed based upon its ability to grow the business.

Business operations based on a centralized architecture are typically vulnerable to a number of risks that could be detrimental to an organization:

- Crucial business implementation is located in a centralized hub that may fail to provide consistent services.
- A central business processing unit may not be capable to sustain an increase of unexpected volume of consumers.
- A centralized business operation would not be able to offer an efficient federated implementation to fulfill business interoperability (see the next section).

Federated Architecture Panel

The federated architecture panel is positioned in the upper-right corner of the key-stone architecture structure classification and decomposition diagram (Figure 7.3). This implies that any of the end-state architecture segments that will be dropped in this panel would range from the mildly to extremely loosely coupled formation and from a somewhat to a very distributed design. These measurements are established upon the decoupling and distribution scales in the diagram.

Federated Architecture Technical Environment

Since the federated architecture is the definitive means for extending message exchange capabilities beyond a single production environment, it is typically employed to transmit information over long network distances. This design's aptitude explains why organizations employ it to address information sharing with other related organizations or with remote partners.

Sharing data across organizations would also necessitate the integration of an enterprise message bus (ESB) to fulfill the concept of federation. But this may not be sufficient. Since the information would travel long distances and span organizations that host distinct operating environments, gateways could be also a part of the integration. A gateway is a message interceptor positioned between two different environments to enable message and security model transformation, and even data format alignments. The outcome of such an undertaking is clear: *facilitating technology interoperability*. Figure 7.7 illustrates a model for federated architecture, in which a gateway and an ESB enable messages to the subscribing consumers.

Instead of employing a true bus technology, some organizations deploy a software proxy in each business region devised to enable technical interoperability. The method

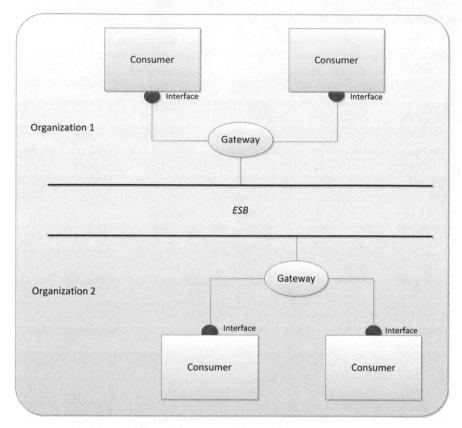

Figure 7.7   Federated Architecture Style

of using brokers to connect each production environment only increases integration challenges. Efficient federation then should be driven by technologies that facilitate architecture expansion and boost message distribution—not by employing local software broker functionalities.

If a single ESB could not accomplish such transmission task, chaining multiple ESBs can carry information over longer distances. This powerful message-routing method is illustrated in Figure 7.8. Note that each business region accommodates an ESB in its production boundary. The chaining mechanism then enables message exchange between organizations.

Federated Architecture Business Perspective

From a business perspective, the federated architecture permits two or more enterprises, each with a distinct business model, to exchange services by employing appropriate middleware and network infrastructure. This concept of *business interoperability* is fulfilled by information sharing across dispersed domains. In comparison, the centralized, mesh, and monolithic architectures are not suited for such business goals. It would be inappropriate, therefore, to federate information with these types of architectures since they do not provide the proper mechanisms for data transmission over such long distances. Any attempt to substitute a true federated design with a centralized

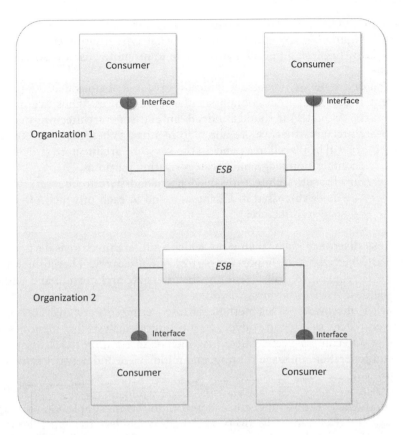

Figure 7.8   Chaining ESBs

or mesh architecture, for example, would result in harsh and irreversible business consequences.

Other business challenges to consider before embarking on federating information across organizations are the tremendous enterprise investments for acquiring proper technologies and personnel to carry out large-scale integration projects. Indeed, this is not a single project. There may be multiple and parallel initiatives across all organizations involved in planning business interoperability. The duration of such implementation could extend over a few years. The outcome is unpredictable and the risk is high. The business strategy, therefore, must be clear and the mission should elaborate on milestones and goals. In this case adopting the incremental software architecture approach could reduce unnecessary risks. Furthermore, small organizations should not pursue federated architecture initiatives because of the large implementation scope.

Discovering and Classifying Sub-Architectures

The keystone architecture structure classification and decomposition diagram is ready. So far, we were able to establish the architecture decoupling (x axis) and architecture distribution (y axis) scales, as depicted in Figure 7.2. At this point, we also understand the reasons for positioning a decomposed architecture segment in a particular diagram panel (Figure 7.3). Now it is also clear what type of architecture each panel represents. How the design in each panel is able to promote business goals is another palpable aspect.

Since an end-state architecture is typically vast, it is obvious that the production environment it represents will contain smaller architectures. Thus, we name them *sub-architectures*. As odd as it sounds, indeed, an end-state architecture may contain nested sub-architectures that we are about to identify. When the time comes, each sub-architecture will be placed in a panel in the keystone architecture structure classification and decomposition diagram for categorization purposes.

To ascertain what sub-architectures make up an end-state architecture, we employ two discovery methods discussed in Chapters 8 and 9, each of which offers distinct views in the end-state architecture:

Business discovery   The manner in which a sub-architecture is devised to fulfill business objectives is an important part of our discovery. Therefore, a business analysis is required to drill down into the end-state architecture and understand how the design drives business solutions.

Technical discovery   This method for discovering sub-architectures contained in the end-state architecture advocates a technical analysis that identifies a number of architectural aspects. These may include integration styles, asset distribution and federation, message routing, and middleware and network infrastructure entities.

Indeed, the task of sub-architecture identification seems simple. Combining both, the technical and the business discoveries methods would lead to identification of various sub-architectures that will be used later to populate the keystone architecture structure classification and decomposition diagram.

For an end-state architecture that has already been implemented and deployed to production, we ought to analyze the tangible environment and understand the integration. Leveraging the tools for topology mapping discussed in Chapter 6 could also assist in identifying relationships between architecture components and ascertaining patterns of design.

So stay tuned.

Note

1. High-availability environment is typically a redundant deployment environment that offers failover capabilities in case a system fails to perform.

CHAPTER 8

Business Analysis Drives End-State Architecture Structural Decomposition

In most cases, implementations of business processes could be discovered in different segments of an end-state architecture. The mission then is to identify sub-architectures in an end-state architecture by analyzing the business activities and the manner in which they achieve business goals. Doing this would ultimately help dissecting an end-state architecture into smaller design sections. This analysis may render answers to the vital questions that follow:

- What lines of business does the sub-architecture support? For example, lines of business of an insurance firm may include car insurance, home insurance, or life insurance.
- What type of business services does the sub-architecture offer? For instance, banking services online may include opening accounts, changing passwords, paying bills, transferring money, and more.
- How does the sub-architecture deliver business services? Does it employ applications, components, and middleware? Does it leverage a Web-based user interface? What data sources are being used to deliver business services?

There might be instances where an end-state architecture, however, would not divulge business implementations in the overall design. This would introduce challenges to the architecture classification efforts. In such case, refer to Chapter 9 that elaborates on end-state architecture decomposition by pursuing technical analysis practices.

Pursuing Business Analysis to Discover Sub-Architectures

One of the most effective business analysis methods for discovering sub-architectures in an end-state architecture environment is tracing business transactions. These message exchanges between architecture elements, such as systems and their encompassed entities, such as applications and components, could uncover one or more sub-architectures in the overall end-state design. The incentive for this discovery effort is to understand how sub-architectures satisfy business needs.

The fact that an end-state architecture can be broken down into business views makes this process utterly compelling. Furthermore, the decisions that drive technical implementations are also uncovered by the manner in which a sub-architecture executes organizational business strategies. This array of discoveries, though, offers a great deal of information about an end-state architecture implementation and its justification to exist.

The list that follows includes a number of business analysis tasks that can assist with finding sub-architectures:

- Identify business transactions and trace message exchange routes between systems, applications, services, and other affiliated components
- Group architecture elements, such as applications, components, and data thought to execute business transactions
- Discover candidate sub-architectures

Group Business Services to Discover Candidate Sub-Architectures

To understand how parts of an end-state architecture are related to business services and how these services form sub-architectures, let us look at Figure 8.1. In this illustration, the online banking Web site consists of business processes delivered by applications and associated components. Middleware and network infrastructure products that enable trading of information between the banking services support these business implementations.

Furthermore, the supporting middleware and network infrastructure elements enable message exchange by leveraging routers and possibly intermediating middleware brokers. There is a reason why these supporting entities are not displayed in Figure 8.1: The focus here is on the business aspects that drive the formation of sub-architectures. Thus the technical aspects are hidden.

But even before tagging sub-architectures, grouping business services, tracing business transactions, and locating data sources would be a good point to start from. In Figure 8.1, we then observe four groups of business services delivered by architecture entities:

1. *Account Reporting Services*. This part of the end-state architecture, shown in the upper-left corner of the illustration, enables bank customers to view their bank accounts' balances, further drill down into each account activities, and even obtain account statements to view debits and credits. A repository, named in the illustration "Data," is also deployed to store reporting information.
2. *Account Management Services*. As depicted in the upper-right corner of illustration, the end-state architecture includes capabilities devised to open and close bank accounts, dispute charges, and set alerts. A database, shared with the account reporting services, is also a part of this business service group
3. *Bill Pay Application*. This portion of the end-state architecture facilitates the scheduling of invoices and bill payments to companies and individuals. This application uses internal data used for billing information.

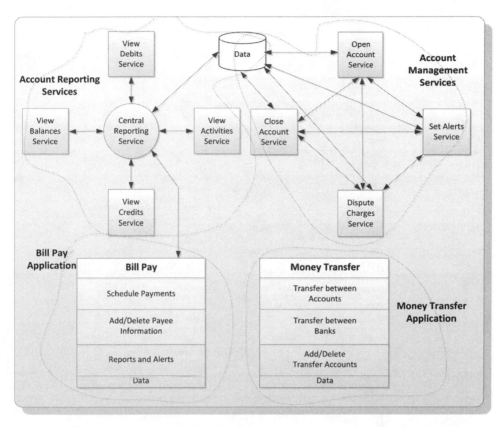

Figure 8.1   Business Services in End-State Architecture

4. *Money Transfer Application*. This business capability enables transferring funds between accounts at the bank or to other banks. An internal data repository is earmarked for this application.

As depicted in Figure 8.1, the business analysis renders four groups of business services. As apparent, data repositories have been also located, providing information to both business services. At first glance, we discover that each group employs a different architecture type to meet business requirements. This is determined by the structural arrangement of the business services and their affiliated components on the network. The next section discusses how business analysis activities pursue the classification of sub-services, and promote end-state architecture decomposition, in the deployed banking environment.

Employ Business Analysis to Discover Sub-Architectures

Now, we are ready to shift our attention from grouping business services to establishing sub-architectures. Specifically, finding out which group of business services make up *candidate sub-architectures* will then be our next step. In view of that,

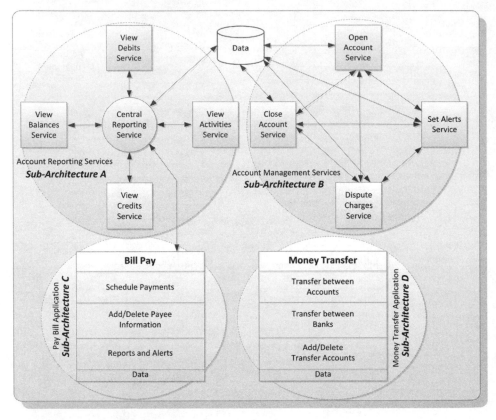

Figure 8.2   Candidate Sub-Architectures

Figure 8.2 not only illustrates the banking applications and services, but also shows the encircled candidate sub-architectures—these are the products of our business discovery efforts.

To summarize the business analysis findings, as illustrated in Figure 8.2, consider the candidate sub-architectures list that follows:

> *Sub-architecture A.* This design contains the account reporting services group, which offers reporting capabilities. The discovered sub-architecture A includes five related services: central reporting service, view debits service, view activities service, view credits service, and view balances service.
>
> *Sub-architecture B.* Recognized as account management services in the sub-architecture B formation is a collection of related services offering account management capabilities. This assortment includes the open account service, set alerts service, dispute charges service, and close account service.
>
> *Sub-architecture C.* The bill pay application, along with its embedded functionality and data, is now a part of sub-architecture C.
>
> *Sub-architecture D.* Similarly, the money transfer application, along with its contained business processes and data, is now a part of sub-architecture D.

The outcome of our business analysis uncovers the four candidate sub-architectures. What make them sub-architectures are the business drivers and the type of business services these designs are devised to offer. It is not mandatory to accept these findings, as these are merely sub-architecture candidates. The final analysis may advocate different sub-architecture formations.

Remember, the goal of the end-state decomposition process is to pursue enterprise-level analyses by discovering and classifying sub-architectures. Therefore, here the inspection of the end-state architecture should center on environments, business transactions, and the collaborative efforts of systems and applications to fulfill business goals. Stand-alone entities such as applications or components should not be the focus of our attention.

Raising the perspective level beyond the application architecture-level, therefore, is the guiding principle for this exercise. This brings us to the conclusion that sub-architectures C and D should be merged into a single sub-architecture for the reason that each represents a single application, not an environment. Yes, let us focus here on the environment rather than on narrow implementations. Consequently, the consolidation of these sub-architectures yields Figure 8.3, in which sub-architecture C depicts the bill pay and money transfer business applications.

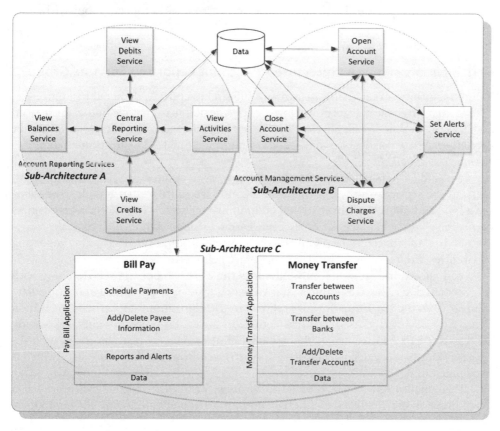

Figure 8.3   Consolidated Sub-Architectures

Pursue Business Analysis to Classify Sub-Architectures

The decisive moment has come. Now we are ready to take a second look at Figure 8.3 and classify the sub-architectures. This categorization activity should not be difficult. At this point, after the business analysis rendered the three groups of banking services, the task for categorizing the sub-architectures is easier than it seems.

So what categories should we apply to our discovered sub-architectures? The obvious answer is easy to guess. The guidelines for categorizing sub-architecture environments have been already defined in the Add Architecture Environment Panels to the Keystone Architecture Structure Classification and Decomposition Diagram section in Chapter 7. There we learned about the four different architecture types that can characterize the sub-architecture environments: monolithic, mesh, centralized, and federated. These landscapes are discussed there in detail along with their business drivers and motivations.

Since these architecture panel environments have been already defined, they serve now as guiding principles for categorization and end-state architecture decomposition. The sub-architecture classification process, though, begins now. In the sections that follow, each sub-architecture is put on the business analysis table and classified according to its architecture attributes, message exchange routes, data sharing, and integration. Remember, however, that business aspects should drive the categorization effort.

Classification of Sub-Architecture A: Account Reporting Services Group

There is nothing easier than categorizing sub-architecture A, depicted in Figure 8.3. The formation of the central reporting service (the dominant service in this formation) and its constituent services—view debits service, view activities service, view credit service, and view balances service—determines the ultimate classification verdict: It is a *centralized architecture*.

It would be impossible to mistake it for any other architecture type. The arrangement of the services on the network and the message route formations clearly resemble a hub-and-spokes architecture—a community center fabric pattern. The business perspective of such classification is even easier to understand: The central reporting service, in the center, generalizes the concept of the offered account reporting capabilities, no matter what kind of reports are being provided.

As depicted in Figure 8.3, not only does the central reporting service along with its associated services, resemble a star network topology, the added reporting data repository to the star formation, as is shown in the illustration, strengthens the notion that we are facing a centralized architecture. In the center of it, the central reporting service acts as a hub, of which the responsibilities are clear: It offers to its subordinate services banking account information retrieved from the data store with which it is connected.

It all makes sense now. Even the business justification for delivering such a design type is straightforward. There is nothing bad about employing the centralized architecture as long as the pressure point, meaning the hub, does not buckle under from the demands of the surrounding consumers. There is no intention here to discuss the technical challenges of such deployment; this will be elaborated upon when time comes in Chapter 9. From a business perspective, however, the stakes are high if the business continuity fails. Therefore, in such circumstances, the business requirements must include nonfunctional specifications, by which performance and availability must be addressed by technical implementations.

Updating the Keystone Diagram with Sub-Architecture A

We all have been waiting for this moment. Now, we are about to drop the classified sub-architecture A along with its containing business applications and services in the proper keystone diagram panel. This is not only the process of the sub-architecture classification, but also the beginning of the end-state architecture decomposition.

All is clear. There is no dispute about matching the keystone diagram panel to sub-architecture A. Indeed, they correspond—both represent a common design type: *centralized architecture*. Figure 8.4 illustrates the recording of the keystone diagram update after affiliating sub-architecture A with the centralized architecture diagram panel.

Note that the centralized architecture panel in the keystone architecture structure classification and decomposition diagram spans from 5 to 10 on the architecture decoupling axis and from 0 to 5 on the architecture distribution axis. Both x-axis and y-axis values for the centralized architecture panel space leave a large space for positioning corresponding centralized types of sub-architectures. In accordance with the business

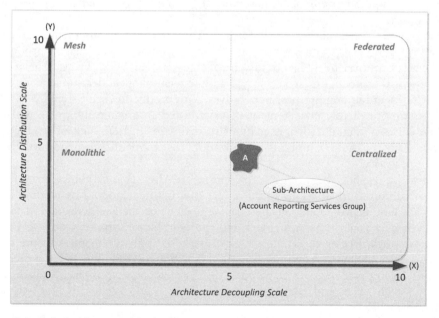

Figure 8.4   Sub-Architecture A in the Keystone Diagram Centralized Architecture Panel

analysis, it seems that sub-architecture A is considered to some extent loosely coupled (near the x axis's 5 value) and fairly distributed (near the y axis's 5 value).

Consider the reasons for positioning sub-architecture A in that specific location in the keystone's centralized architecture diagram panel:

> *Architecture decoupling consideration.* Sub-architecture A is somewhat loosely coupled (axis x) because its business applications and services are *separated*, exchanging business transactions through message routes. Centralized architectures like this are characteristically not extremely loosely coupled.
>
> *Architecture decoupling consideration.* The *dependency level* of the comprising entities in sub-architecture A is objectively high and thus the design is considered slightly loosely coupled. Star formations are typically classified this way because of the tightly formed relationship between the hub and its consuming entities.
>
> *Architecture distribution consideration.* Sub-architecture A is not federated since it does not span organizations or production environments. Yet its design is somewhat distributed, as it is typical for centralized architectures to reside in a single production environment.

Classifying Sub-Architecture B: Account Management Services Group

Perhaps the most common architecture type found in most production environments is the point-to-point style, a community fabric pattern. In this book, we name it "mesh," and it is easy to understand why. At times, the web of message routes is so vast and complex that organizations would not even consider simplifying it. The cluttered arrangement of enterprise production assets, such as applications and middleware, seems so random that operation engineers have very little knowledge about the environment they support.

So how is the mesh architecture formed? Year after year, deployment of layers on top of layers and endless integrations and configuration initiatives make a production environment unmanageable and uncontrollable—a real Wild West. This unruly landscape is the product of arbitrary and ad hoc technological decisions, made while rushing to meet burning business imperatives. This production ecosystem is a result of long-running negligible management that permitted an organically grown real-time deployment environment that is arduous to maintain. Indeed, lack of strategy and shortsightedness can commit an organization to exponential expenditure that is difficult to justify.

Now, let us shift the attention to Figure 8.3. After a quick glance at its design style, sub-architecture B seems to fall under the mesh category. The tactic for executing account management business services divulges the inefficiency and lack of style. Not only could the deployment and configuration efforts of such a formation on the network decelerate time-to-market, but also applying changes to the architecture would be time-consuming. Environments like this only increase maintenance and monitoring cost because almost any design elements in sub-architecture B are linked to each other. Indeed, many organizations should avoid this point-to-point implementation.

Ironically, it is easy to decipher sub-architecture B. The business relationships formed by the connecting message paths tell the story, giving a clue about the intent of the design to meet business objectives. Simply put, this is about the management of bank accounts and the capability to open and close them. Setting alerts and dispute charges are other features offered by this sub-architecture.

Sub-architecture B does not offer architecture elasticity. Design elasticity is about the ability to apply quick changes to an integrated environment. It is also about the capability of the business to deliver products to consumers rapidly. In fact, there is nothing nimble about the promise of the design. By all accounts, business agility is not even considered.

Updating the Keystone Diagram with Sub-Architecture B

It's time to drop sub-architecture B into the proper keystone diagram panel. This is not a challenging task. Obviously, the mesh panel environment is the best match, since both bear the characteristics of the point-to-point architecture type. Figure 8.5 illustrates the keystone diagram after sub-architecture B was placed in the mesh panel. Note that sub-architecture A had been positioned in the diagram too. It is located in the centralized architecture panel.

Note that in the keystone classification diagram the mesh architecture panel spans from 0 to 5 on the architecture decoupling axis and from 5 to 10 on the architecture distribution axis. Both x-axis and y-axis values for the mesh architecture panel allow a sizeable area for placing the corresponding sub-architecture B. As shown in Figure 8.5, sub-architecture B's location in the mesh diagram panel implies that its design is considered tightly coupled, valued 2.5 out of 10 on architecture decoupling axis. On the other hand, the business analysis calls for placing sub-architecture B near value 5 on the architecture distribution axis.

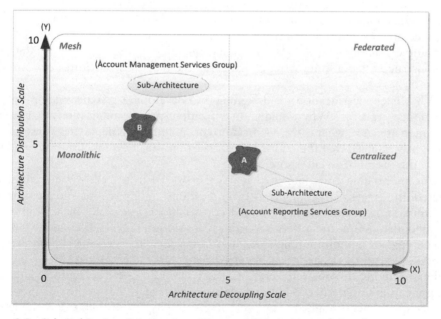

Figure 8.5   Sub-Architecture B in Keystone Diagram Mesh Architecture Panel

Consider the reasons for positioning sub-architecture B in that specific location in the keystone diagram panel:

Architecture decoupling consideration. For the most part, sub-architecture B is fully connected since all the services in the design are linked to each other and the data repository. Such high dependency between the services, due to the point-to-point message paths arrangement, puts sub-architecture B in the tightly coupled range.

Architecture distribution consideration. In the overall design, the sub-architecture B's services seem not to spread over a long network distance. Therefore, the design is not considered highly distributed.

Architecture decoupling and distribution considerations. Properly operating mesh types of architectures are ordinarily not too distributed, nor are they excessively loosely coupled. Note the emphasis is on designs that yield acceptable performing systems. As discussed earlier, large deployment environments made up of massive mesh architectures that span multiple production environments are destined to fail.

Classifying Sub-Architecture C: Pay Bill and Money Transfer Application Group

There is not much surprise in finding that many organizations still host, maintain, and monitor monolithic systems or applications. The early era of computing left us with myriad tightly coupled implementations, often referred to as legacy systems, that are impossible to break down into smaller services. Ancient technologies would not facilitate the creation of reusable and distributed components. Nor did architecture best practices and policies foster agile implementations.

This was part of the computing history. Now, with advanced technologies and a better understanding of how to boost performance and master distribution of assets, we should be able to avoid monolithic architectures and environments. With the superb technological advantages of today, it is mind-boggling to run across newly designed and constructed monolithic systems that carry the technical signatures of yesterday. Isn't it?

What is the justification for designing and developing systems resting on past architecture practices? Why would an organization sponsor applications that are too big to manage? And what is the justification for building and deploying a system that is so tightly coupled that the efforts to externalize its business functionality would be beyond the means of an enterprise?

The monolithic environment that was discovered in the end-state architecture depicted in Figure 8.3 contains two applications: bill pay and money transfer. The illustration reveals tightly coupled constructions, each of which maintains a dedicated data store and offers reporting capabilities. This self-contained design is archetypal to monolithic implementation, of which the dependency on external business applications or services seems nonexistent.

Furthermore, in sub-architecture C the code base seems to be located within the application's single tier. Additional tiers are not found, nor is the distribution of software components applied. The most staggering aspect of such sub-architecture, though, is that the data is not shared with the account reporting or account management capabilities delivered by sub-architecture A and B.

With such a design style, the execution of business goals is utterly challenging. The tightly coupled implementation would not permit separation of business concerns. That is, applying modifications to the already deployed application would require additional resources and budgets. But the difficulties of applying rapid alterations to an existing application functionality would not always harm the business in a serious manner. Most organizations have learned how to address such problems. The most damaging aspect to the business, nevertheless, is the inability to alter quickly a monolithic implementation when business strategies and visions change.

The symptom of business stagnation because of technical limitations can indeed impede commerce growth.

Sub-architecture C also offers a view into the environment formed by the two monolithic banking applications. The bill pay and money transfer implementations weigh on the production landscape they create. In other words, the term "monolithic" also applies to the space shaped by the systems or applications of that kind. Such an environment with agility limitations negatively affects any business implementation.

One would argue that since the monolithic applications in sub-architecture C already contain all the components they need to operate independently without relying on external applications and resources, the integration efforts in production must be minimal. This assertion holds some truth. However, the challenges of cumbersome and inflexible design overshadow the benefits of quick and minimal integration such as configuration and message routing.

Updating the Keystone with Sub-Architecture C

The time has come to place sub-architecture C, the last part of the design depicted in Figure 8.6, into the appropriate keystone diagram panel. There is nothing hard about

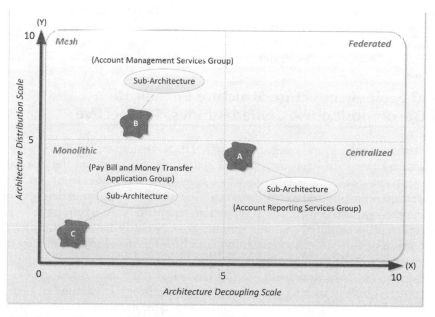

Figure 8.6   Sub-Architecture C in Keystone Diagram Monolithic Architecture Panel

this task. The business analysis discussed in the previous section already concluded that the bill pay and money transfer applications create a monolithic sub-architecture environment. They are sizeable, self-contained, tightly coupled, hard to maintain, and difficult to alter. The production landscape they imprint is similar to the monolithic design panel of the keystone diagram. Therefore, let us place sub-architecture C in its corresponding monolithic diagram panel. Figure 8.6 illustrates this update of the keystone diagram.

As shown, the monolithic design panel in the keystone diagram stretches from 0 to 5 on the architecture decoupling axis and from 0 to 5 on the architecture distribution axis. Both x-axis and y-axis values allow considerable space to place monolithic architecture. It all depends on the extent of coupling and distribution of the sub-architecture. In our case, sub-architecture C is positioned near the value 0 of both axes: architecture decoupling and distribution scales. This placement reveals the true characteristics of a monolithic design.

Consider the reasons for positioning sub-architecture C in that specific location in the keystone diagram panel:

Architecture decoupling consideration. The bill pay and money transfer monolithic applications do not heavily interact with outside applications or data sources. Figure 8.3 indeed reveals that only the bill pay application communicates with the central reporting service in sub-architecture A. This style is then considered extremely tightly coupled because the bill pay and the money transfer applications contain most functionality needed for their operations

Architecture distribution consideration. Because sub-architecture C contains two monolithic applications, each of which consists of one tier only, their internal components are not distributed.

Architecture decoupling and distribution considerations. Monolithic applications are typically tightly coupled and in many instances undistributed. However, to mitigate the business risks that come with monolithic implementations, leveraging adapters are considered to ease the externalization of functionality. Adding proxies or increasing message routes could also increase the applications' agility and promote loosely coupled design.

Grand-Scale Architecture Structure Classification and Decomposition: A Unified Business Perspective

So far we have analyzed and categorized parts of the end-state architecture and learned how business goals are being satisfied. This analysis also rendered the discovery of business processes and the manner by which business services offer solutions. We also employed the keystone architecture classification and decomposition diagram and its panels to catalog various pieces of the end-state architecture. As a result, the end-state architecture is decomposed into sub-architectures. Now, we have a better idea about the direction of the end-state architecture and how business services employ design capabilities in a production environment.

Now, we must conclude with a unified business categorization of the end-state architecture. There is nothing complicated about the proposed method to categorize the overall enterprise design. New architecture type names are not about to be introduced either. Instead, the grand-scale architecture classification is presented in a single graph, identifying the overall business dominance and criticality of each discovered sub-architecture (largely discussed in the previous sections): monolithic, centralized, mesh, and federated.

The terms "dominance" and "criticality" convey how vital certain design styles are to the overall end-state architecture. For example, the grand-scale architecture classification diagram will clearly quantify the dominance and criticality of a centralized sub-architecture design in the overall end-state architecture view. If an end-state architecture is dominated by monolithic sub-architectures, this too could be detected in the unified business perspective.

One may argue that the introduced unified categorization method does not actually render an overall end-state architecture type. In other words, the claim might be that an end-state architecture that includes dominant sub-architectures would not reveal its overall category. To understand the unified categorization method, let us continue until the concept of classification is wholly clear.

Grand-Scale Architecture Structure Classification and Decomposition Diagram

Without further ado, let us have a look at Figure 8.7. A quick glimpse at the grand-scale architecture classification and decomposition diagram unveils a look-alike lake shape that spreads from the center of star, at value 0 where its arms meet, flowing outward toward the end of the arms. As depicted, each arm shows the business dominance and criticality value of a sub-architecture on a scale of 0 to 100. Obviously, the value 0

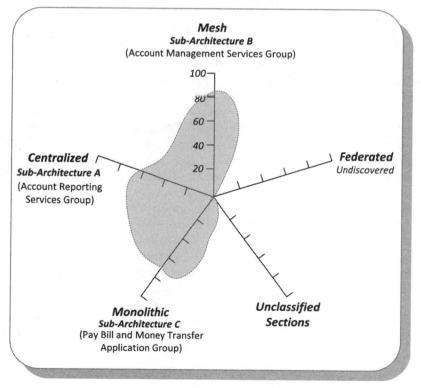

Figure 8.7   Grand-Scale Architecture Classification and Decomposition Diagram

indicates that the sub-architecture is noncritical and its dominance level is minimum or nonexistent. A score of 100 points, on the other hand, specifies the maximum dominance and criticality values. In addition, each star arm is labeled near its tip with a sub-architecture design type: monolithic, centralized, mesh, federated, or unclassified.

The unclassified sub-architecture star arm, however, was added to the grand-scale diagram to represent parts of the end-state architecture that we were unable to categorize. It is common to observe such undefined areas in almost every end-state architecture. Many reasons could contribute to undecided sub-architecture classifications, most of which are lack of fabric patterns and message-path style identification. Among others, the more important cause is the inability to understand how the design drives business solutions. This is affiliated with architecture complexity and design chaos factors.

Composing a Grand-Scale Architecture Classification and Decomposition Diagram

To compose the grand-scale architecture classification and decomposition diagram, we would need to refer back to Figures 8.3 and 8.6. The former, as discussed throughout this chapter, illustrates the business perspective of the end-state architecture, in which sub-architectures A, B, and C are the chief players in the overall end-state architecture. There are almost no areas in this design that are classified as undefined.

The keystone diagram panels in Figure 8.6 reveal other pieces of information needed for creating the grand-scale architecture classification and decomposition diagram. This illustration tells how loosely coupled and distributed the sub-architectures are in the end-state architecture. Sub-architecture categories, however, are the most important facts learned from the business analysis.

Now, let us review again Figure 8.7 and understand how the overall classification of the end-state architecture is determined. As mentioned earlier, the decision that drives the creation of the look-alike lake formation is based upon how dominant and vital the design of a sub-architecture is in the end-state diagram. Remember that this determination is founded upon the criticality of the business solutions offered by a sub-architecture. Other factors may be driven by the magnitude of the business processes and services a sub-architecture provides. Taking these aspects into consideration when constructing the grand-scale diagram can help with quantifying the dominance of a sub-architecture.

Ultimately, the overall view of an end-state architecture is formed, rendering a visual class of the grand design.

Consider the reasons for determining the scaling of each sub-architecture in the grand-scale architecture diagram depicted in Figure 8.7. We start with the monolithic sub-architecture C, located on the bottom of the diagram. It is the most tightly coupled and non-distributed design. The list then continues, moving up in a clockwise direction toward the lesser-coupled and more distributed sub-architectures. Figure 8.8 depicts this orderly review:

Monolithic sub-architecture C   Bill pay and money transfer applications in sub-architecture C are extremely important to running a banking business. Without such services, a customer would not be able to move funds from bank accounts or institutions to others. It is then assigned 70 out of a total of 100 points.

Centralized sub-architecture A   Next, this part of the end-state architecture contains the account reporting services. The design offers business solutions for

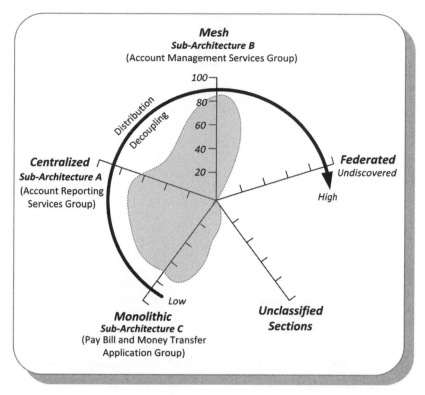

Figure 8.8   Distribution and Decoupling Scales in a Grand-Scale Architecture Classification Diagram

reporting account balances and statements. Obviously, the provided services are fundamental features of any banking operations. The value of about 62 on the dominance and importance scale for the centralized architecture type justifies this assessment.

Mesh sub-architecture B   One of the most important features of a banking implementation is the ability to maintain checking and savings accounts. Opening and closing customer accounts are among these offerings. Therefore, the dominance and importance of the account management services led to a value of 85 out of 100.

Federated   The end-state architecture does not contain any sub-architecture that is classified as federated. The value on corresponding scale is then 0.

Unclassified   The only message path that is not included in any sub-architecture is between the central reporting service and sub-architecture C (monolithic environment). This is an unclassified element that in the grand-scale architecture classification diagram is slightly more than the minimum 0 value, perhaps 1 or 2 out of 100.

Capturing End-State Architecture Generations

Tracing an end-state architecture evolution is one of the most significant business analysis aspects. As time goes by, new products are being deployed to production,

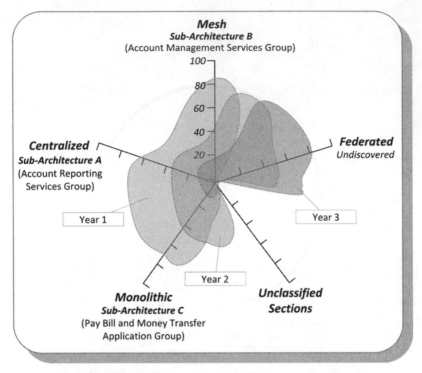

Figure 8.9   End-State Architecture Generations

topology maps change, and sub-architectures gain or lose their dominance. Some sub-architectures become more critical for the business. Others contribute less to an organization. Modification of business priorities or alterations of business strategies indeed affect an end-state architecture direction.

Figure 8.9 illustrates the architecture evolution concept. In the depicted example, the design progression spans three years, during which significant business changes take place:

- Monolithic implementations are losing dominance and their importance level decreases. As apparent, in the third evolution year, the monolithic environment shrinks to 10. This may imply that the organization retired some monolithic applications or reduced its dependency on such outdated architecture.
- Similarly, centralized architecture formations decrease too. In the third year of progression the value decreases to 10. Perhaps the corresponding organization reduced hub-and-spokes design styles.
- The mesh type of design implementations plunged down from 85 in the first year to almost 20 in the third year. The organization was able to reduce the point-to-point architecture dependencies.
- The evolution clearly shows that the federated architecture implementations increased from 0 in the first year to about 80 in the third one. This denotes that the overall architecture expanded and introduced changes to the dominance of the monolithic, centralized, and mesh designs.

CHAPTER 9

Technical Analysis Drives End-State Architecture Structural Decomposition

There is no shortage of technical implementations and installed products in a production environment. And there is no dearth of sub-architectures in a sizeable end-state architecture. The design styles could be spotted anywhere. But with increasing product deployments, the variations of sub-architecture styles are growing as well. Not all patterns, however, of enterprise asset arrangements on a network could be classified. In fact, many formations are not even understood by production engineers. This inability to categorize sub-architectures only increases operational confusion and creates business continuity perils.

The chief technical analysis mission then would be to decompose an end-state architecture into sub-architectures buy classifying them. This process may be applied to a proposed enterprise grand design or an operating production landscape. Ascertaining how the various products and technologies carry business functionality would then be a good starting point. In other words, the end-state decomposition effort ought to be driven by *technical capabilities*.

Remember, here we do not pursue sub-architecture classification and end-state architecture decomposition from a business perspective.

Technical capabilities demonstrate the power of the technologies driven by enterprise architecture to provide solutions. Only a technical analysis could delve into sections of an end-state architecture and deduce if part of an environment meets design specifications. A successful examination of this kind should render answers to the vital questions that follow:

- How should one divide an end-state architecture into sub-architectures?
- What are the technologies used to maintain adequate technical capabilities?
- What are the system fabric patterns[1] that are employed in the discovered sub-architecture?
- Are there any unrecognized design formations in the end-state architecture?
- How should unrecognized design formations be categorized?
- What are the middleware and network infrastructure products supporting the systems and/or applications in the end-state architecture?

It is important to remember that the decomposition effort of an end-state architecture into sub-architectures is a fundamental practice that enterprise architects ought to employ to deliver a powerful enterprise design. In fact, as a part of the end-state architecture design efforts, such decomposition can yield immense knowledge about organizational production environments and the driving business imperatives.

A Quick Guide to Discovering Sub-Architectures

Pure technical analysis, without taking into consideration business concerns, to discover sub-architectures in an end-state architecture seems like an easy task. However, this production environment breakdown, even without a deep exploration of business aspects, calls for the examination of many technical factors. The technical analysis for discovering sub-architecture, therefore, should be a thorough and systematic process of ascertaining *the technological capabilities* employed to enable business services.

So what is the overall mission? The sub-architecture discovery task is then to isolate sections of the end-state architecture environment into sub-architectures and identify their architectural roles and responsibilities. In other words, the purpose is to discover their contribution to the overall integrated environment. These parts of an end-state architecture are referred to as technical views. Once these perspectives have been recognized, categorizations of the sub-architectures begin.

The list that follows includes a selection of technical analysis activities leading to the discovery of sub-architectures:

Technical profiling   Start by identifying the contribution of chief components in the end-state architecture. Namely, study their *technical capabilities* by profiling their impact on a production environment. If the middleware plays a major role in the overall architecture, understand what the involvement of each element is. For example, if an ESB is used to deliver information, find out its features. If a rules engine is leveraged to execute processes, study its technical capabilities. The section Carry Out Technical Profiling to Discover Architecture Capabilities discusses in detail this aspect.

Fabric patterns   While pursuing the technical profiling, also identify system fabric patterns, as discussed in Chapter 4, in the end-state architecture proposition. If the architecture has already been implemented, use proper tools to map these patterns in the production environment (see Chapters 5 and 6 for mapping tools).

Architecture capabilities   Group architecture capabilities empowered by systems, applications, middleware, and network infrastructure products. The technical profiling and system fabric patterns should drive this activity.

Sub-Architectures.[2]   The discovery of architecture capabilities should lead to the identification of sub-architectures in the overall end-state architecture.

Enterprise End-State Architecture Technical Case Study

We are about to view an end-state architecture diagram illustrating a case study to be used for our technical analysis. Let us have a deep look at Figure 9.1 and attempt to understand it. But before breaking it down into sub-architectures, the analysis should render concepts and the direction of the overall design. This means that by studying

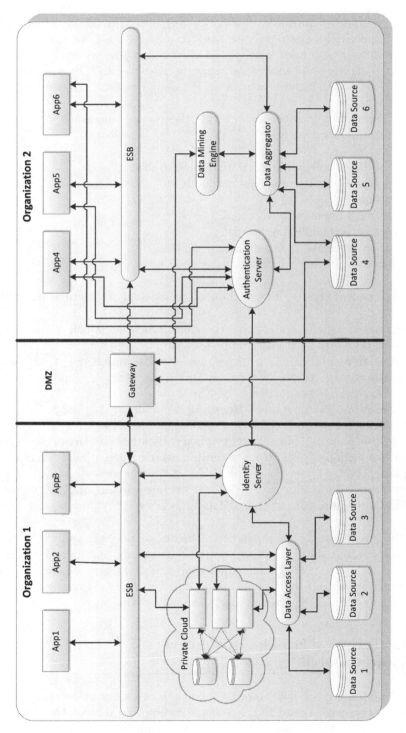

Figure 9.1   A Technical Environment of End-State Architecture

the architecture's major components, one will attain a clear view of what the design is trying to accomplish.

For this exercise, Figure 9.1 illustrates a technical environment, from which the business aspects were completely omitted. Any business affiliation or references to actual business transactions were purposely hidden. Any mention of business requirements or citations of application names were avoided. Therefore, the focus should merely be on the technical aspects of the design without involving any other unaffiliated concerns.

For our preliminary technical analysis, ask these simple questions to understand the environment and its elements:

- What is the overall architecture attempting to achieve?
- Does the end-state architecture illustrate more than one production environment?
- Where are the applications located?
- Where are the middleware products?
- Where are the network infrastructure elements?
- What are the leading system fabric patterns?

The inspection of Figure 9.1 yielded the environmental observations that follow:

- Identified are two production ecosystems, each of which is part of an organization: organizations 1 and 2.
- Organization 1 consists of three applications, numbered 1, 2, and 3. Organization 2 consists of three applications, numbered 4, 5, and 6.
- Each organization hosts a dedicated ESB.
- Organization 1 manages three data sources, numbered 1, 2, and 3.
- Organization 2 manages three data sources, numbered 4, 5, and 6.
- In addition to other design elements found within the boundary of organization 1, its production environment also hosts a private cloud, data access layer, and identity server.
- Organization 2 includes these additional architecture components: data mining engine, authentication server, and data aggregator.

After the initial discovery of the design elements, we ought to study their associations. This inspection should elaborate on the relationships originated between the chief architecture components. Understanding the general integration scheme by tracing the connecting message routes would be another key aspect to investigate. For this purpose, refer to Chapter 4 for identifying system fabric patterns.

Carry Out Technical Profiling to Discover Architecture Capabilities

Without understanding the chief features of end-state architecture elements, no one would be able to grasp what the design is trying to accomplish. Technical profiling is the discipline, therefore, that can shed light on how an architecture employs certain technologies to enable information exchange in a production environment. Profiling is also about discovering the technical capabilities of the inspected components. If an ESB is employed to transmit messages to consuming applications, for example, additional studies are required to discover its underpinning functionality.

In many instances, production environments underutilize middleware or network infrastructure products, a common reality that yields unnecessary expenditure and consumption of resources. Technical profiling, therefore, should be employed to assess if architecture components are essential and the cost is justified.

Another important technical profiling goal would be to assess overutilization of software or hardware components in a production environment, such as brokers or software intermediaries. Overwhelming employment of architecture elements could impede application performance and harm business continuity. Think about unwarranted or extreme utilization of security servers for example. What about the needless deployments of data repositories? And what about servers that provide redundant services?

Let's roll up our sleeves and get to know the functionality and the purpose of the main design components in Figure 9.1. The sections that follow describe their features and the purpose they serve in the end-state architecture.

Enterprise Service Bus Enables Interoperability

There are umpteen pieces of literature describing ESB features and functionality on the market. In our particular case study, depicted in Figure 9.1, the chief use of the two ESBs employed by organization 1's and 2's production environments is to enable information sharing. Since the business requirements are abstracted, the assumption is that there could be any type of data exchanged between these institutions. This traded information may pertain to client profile, bank accounts, product and manufacturing, news, security, health care, and so many other industries.

A typical ESB offers numerous features. As technology progresses, an ESB concept morphed from a mere information queuing concept into an enterprise middleware product. This evolution contributed to the messaging strategy of the enterprise. One of the most compelling uses of an ESB in production is to enable interoperability. To understand this term, think about two organizations, each of which is founded on distinct business models and technologies. To enable communication between the two, an ESB would be an attractive solution.

Figure 9.1 represents such business and technical requirements. Technical and business interoperability then is vital for the information sharing in our case study. Let us stop for a minute and find out some of the many features these two ESBs offer to the overall end-state architecture:

- Message queuing
- Message mediation and interception
- Message routing and workload management
- Orchestration of messages
- Message and information transformation and mapping
- Protocol conversion
- Data augmentation
- Security model transformation
- Rule engine capabilities

One may wonder why an end-state architecture would support the employment of two ESBs, each hosted in a different production environment, as depicted in Figure 9.1. The technical term for linking two or more ESBs is named "ESB chaining." This scenario would reduce the message load on each ESB. But one of the most significant reasons is related to the architecture federation capability. The federated architecture style is devised to avoid hub-and-spokes or even mesh formations over long network distances. Breaking down these archaic centralized and point-to-point formations would enable multiple organizations to join the federated information exchange capabilities. Read more about chaining ESBs in the Federated Architecture Technical Environment section of Chapter 7.

Data Access Layer Offers Environment Isolation

Our technical profiling continues here by analyzing the contribution of the distributed data access layer (DAL) in Organization 1, as shown in Figure 9.1, This middleware implementation is positioned in front of the data sources 1, 2, and 3. DAL's array of functionalities is devised to shield the data sources from direct access. In design software terms, such isolation is named data abstraction. DAL's chief duties focus on executing database calls on behalf of its consumers. In our case study, the private cloud, identity server, and the ESB are the related message exchange entities.

Hidden from consumers, DAL maintains relationships with the protected data sources (1, 2, and 3). This denotes that the calls to the data repositories are designed to perform essential data manipulations: create, read, update, and delete, often referred to as CRUD operations. These data brokering capabilities offload responsibilities from consumers by centralizing data access needs.

The abstraction of data is obtained by hiding the actual data structures from consumers. Requests for data sent to DAS may return simplified formats of tagged information. DAS can return a variety of human-readable or machine-oriented formats after a consumer issues a database query. These typically include references to class structures, XML,[3] or JSON.[4] No matter in which structure the information is returned, the consumer is not aware or concerned with the actual calls to the data store. There are instances that the consumer does not even know the specific data store and its location.

The employment of a DAS in an architecture is a sign of design maturity because the technical solution it proposes is *enterprise-level separation of concerns*. But any solution of its kind that deploys software intermediaries typically dodges performance issues on a large scale. In addition, a distributed broker such as DAS becomes a single point of failure concern. A consideration must be given, therefore, to scalability measurement to circumvent data access discontinuation.

To sum up the DAS functionality, consider the items on the list that follows:

- Data abstraction
- Data isolation
- Data calls brokering
- Data access brokering
- Data manipulation (CRUD operations)
- Information formatting and mapping
- Data source management

Identity Server for Enterprise Asset Management and Profiling

Another effort of our technical profiling includes the inspection of the identity server that is deployed to the production environment in organization 1, depicted in Figure 9.1. Assets in a production environment must be identified and registered. People who access these enterprise systems or their contained applications, and databases must be known and classified into interest groups. Data repositories must be listed along with their related access keys. Hence, the identity server offers the ability to detect and profile any enterprise asset in a production environment.

There are numerous security and management reasons why organizations employ identity servers. One of the most important is the enforcement of enterprise policies when it comes to standardization of technologies. Unapproved technologies that are not registered with the identity server would not be allowed to operate in production. Another justification for using an identity server would be to foster reuse of assets, such as data sources and applications, across an organization. The profiling of network devices is yet another incentive to employ the identity server.

Not all enterprises employ identity servers. The management of such operation is typically costly. The introduction of such an intermediary to a production environment that is already saturated with umpteen proxies would only increase message routes and potentially hinder the performance of business transactions.

Some identity management products even come with credential management and user authentication capabilities. These features are similar to those of the authentication server employed by organization 2.

The list that follows captures the chief technical capabilities of the identity server:

- Organizational centralized control for asset management
- Asset identification
- Personnel identification
- Data access management for repositories
- Identity management for heterogeneous production landscapes
- Credential management and provisioning
- Policy management enforcement
- Profiling of network devices

Private Cloud Abstracts Services and Technology

The last architecture item on the organization 1 list is the cloud computing formation. The reasons to host a cloud are vast. We thus focus on the use depicted in Figure 9.1. Note that this cloud is classified as a private entity. This means that the services provided by the cloud are for internal use to organization 1.

But this is not entirely correct. As shown, the private cloud is also linked to the ESB deployed to share information with organization 2. What makes it private, though, is the fact that it operates from organization 1's boundary; and the services it provides are also invoked by the internal identity server, ESB, and data access layer. Furthermore, the cloud information is shared through the ESB with organization 2 only. This confines the cloud services to the two organizations, enough to name it private.

An enterprise end-state architecture that proposes a cloud, such as seen in organization 1, clearly aims to abstract the employed technologies. But the abstraction level goes much beyond pure technical aspects. This is also about design considerations, such as abstracting the models of database structures, hiding the cloud internal architecture, and isolating implementations. In other words, consuming applications and other enterprise users do not have to know *how* the services are provided to them. The only concern would be to understand *what* services they utilize. The "what" aspect is also related to data exchange formats, response time and availability, and other service level agreement (SLA) parameters. In a nutshell, the decision to include a cloud in an organization is driven by promoting enterprise design abstraction to foster asset reuse and consolidation.

Aside from hiding the implementation and the data, clouds also provide operational offerings to consumers. Traditionally, a cloud may offer three chief services: software as service (SaS), platform as service (PaS), and infrastructure as service (IaS).

Consider the chief functionalities that the private cloud entity offers to consumers in organization 1:

- Abstracts data, implementation, and design from organization 1's consumers
- Isolates technology implementations from the enterprise
- Interacts with the data access layer for information exchange or augmentation
- Links to the ESB to enable data sharing with organization 2
- Registers as a participating entity with the identity server to comply with organizational standards

Gateway Facilitates Interoperability

There is no need to employ a gateway to enable interoperability. An ESB functionality alone could provide identical services to enable communication between heterogeneous computing environments. In Figure 9.1, the depiction of the gateway that links organizations A and B suggests that it may augment both ESBs' offered features. The technical analysis should not rely on assumptions such as this. We ought to understand why a gateway is positioned between the ESBs and what the extra features are. In this case, more documentation and explanations should be provided to address the raised concerns.

Delving into the justification of the gateway deployment should render a list of features that are essential for the technical analysis and classification of sub-architectures. For now, let us understand what a gateway is and why organizations leverage its functionalities. Generally, a gateway is another message interceptor type, a mediation service deployed to enable business and technical interoperability. As depicted in Figure 9.1, the specified gateway is located in the demilitarized zone (tagged as DMZ), enabling the chaining of the ESB in organization 1 to its counterpart in organization 2.

Organizations prefer to build proprietary gateways, homegrown products that possess the intelligence to link two branded lines of business or production ecosystems. Off-the-shelf products are difficult to find to fill this very special gap.

The listed functionalities are typical to gateway implementations:

- Data formatting
- Communication protocol conversion
- Locating services or applications

- Security model conversions
- Synchronization of requests and responses, in case asynchronous and synchronous are used to deliver messages
- Increasing business and technical interoperability between lines of business

Authentication Server Manages Access

The next step in our technical profiling process is to understand what the authentication server's features are and how they contribute to the deployed environment in organization 2, depicted in Figure 9.1.

The authentication server is utterly central to organization 2's production environment, an integral design component that manages access to enterprise assets. The server authenticates user and process credentials to grant a variety of access privileges to production facilities, systems, and related applications. Authorized parties are then allowed to access deployed services in certain capacities and permission levels. Moreover, repudiating services from consumers triggers monitoring alerts that are addressed urgently to protect organizational assets.

After looking deeper into the end-state architecture illustration in Figure 9.1, it is apparent that applications 4, 5, and 6 are linked to the authentication server in organization 2. The ESB and the data aggregator are linked to it too. Even the identity server in organization 1 exchanges messages with the authentication server. This formation creates a tight dependency between the message exchange parties. In this scheme, the authentication server along with its direct consumers resembles a star formation, a centralized design style. This arrangement on the network implies that the server offers vital services that almost every architecture element must use.

Remember the chief contribution of the authentication server to the end-state architecture:

- Access control management
- User and process authentication
- User and process authorization

Data Aggregator for Data Collection

When it comes to data gathering responsibilities, the data aggregator is an essential design component for information collection. The data is being collected from a wide array of sources, such as data warehouses, applications, third party information providers, enterprise repositories, and more. Furthermore, on an enterprise architecture-level, the duty of data assembling should not be pursued by business applications. Assign this task to middleware products, such as data aggregators, that specialize in information collection from a variety of data sources.

One of the leading concepts in this field is customer data integration (CDI). It is all about the simple principles of data consolidation and repurposing. This means that the aggregator not only collects the data, but can also create different information views for diverse consumers. But the manipulation of data is not one of the strongest data aggregator's features. Again, it is merely devised to retrieve and combine different types of information requested by consuming processes or users.

Figure 9.1 illustrates direct and indirect links the data aggregator forms with the organization 2's consumers. Obviously, the aggregator collects data from data sources 4, 5, and 6. It also establishes communication with the ESB, through which the collected data is passed to application 4, 5, and 6. Furthermore, the data aggregator trades messages with the authentication server and data-mining engine.

The employment of a data aggregator such as this is only justified if there are a large number of data sources that require a unified view. Information repurposing, as mentioned earlier, is also a reasonable goal. The list that follows reiterates the data aggregator requirements:

- Data integration
- Data repurposing
- Data unification
- Creating multiple data views

Data Mining Engine for Information Repurposing

The work of technical analysis to profile the end-state architecture components is about to conclude with the inspection of the data mining engine. Depicted in Figure 9.1, the engine operates in organization 2's boundary. The information that is funneled from the data aggregator into the data mining engine undergoes substantial formatting and further repurposing for consumers. This is an analytical process designed to find relationships between data variables and relate them to consumers' requirements.

In the field of data mining, this activity is named "pattern matching" and is devised to relate data sets. If the gathered information is related to real estate, for example, a consumer may request affiliated data about housing in certain regions. Comparing cultural differences and living preferences of diverse neighborhoods could be the outcome of the data mining effort.

Consider a few important features of the data-mining engine:

- Relates data that is retrieved from various data sources
- Groups information in cluster formations
- Categorizes data in different groups to satisfy consumer preferences and quick retrieval

Grouping Architecture Capabilities to Discover Sub-Architectures

The technical profiling discussed in the previous sections elaborates on the contribution of each production entity, such as servers and middleware products, to the overall end-state architecture. We learned about their architecture capabilities by ascertaining their features and the services they offer. Discovering the message exchange routes used to trade business transactions is another activity that explains the behavior and interaction with the environment of these design entities.

Now, we are going to pursue another exciting process for discovering sub-architectures in the overall end-state architecture for the purpose of classification and decomposition. Figure 9.1 illustrates our starting point. Next, the milestones leading to the categorization goal are about breaking down the enterprise grand design into groups of architecture capabilities, each of which ought to prove viable solution delivery mechanisms. Again, these technical capabilities must justify the existence of each end-state architecture part.

In simple words: The end-state architecture decomposition work is about discovering sub-architectures and classifying them based on their contribution to the overall design. After doing this, we should be able to place the sub-architectures in the proper keystone architecture structure classification and decomposition diagram panels. To a certain extent, this activity is akin to the placing of sub-architectures in diagram panels based on business analysis, as discussed in Chapter 8.

Still driven by technical analysis activities, the sections that follow pinpoint two chief sub-architectures (A and B), each of which demonstrates different technical capabilities in the end-state architecture.

Classifying Sub-Architecture A: A Technical Perspective

With no time to spare, let us inspect Figure 9.2, in which sub-architecture A spans the two organizations 1 and 2. The list that follows itemizes the components that offer collaborative technical capabilities:

- Sub-architecture A's components in organization 1:
  - ESB
  - Applications 1, 2, and 3
  - Services in the private cloud
  - Data access layer
  - Identity server
- Sub-architecture A's components shown in organization 2:
  - ESB
  - Applications 4, 5, and 6
  - Authentication server
  - Data aggregator
- Gateway connecting the two ESBs in organization 1 and 2

Note the grouping of technical capabilities that exists in two different organizations. In our case, we selected the two ESBs and their related consuming entities to represent the technical offerings and features of sub-architecture A. This assembly is justified since these capabilities are tied together; and they collaborate to provide a solution to a mutual problem that the two organizations are concerned about.

Sub-Architecture A: A Federated Strategy

What is the architectural strategy that drives the linking of the two ESBs and the mediating gateway to each other, as illustrated in Figure 9.2? Why would an organization build such a technical bridge? The quick answer is business and technical interoperability. This concept expands much beyond the boundary of an isolated application or a single data repository. It is not about the consumers of one organization

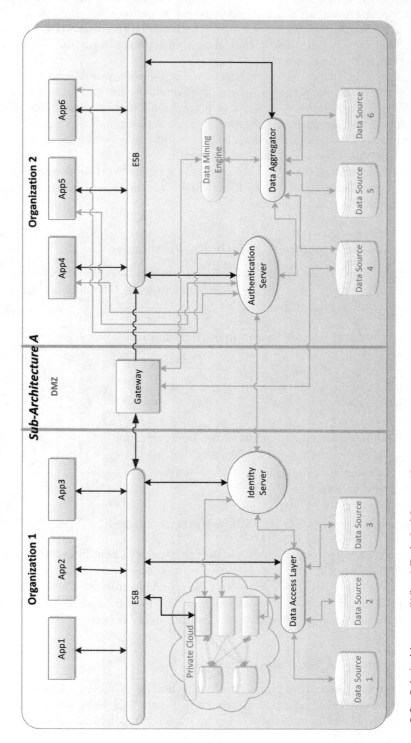

Figure 9.2   Sub-Architecture "A" —A Technical Perspective

either. It is a collaborative approach to achieve information sharing. It is about offering cross-domain knowledge, by which each pool of organizational expertise opens for exchange with another.

So how should sub-architecture A be categorized? These imperatives classify sub-architecture A as a *federated design style*.

Indeed, the exchange of information between organizations is a powerful concept if the technical capabilities can carry out such task. The requirement for business and technical interoperability is sound because neither production environment nor organization can talk to each other without proper message transportation mechanisms. The strategy, therefore, calls for linking domains, departments, divisions, businesses, or enterprises to enable information federation. The strategy also appeals for enabling two or more organizations with distinct business models to understand each other. In addition, the strategy requires abstracting the technologies that each organization supports to allow flawless business transactions. Technological abstraction means that there would be no need for an organization to understand the supported technology of the other. They can be different, and indeed they are in most cases.

The federated architecture strategy is a major undertaking. There are umpteen parallel initiatives that must be accomplished to enable interoperability. Building such an information highway calls for applications and middleware products to join the venture. This implies that that the employed ESBs products must provide connectors to enable an easy and rapid integration.

Why Chain ESBs?

Why is each organization (1 and 2) in sub-architecture A (as depicted in Figure 9.2) required to host a dedicated ESB? Would employing a single ESB for enabling architecture federation be sufficient? Would a single, properly scaled ESB satisfy performance requirements? The single answer for these questions lies in the anticipated volume level of the message exchange. If the information load that travels through a single ESB may hinder its overall performance, it would be wise to employ a separate ESB for each production environment or organization that participates in the federated architecture.

The justification for deploying an organization-dedicated ESB does not only depend on the projected volume. In many instances, no one can predict the pressure on an ESB without knowing in advance how many consuming applications and users would subscribe to its messaging services. Therefore, the discipline of capacity planning comes in handy to help forecast future usage trends. Again, not only the workload counts, but the increased number of subscribers could introduce a performance challenge.

Perhaps one of the most compelling reasons to chain two or more ESBs in a federated architecture environment is to break the traditional centralized architecture formation. The star, community center (discussed in Chapter 4), and hub-and-spokes are only a few names that represent the concept of design centralization. This arrangement of enterprise assets may apply excessive network pressure on a single point of failure, namely the hub, and introduce performance challenges. To avoid such an architectural error, the federated design fosters the distribution of assets over long network distances by leveraging chained ESBs.

The danger of using a single ESB to link two or more organizations is then clear: Such design would form a disastrous hub-and-spokes architecture formation that may buckle under the pressure of high volume of message exchange. In this case, the ESB transforms into an actual hub without utilizing its capability to boost the distribution of organizational assets. To further help avert the performance issue, the depicted gateway in Figure 9.2 enables the expansion of the architecture by introducing another layer of isolation in the design.

On the other hand, an inappropriate federated design that supports multiple ESBs, intermediaries, and proxies would actually lengthen the message transmission path. Again, the peril of performance degradation must be considered. The rule of thumb, therefore, suggests striking the right balance between an overly distributed federated architecture and a centralized design. Both must be tested carefully to understand the implications.

Updating the Keystone Diagram with Sub-Architecture A

Now, we are ready to place sub-architecture A, depicted in Figure 9.2, in the corresponding keystone architecture structure classification and decomposition diagram panel. The technical analysis in the previous section clearly indicates that sub-architecture A matches the profile of the federated architecture environment diagram panel.

As discussed in the Federated Architecture Panel section in Chapter 7, the federated architecture that is presented by the keystone panel shares most attributes with the sub-architecture A. Both depict a distributed asset formation and illustrate a loosely coupled design. Obviously, it all depends on the placement of sub-architecture A in the federated panel. Let us have a look at Figure 9.3 to understand why sub-architecture A was placed in the upper-right corner of the federated design diagram panel.

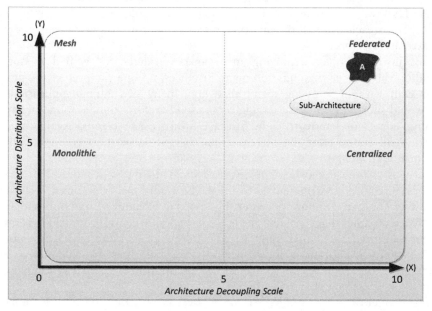

Figure 9.3   Placing Sub-Architecture A in the Keystone Diagram Federated Architecture Panel

As is apparent in the illustration, the federated design panel occupies the keystone diagram space that ranges from 5 to 10 on the architecture decoupling axis and from 5 to 10 on the architecture distribution axis. This area is large enough for placing the federated sub-architecture A. The exact insertion in the panel, though, is significant to the understanding of how loosely coupled and distributed the design is. Sub-architecture A then is positioned on the architecture decoupling far-right scale (near the axis value 9) and high on the architecture distribution axis (near the value 9, too). By all measures, this analysis reveals that sub-architecture A is extremely loosely coupled and exceedingly distributed. This classification seems correct: When viewing again the end-state architecture diagram in Figure 9.2, it becomes apparent that sub-architecture A , spans two organizations (1 and 2), and includes a growing number of consumers, applications, middleware, and servers. Indeed, it is extremely distributed and loosely coupled.

Consider a number of reasons for positioning sub-architecture A in that specific location in the keystone diagram federated design panel:

Architecture decoupling consideration. Federated architectures like sub-architecture A enable business transactions over long network distances. This arrangement on a network must be supported by a variety of software and/or hardware intermediaries to expand the architecture and transmit information from start to end-points. Such a formation encourages the design of a loosely coupled enterprise environment, in which brokers and gateways play significant message exchange roles.

Architecture distribution consideration. The increase of brokers and intermediaries makes sub-architecture A a collaborative implementation, of which unaffiliated consumers leverage the bus technology to share information. In the context of the two organizations, 1 and 2, the distribution of assets and the formed relationships is considered vast.

Architecture decoupling and distribution considerations. There is always a correlation between a distributed and loosely coupled architecture. The more distributed the design is, the more loosely coupled it may be. This seems an odd link between the loose coupling and distribution design concepts. It is also a necessity, though. To achieve a high degree of distribution it would be compulsory to use extreme decoupling mechanisms by employing intermediaries and breaking down large implementations into smaller components.

Classifying Sub-Architecture B: A Technical Perspective

Next, let us break down the discovered sub-architecture B, as illustrated in Figure 9.4. The four chief components of this design are located in organizations 1 and 2.

- Sub-architecture B's components in organization 1:
  - Data access layer
  - Identity server
- Sub-architecture B's components in organization 2:
  - Authentication server
  - Data aggregator

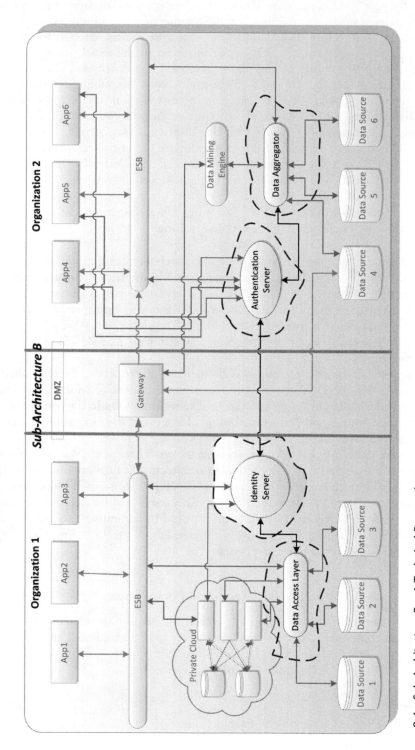

Figure 9.4 Sub-Architecture B—A Technical Perspective

As illustrated in Figure 9.4, each of the main components exchange messages with related consumers. Consider the further breakdown.

- Consumers of the data access layer in organization 1:
  - Data sources 1, 2, and 3
  - Two services in the private cloud
  - ESB
  - Identity server
- Consumers of the identity server in organizations 1 and 2:
  - Data access layer in organization 1
  - A service located in the private cloud in organization 1
  - ESB in organization 1
  - Authentication server in organization 2
- Consumers of the authentication server in organization 1 and 2:
  - Identity server in organization 1
  - Applications 4, 5, and 6 in organization 2
  - ESB in organization 2
  - Data aggregator in organization 2
- Consumers of the data aggregator in organization 2:
  - Data sources 4, 5, and 6 in organization 2
  - Authentication server in organization 2
  - Data mining engine in organization 2
  - ESB in organization 2

Figure 9.4 depicts sub-architecture B with its related and linked design elements. This sub-architecture is distributed across organizations 1 and 2. Indeed, we face a vast distribution of software and hardware across two production environments that offer services to a wide range of subscribers. Then, how do we categorize such architecture? What would be the keystone diagram panel that sub-architecture B is associated with? Attend to the sub-architecture categorization discussion in the sections that follow.

Sub-Architecture B: A Chain of Distributed Community Centers

The design formation illustrated in Figure 9.4 indeed seems odd. However, it is common to many organizations. The intuitive approach to designing a distributed and centralized architecture typically results in the technical view discovered in this illustration. There, the arrangement of the organizational assets on the network leaves no doubt that we are viewing a chain of hub-and-spokes formations. This design resembles a collection of community center fabric patterns.

In fact, many enterprise production environments contain chains of star formations just as we observe in Figure 9.4. This is both a common and an unfortunate practice. There is nothing easier than slapping a number of design elements on the design table and linking them to chained hubs. This is also an unplanned method for distributing information over a long-distance network. In fact, there is almost no justification for linking communities of consumers to a chain of hubs, expecting such design to deliver a federated, reliable, and rapid performance across an organization or production environments.

Sub-architecture B is indeed a strange breed of convoluted design that arranges subscribing consumers around processing centers to deliver a distributed solution. Such style burdens a production environment with hub-and-spokes formations. It is also needless to deploy a chain of such formations across two or more organizations, as depicted in Figure 9.4. A hub-and-spoke architecture should not expand an architecture beyond a confined network. Perhaps it should be limited to a single production environment or organization.

To maintain the distributed chained structure the identity server in organization 1 is linked to its counterpart, the authentication server in organization 2. This is yet another example of an ill-designed integration, by which a point-to-point relationship is formed in lieu of leveraging both ESBs, the formal organization information highway, to exchange information. By creating a direct message route between the two, the effectiveness of architecture federation diminishes; the design complexity increases by deviating from standard integration practices.

Is the chained community centers design style a technological strategy to deliver solutions? Regrettably, not all solutions proposed by an end-state architecture are driven by overarching enterprise strategies. And not all implementations that have been deployed to production are steered by long-term organizational plans. Unfortunately, layers of integration initiatives form somewhat arbitrarily. The chained community centers architecture depicted in Figure 9.4 is one of those that was created to address interoperability without a strategic vision.

Although sub-architecture B is not an advisable design, still, the formation of the chained community centers, depicting a collection of star topologies, plays a major role in the overall end-state architecture. No one should disregard the vital contribution of the entities that make up such a fabric pattern. To simplify its complexity, organizations 1 and 2 should consider revamping the design by transforming it to a true federated architecture.

Updating the Keystone Diagram with Candidate Sub-Architecture B

How can such a problematic chain of hubs and their related consumers be matched up with the proper keystone architecture structure classification and decomposition diagram panel? The analysis provided in the previous section left very little doubt about which design category that sub-architecture B is related to. Plainly, sub-architecture B should be classified as a *centralized design* despite the series of hub-and-spokes formations that span organizations 1 and 2, as depicted in Figure 9.4.

But classifying sub-architecture B merely as a centralized design would not do justice to its overall structure and the technical interoperability it attempts to fulfill. A second look at sub-architecture B would render a second opinion: The design is not only a centralized one; it also offers information sharing by the distribution of its components. Such dispersal of server and software assets that span organizations 1 and 2 also falls under the *federated architecture* style category.

Strange? Indeed.

Figure 9.5 illustrates this finding in the updated keystone architecture structure classification and decomposition diagram where sub-architectures A and B are shown. Recall that sub-architecture A is classified as a pure federated design. However, sub-architecture B appears to stretch over the two keystone diagram panels: federated and centralized. There is nothing surprising about a sub-architecture such as this,

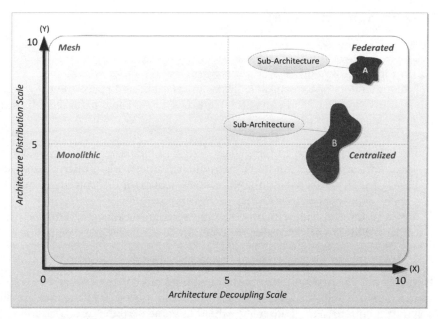

Figure 9.5   Sub-Architecture B in the Keystone Classification Diagram Centralized Architecture Panel

which is categorized as a combined design style. Similar circumstances are common in most production environments.

A quick analysis of the keystone architecture structure classification and decomposition diagram reveals that sub-architecture B is loosely coupled (located near the architecture decoupling axis at value 8). It is also fairly distributed, situated between the architecture distribution axis values 3.5 to 7. The position of sub-architecture B on the two panels indicates the complexity and to a certain extent unclear design categorization. Perhaps this is a hybrid architecture style. Again, consider this as common network arrangement, one that could be avoided or improved upon.

The list that follows further elucidates the reasons for locating sub-architecture B on the two keystone diagram panels:

Architecture decoupling consideration. As much as sub-architecture B is a community center formation, it is also a distributed structure devised to exchange messages over a long network distance. The spread of its components over the network makes it loosely coupled despite the chain of its hub-and-spokes formations.

Architecture distribution consideration. Sub-architecture B ranges from a mild to a highly distributed design, as shown on the architecture distribution axis. Some of its components are local to organizations A and B, where they play a centralized role to enable local message exchange in their corresponding production environments. But sub-architecture B is also highly distributed as it serves the two organizations. This mix of centralization and distribution positions sub-architecture B in between the federated and the centralized keystone panels.

Architecture decoupling and distribution considerations. As noted, there is a strong dependency between centralization and federation. Paradoxically, these two design styles negate each other. Organizations should avoid such design practices to reduce architecture complexity and maintenance cost.

Overlapping Sub-Architectures

The entire end-state architecture environment cannot always be broken down into sub-architectures for the purpose of classifications. And slicing an end-state architecture into design parts is not always clear-cut. In other words, a collection of sub-architectures does not resemble a jigsaw puzzle—design spaces tend to overlap. This unclear division of an end-state architecture is due to some natural compositions formed in the production fabric:

- Two or more sub-architectures share design elements, such as servers, applications, software proxies, middleware products, or network infrastructure devices.
- Message paths may cross sub-architectures, making it difficult to discover clear design boundaries.
- A sub-architecture may span two or more organizations, domains, or partner entities. This further increases the complexity of the design, leaving untouched technical analysis areas.

To top it off, the process of discovering sub-architectures is subjective. No two individuals ever decomposed an end-state architecture in the same manner. At times, it is even difficult to gain consensus when it comes to the categorization of a sub-architecture. The various design interpretations and the resulting analysis could be far away from each other.

Figure 9.6 illustrates the design spaces of sub-architecture A and B. This muddled presentation of the two overlapping architectures illustrates the difficulty of separating parts of an end-state architecture into clear classification sections. Therefore, the rule of thumb is to avoid charting the two sub-architectures in one diagram. The other approach would be to decompose an end-state architecture into smaller pieces to avoid the vast overlay of design components.

Grand-Scale Architecture Structure Classification and Decomposition: A Unified Technical Perspective

Similar to the establishment of the unified business perspective in the Chapter 8 section titled Grand-Scale Architecture Structure Classification and Decomposition: A Unified Business Perspective, here, too, we are commissioned to set off to the last step of the end-state architecture categorization and structural decomposition. This process, however, is all about classifying the end-state architecture by assessing its overall technical capabilities.

But before moving on to the creation of the grand-scale architecture structure classification and decomposition diagram, let's stop for a few moments and summarize our accomplishments so far. In the previous sections, we learned how technical analysis could drive the discovery of sub-architectures. These technical views decompose an enterprise end-state architecture into smaller design areas. To be able to discover the sub-architectures, the analysis process calls for technical profiling of the various servers, applications, and middleware products that make up an end-state architecture. By grouping their related technical capabilities, sub-architectures are then established.

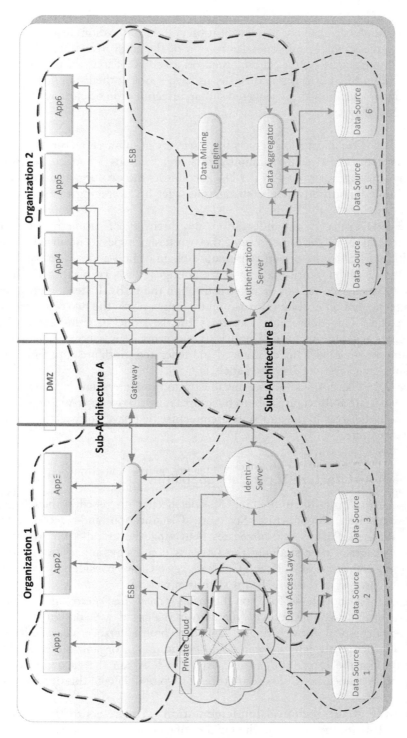

Figure 9.6 Overlapping Sub-Architectures A and B

Review Sub-Architecture Discovery Artifacts

We are now about to create a unified technical perspective of the end-state architecture. This activity renders a grand-scale classification and decompostion diagram that can shed light on the strategy and general direction of the enterprise architecture. The process for doing this is simple. It only requires a review of four artifacts that have been produced in the previous sections. Let us have a look at the listed figures in this chapter to understand how the discovered sub-architectures can be employed to found the grand-scale diagram:

> **Figure 9.2.** This illustration depicts the discovery of sub-architecture A that represents a federated design spanning across organizations 1 and 2. Moreover, a gateway (broker) positioned in the DMZ connects the two organizations' ESBs. Consuming applications then exchange messages by leveraging the information highway enabled by the ESBs.
>
> **Figure 9.4.** Visible in this illustration, the discovery of sub-architecture B is characterized as a hybrid category of the two design types: centralized and federated. Specifically, the design represents a chain of hub-and-spokes formations (community center fabric patterns), straddling across organizations 1 and 2. As shown, messages are not exchanged through the ESBs. Instead, a proprietary bus implementation enables information trading between the two organizations.
>
> **Figure 9.5.** This deliverable illustrates the keystone diagram and the two ascertained sub-architectures A and B. The former represents a federated and the latter a combined style: centralized and federated. Both are apparent in their corresponding keystone diagram panels.
>
> **Figure 9.6.** Take a quick look at this illustration to understand in which section of the end-state architecture sub-architectures A and B overlap. And on the other hand, note the areas in the end-state architecture that have not been identified as sub-architecture.

Determining Architecture Technical Capabilities

The method for creating the unified business perspective discussed in the Chapter 8 section, Grand-Scale Architecture Structure Classification and Decomposition: A Unified Business Perspective, advocates delivering the grand-scale architecture classification diagram after studying the business dominance and criticality of the discovered sub-architectures A, B, and C. These key business considerations drive the categorization process of the overall end-state architecture.

In this chapter, though, we focus on the *technical capabilities of each sub-architecture*, subsequently drafting a *unified technical capability* of the grand-scale design.

The leading aspect for creating a unified technical perspective is indeed the capability of a design to deliver technological solutions to organizational problems after determining the capabilities of its parts. But how can the capability of each sub-architecture be measured? There are three key components to this determination:

Magnitude of the technical implementation   This refers to the size of the deployed sub-architectures and the number of consumers they service.

Organizational dominance   Is the employed technology part of an organizational strategy? Is the technology being reused and leveraged across the organization? Is the technology being employed to exchange information with other organizations and business partners?

Technical criticality   How important is the technology to current and future implementations? Does an organization rely heavily on the technology? Can the technology be replaced with advanced ones?

Creating the Grand-Scale Architecture Structure Classification and Decomposition Diagram

Figure 9.7 depicts the grand-scale architecture structure classification and decomposition diagram, a unified technical view of the end-state architecture. The illustration displays a star formation with five arms, each of which is devised to represent the technical capabilities of a sub-architecture. Note that the technical analysis rendered only the two sub-architectures A (federated) and B (centralized and federated), while some of the mesh formations did not turn into a sub-architecture.

Moreover, the star arms in Figure 9.7 meet in the center of the diagram at value 0. As apparent, the maximum value that could be assigned to a sub-architecture technical capability is 100. Now, let us have a closer look at each of the arms to understand what they represent and how the technical capabilities values were assigned.

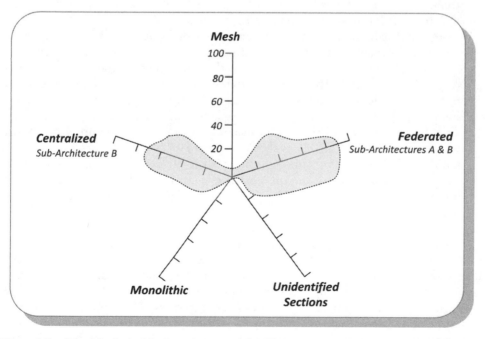

Figure 9.7   Grand-Scale Architecture Structure Classification and Decompostion Diagram—A Technical Perspective

We start the review with the monolithic sub-architecture capability, moving clockwise and concluding with the arm named "unidentified sections":

Monolithic sub-architecture The technical analysis has not led to the discovery of monolithic implementations in the end-state architecture. Thus, the technical capability value is set at 0.

Centralized view of sub-architecture B This sub-architecture is deployed across the two organizations A and B. The magnitude of the chained hub-and-spokes formations is vast, and so is its dominance in the overall end-state architecture. Indeed, looking back, Figure 9.4 shows that this large formation offers technical capabilities in four different architecture concerns: data access layer, identity server, authentication server, and data aggregator. An increasing number of consumers in both organization boundaries benefit these technical offerings. Therefore, the technical capability for sub-architecture B is set at 70 out of 100 on the diagram arm named centralized, as shown in the grand-scale architecture structure classification and decomposition diagram in Figure 9.7. But sub-architecture B is also federated akin to sub-architecture A. See their combined technical federation capability evaluation below, after the mesh formation paragraph.

Mesh formation After reviewing Figure 9.6, in which both sub-architectures A and B occupy almost all the end-state architecture space, it was determined not to categorize the point-to-point design style (mesh formation) as a sub-architecture. The mesh structure is located in the private cloud in organization 1. Since this mesh portion of the architecture does not utterly influence the overall end-state architecture, the value is then set at 8 out of 100, as depicted in the grand-scale architecture classification diagram in Figure 9.7.

Combined federated views of sub-architectures A and B This implementation is about enabling information sharing across organizations 1 and 2. Business and technical interoperability, however, is the chief benefit of the design. There is very little doubt about the dominance and the criticality of sub-architecture A and B. Its magnitude is vast as it stretches across the two organizations, enabling consuming applications and middleware to exchange information on both sides of the aisle. For these reasons, the technical capability of sub-architecture A combined with B is set at 90 out of 100, as shown in Figure 9.7.

Unidentified sections Although the mesh implementation that is spotted in the private cloud in organization 1 has not been classified as a sub-architecture, it should not fall under the unidentified section. Therefore, the value assigned is 0 in Figure 9.7.

Finally, something must be said about areas in an end-state architecture that are not established as sub-architectures despite the discovery of their design styles. Such a determination was made with the mesh formation in the grand-scale architecture structure classification and decomposition diagram, depicted in Figure 9.7. Not all design style discoveries will eventually end up as sub-architectures. The formations that offer substantial implementation value will appear in the diagram as a vital sub-architecture influencing the overall end-state design. Others will simply be mentioned as a mere implementation.

Moreover, other areas in the end-state architecture are named unidentified sections because their design style could not be determined by the technical analysis. Such indecisive analysis and classification is common to many production environments.

End-State Architecture Evolution Diagram

One of the most strategic aspects of an end-state architecture is to communicate to the business and IT organizations the future progression of the grand scale design. Perhaps, more than an intent to predict how an end-state architecture would look on paper, the chief goal of such exercise would be to emphasize a technological direction. This may include setting up milestones and goals for the end-state architecture evolution. Consider the questions related to such organizational guidance:

- What type of technologies would be acquired?
- What class of architecture styles would be employed?
- What would be the magnitude of the consuming community?
- How many lines of business would the end-state architecture span?

Although, no one could ever predict the future, these intents are required. Again, this is considered organizational strategic thinking, not business or technological predictions. Figure 9.8 illustrates the end-state architecture evolution diagram. As shown, the depicted progression stretches over three years. The second and the third year

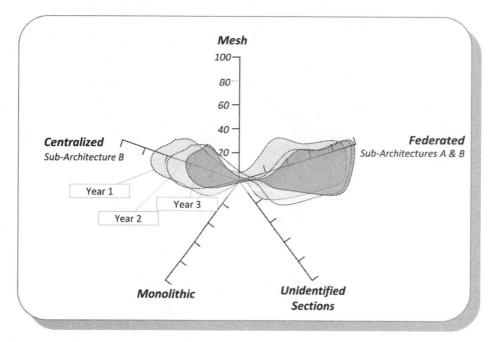

Figure 9.8   End-State Architecture Evolution Diagram

clearly stress the need for reduction of centralized formations, moving away from the hub-and-spokes design toward a more federated end-state architecture.

Notes

1. System fabric patterns are discussed in Chapter 4.
2. As recalled, in Chapter 8, the business analysis first rendered four candidate sub-architectures, three of which materialized into concrete and final sub-architectures. The process of end-state architecture decomposition, however, does not necessarily mandate the discovery of candidate sub-architectures. Practitioners may choose to skip this activity and directly establish concrete sub-architectures, as demonstrated in this chapter.
3. http://www.xml.org
4. http://json.org

CHAPTER 10

Business Views Drive End-State Architecture Decomposition

Areas of business ownership and sponsorship could dominate the decomposition of an end-state architecture proposition, a blueprint that has not been implemented as of yet. If the incremental software architecture method is perused to detect system failures in an operating production ecosystem, the decomposition process could be driven by ascertaining business-dominated segments. In both instances, business boundaries are drawn to break down an end-state architecture into business views.

There is a compelling reason for doing this: An architecture of such enterprise scale is typically sponsored by business organizations seeking to launch products to fulfill organizational strategies. Consequently, the imprints of business goals are noticed in the overall enterprise design. This would also include noticeable areas of business ownership in a production environment.

Therefore, there is an essential motive to look at an end-state architecture through a business lens. The formed business views could reveal sections in the overall design that are not only owned by business domains, but also controlled by management, which sees an enterprise architecture from a different perspective. Business views, therefore, could paint an end-state architecture in a different light—not necessarily a technical one.

The decomposed end-state architecture segments would be more about revenue and return on investment rather than technological capabilities. The subdivided grand-scale design would be more about the business vision and mission rather than the technical structure formations of applications or services. The subdivided end-state architecture would embody customer preferences and customer support rather than technical capabilities. Business change would be more visible in the end-state architecture.

The sections that follow discuss this trend of business-driven architecture decomposition. It comes in handy when an enterprise architecture is devised. It is helpful when a project is launched. It is valuable when the business changes its course. It is useful when a business model is modified. Therefore, the focus of this chapter is on three fundamental business aspects that influence the outcome of end-state architecture decomposition:

1. Formations of business structures
2. Distribution of business structures
3. Business change that introduces areas of volatility in production

End-State Architecture Decomposition Driven by Business Formations

Decomposing an end-state architecture into business-oriented segments seems a logical task to pursue because in most successful organizations, business units are well defined, and by nature, well structured. For example, the products offered to insurance customers, such as life insurance, car insurance, and home insurance, tend to influence the business structure. Each of these business domains is an area of knowledge and a service providing entity in its own space and expertise.

In this chapter, we refer to a business domain as an execution arm of the enterprise, a unit founded to incur revenue. It may sound simple; yet, it is a powerful concept of organizational survival. Without business domains, often referred to as lines of business, an organization would not be able to produce and launch superb products. Clearly, without products the business would not exist. Therefore, a domain is a nucleus of every business that is striving to survive and compete in challenging, and at times, unforgiving market conditions. It is common to spot multiple domains in a firm that logically and physically separate the business into areas of expertise. It is also common for domains to collaborate with each other to deliver business services.

In the sections that follow, domains are being conceived as *structural and contextual* business entities of an enterprise. In the context of this chapter, the term "structural" means that a line of business, such as life insurance, has tangible boundaries and a geographical location: A life insurance business domain may be located in a U.S. region or somewhere in Europe. This domain may also possess software and hardware assets, such as applications and servers that run on a dedicated network in its own production environment. More likely, a layer of executives that issue policies and drive commerce would manage it.

On the other hand, "contextual" refers to a domain's occupation and the services it offers. Issuing life insurance policies is the livelihood of the domain. Its offerings may vary from temporary life insurance to lifetime coverage products. Questionnaires, underwriting, and policy issuance are other services that such a domain must provide to its customers.

An end-state architecture, therefore, may be decomposed into structural or contextual aspects of a business. The architecture may be partitioned into domain physical locations. A more granular design breakdown could be achieved by segmenting a domain into groups of systems or applications. On the other hand, architecture contextual subdivision may focus on a domain's specialties and the type of services it offers.

Structural Decomposition of Business Layers

Flaking off layers of business, like peeling a union, is a useful end-state architecture decomposition method. To understand what type of a business structure it might be, let us have a look at Figure 10.1. This illustration depicts three banking organization layers, arranged in a hierarchical structure. The depicted entity on the bottom, referred to as business credit domain, is the largest domain. It contains a smaller child entity named small business credit domain. The latter also consists of a single child titled small business credit card domain.

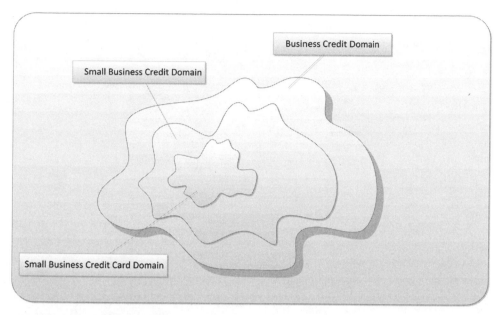

Figure 10.1   Business Layers Example

This is a typical tightly coupled and hierarchical business structure geographically located in one location. From a management perspective, the three domains may represent a division with nested child subdivisions or departments. Moreover, the reporting structure may vary in such a business formation. Each domain may operate autonomously with a staff that reports to the specific domain management. Other enterprises would favor a different management control style: The parent domain may consist of executives that drive the operations of the child domains.

In this end-state architecture decomposition exercise, the management structure should not be the leading factor. The design separation goal should be merely about physical isolation, not contextual. Therefore, the tangible business assets that belong to a domain should be the aspects that drive the decomposition effort. These are affiliated architecture entities, such as domain-specific systems, applications, or even middleware products. By doing this, business executives would be encouraged to play a visible role and be more involved with the state of their software and hardware assets in production.

Figure 10.2 illustrates the concept of business layer decomposition, in which the three business domains are separated into three groups of applications. Each domain is also established as an end-state architecture segment:

1. Business credit domain (end-state architecture segment 1): Mortgage management application, student loans application, appliance loans application, and car loans application
2. Small business credit domain (end-state architecture segment 2): fast small-business loans application, online loan application, temporary cash flow loans application, and merchant cash advances application
3. Small business credit card domain (end-state architecture segment 3): gold credit card for business application, online small business credit card application, and silver credit card for business application

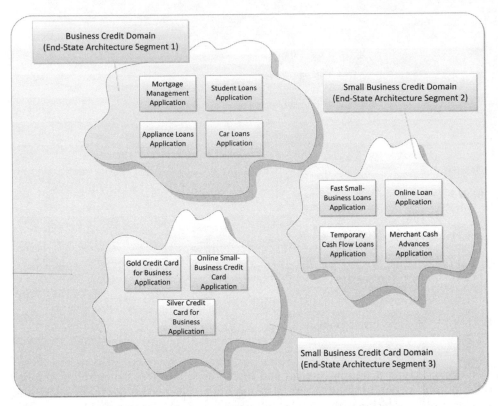

Figure 10.2   Structural Decomposition of Business Layers

As apparent, this depiction is merely schematic. For the purpose of simplification, it does not include the supporting messaging, provided by middleware products, or network infrastructure capabilities. The illustration focuses, therefore, only on business structural aspects of the end-state architecture, disregarding many technical design components. Here, the idea of breaking down a layered business comes across easily when non-business aspects are omitted.

In the real world, where the business is more intricate, comprised of layers upon layers of organizations and their supporting domains, the work of end-state architecture decomposition could be lengthy. The benefits, however, typically outweigh the investment. Splitting off the design into smaller business structure could enhance the business knowledge of management, architects, and developers. The term "business knowledge" pertains to information about how the various business domains incur revenue, their strategy, and vision. But the most important benefit of this exercise is that it introduces architecture segments for the impending incremental software architecture verification process (see Chapters 12–15).

One would argue that an end-state architecture decomposition such as this would not require extensive analysis efforts. And if each business domain indeed represents an end-state architecture decomposed segment, why go through such a lengthy process? Isn't it obvious that each domain and its business capabilities, such as systems and applications, end up being an end-state architecture segment anyway? The answer to these questions is resoundingly clear: It is not always obvious. Another rebuttal would reject the notion that each business domain should be considered as an end-state architecture segment. Examination of business granularity should determine if indeed all of a domain's offered capabilities should be included in a single architecture segment.

The term "business granularity" pertains to the magnitude of a business domain in terms of business processes and business services. The larger is a domain and the more services it offers, the greater the chance that such a domain would be further subdivided into separate sub-domains. This refined decomposition would ultimately form smaller architecture segments. So how would a domain be sliced into smaller portions? The course of domain subdivision should continue. That is, the driving efforts should be to group the domain business services into subgroups, each representing a smaller end-state architecture segment.

Structural Decomposition of Business Tiers

Another method for decomposing an end-state architecture is by discovering business tiers. Here again, domains drive the formation of the business structure. This discussion defines a tier as an autonomous and distributed business domain. That is, a domain that is separated from other domains in the enterprise is considered as a business tier. Still, it collaborates with its peers to accomplish business goals.

The idea of distributing business domains is deeply entrenched in the culture of many enterprises. Restaurant franchises, for example, must dispense their business operation across countries or continents. In the same way, shipping companies must maintain a presence in multiple regions to reduce transportation costs. The list is long. The concept of business tiers, however, has been practiced by countless enterprises throughout the history of commerce.

Now, the work of end-state architecture analysis is about discovering the business domains residing in local regions or remote geographical locations. Another important task would be to identify the relationship between the various scattered domains. Once the distribution scheme of the business is uncovered, the end-state architecture decomposition efforts begin.

So what is the work of end-state architecture decomposition? Here, each autonomous business tier is founded as a section of the architecture. This assertion may not be entirely correct if a business tier contains a large amount of business processes or supports too many applications. In this case, breaking down a business tier into smaller groups of business services would yield smaller end-state architecture segments.

One important thing to remember is that end-state architecture decomposition is always about segmenting a design. Therefore, the aim of breaking down a business into smaller units of execution must be accompanied by understanding what assets they possess. Partitioning a design into smaller parts would enable later on an efficient architecture verification effort (Chapters 12–15).

It is time to look at the example depicted in Figure 10.3. As illustrated, there are three regions of a car manufacturer: U.S., Europe, and Asia. Each produces four types of cars. To simplify this view, note that the supporting elements of the architecture, such as middleware and network infrastructure, are not present. Nor are visible the message routes that connect the car manufacturer's applications. The focus here is then

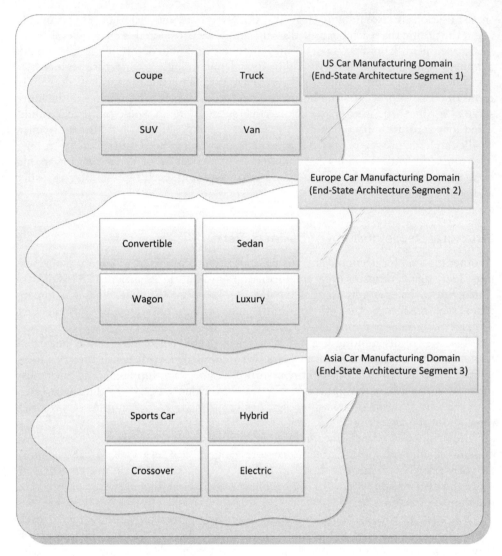

Figure 10.3   Structural Decomposition of Business Tiers

on the distribution of business domains across three continents, and most important, architecture decomposition into three domain tiers. Each tier is also founded as an end-state architecture segment:

1. Business Tier 1: U.S. car manufacturing domain—end-state architecture segment 1
2. Business Tier 2: Europe car manufacturing domain—end-state architecture segment 2
3. Business Tier 3: Asia car manufacturing domain—end-state architecture segment 3

After a quick examination, it is clear by now that each tier in Figure 10.3 is also established as an end-state architecture segment. And each of these segments includes a group of business capabilities, delivered by its related applications and/or components. Would they be too large to handle? Not every decomposed segment, however, must agree with a business tier boundary, as mentioned earlier. In some cases, outsized architecture segments may be too difficult to handle during the upcoming incremental software architecture verification process.

The work of decomposition, then, could focus on establishing finer-grained end-state architecture segments. Fine-grained means smaller groups of business capabilities. In this case, a business domain tier could be further subdivided into smaller design segments that would be easier to verify later.

Structural Distribution of Business Domains

The concepts of business layers and tiers have been discussed in the previous two sections. We also learned that each segment of the decomposed end-state architecture could represent a single business domain layer or tier. This is simplified mapping, however. It is a mere example. The result of such architecture subdivision may render large design segments that may be challenging to handle during the impending verification process. This decomposition activity, consequently, may call for a further domain breakdown until the outcome introduces fewer verification difficulties.

Understandably, the discovery activity of various business domains is an important prerequisite, a task that must be accomplished before any end-state architecture decomposition activity. But how and where can business domains be found? By now, we are aware that business domains are characteristically arranged in tightly coupled formations, such as layers. They can also be distributed, like loosely coupled tier structures. Expending on the distribution aspect, the next sections, therefore, discuss patterns of business domains formations, distributed over geographical locations. This aspect could ease their identification and enable efficient end-state architecture decomposition. Simply put, the more we know about how domains are typically distributed, the easier it will be to discover them.

Decomposing Centralized Business Domains

One of the most common business structures is the centralized business domain. This resembles the community center fabric pattern, discussed in Chapter 4. The arrangement of domains in a star-like shape, where the central domain controls its subordinates, explains the business interaction and relationship between lines of business in an enterprise. It must be emphasized, though, that these are business associations between business units of an organization, not links between nodes on a network.

The centralized business domain is a classic chain-of-command business pattern. Business decisions and strategies that are fashioned in the central domain affect the entire organization. Enterprise policies and best practices are propagated down to the surrounding business units. Indeed, this fosters a unified, and at times strict, protocol of communication. Yet, the enforcement of firm-wide guidelines is also its Achilles heel. A centralized business organization offers little comfort to business executives eager to launch business products on time and on budget.

A centralized architecture style serves a centralized business formation well. Both resemble the hub-and-spokes communication style, a pattern that is easy to remember. Therefore, lines of business that make up a centralized business domain would be easy to identify. The process of discovering domains that are distributed in such a style calls for ascertaining the dominant domain, typically the central business unit.

The next activity is to trace all the connected business domains. Once the centralized business domain structure has been identified and all domains in the formation have been located, the end-state architecture decomposition actually concludes. Each business domain and its systems, applications, middleware, and network infrastructure could become an end-state architecture segment. Akin to the previous sections, if an architecture segment were found to be too large, a further decomposition activity would be required to reduce its boundary.

Figure 10.4 depicts an end-state architecture decomposition of a centralized business domain. This illustration identifies a central banking office domain and its reporting five sub-organizations:

1. End-state architecture segment 1: chief financial officer domain (central management business unit)
2. End-state architecture segment 2: global banking domain
3. End-state architecture segment 3: global marketing domain
4. End-state architecture segment 4: investment banking domain

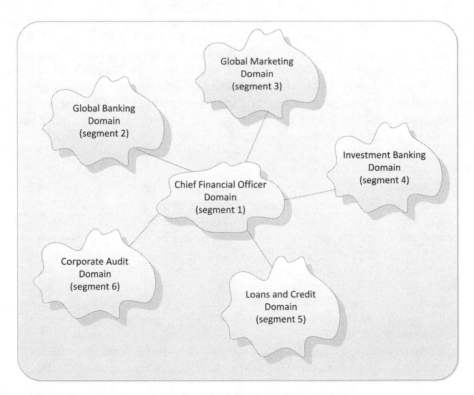

Figure 10.4   Decomposing a Centralized Business Domain Formation

5. End-state architecture segment 5: loans and credit domain
6. End-state architecture segment 6: corporate audit domain

Here again, the question about the direct mapping between a business domain and an end-state architecture segment might arise. As indicated in the previous sections, it is increasingly clear that if this end-state architecture decomposition activity renders large design segments, it would be possible to subdivide each domain layer into smaller sections. The reduction of segment size may simplify the forthcoming incremental software architecture verification process.

Decomposing Federated Business Domains

Another distribution scheme of a business structure is the federated business domains.[1] A federated business formation contrasts with the centralized business domain structure discussed in the previous section. The former does not depend on a centralized governance body. Instead, it forms a chain of domains that share vital information across multiple lines of business and organizations. Business imperatives shape such distribution. This formation is driven by a crucial business strategy that calls for achieving business interoperability and the need for forming solid communication with peer enterprises and partners.

The rapid evolution of business and the expansion of commerce calls for the establishment of a federated business domain structure to satisfy growing demands of consumers. The structural chain of the federated business scheme, therefore, forms a decentralized business model. Here, domains are linked to each other for a chief purpose: efficient transmission of data over a loosely coupled, perhaps even a long distance, area of business operations. Breaking off the centralized business model, the federated model is rooted in the requirements to connect lines of business across longer geographical distances.

As indicated in the previous sections, the first logical step would be to discover the domains that are part of the federated model. Once all business units have been detected, each could be recognized as an end-state architecture segment. It must be mentioned again that an architecture segment is not merely about the components of the design. It is about the assets and services of each domain. It is about the business capabilities delivered by systems, applications, components, and supporting infrastructure. And it is about the message exchange routes that link systems and applications to enable business transactions.

Figure 10.5 exemplifies the concept of an end-state architecture decomposition applied to a federated business environment in the pharmaceutical industry. The federated business structure spans three U.S. regions, each of which contains two domains. These linked lines of business execute the pharmaceutical business process:

1. U.S. region 1: Pharmaceutical research domain (end-state architecture segment 1), product development domain (end-state architecture segment 2)
2. U.S. region 2: Supply-chain management domain (end-state architecture segment 3), manufacturing (end-state architecture 4)
3. U.S. region 3: Marketing/sales domain (end-state architecture segment 5), healthcare services domain (end-state architecture segment 6)

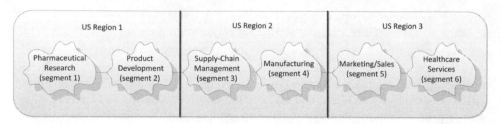

Figure 10.5   Decomposition of a Federated Business Domain Formation

Note that in Figure 10.5, the chained business domains are structured to process business activities that *do not require* a centralized formation. Each line of business or a business unit is responsible for different activities. The federated structure, therefore, enables the domains to share enterprise information and leverage the overall expertise of the organization. Moreover, the end-state decomposition activity established each domain as a design segment, in which systems and applications deliver business services. As with all formations discussed so far, here, too, the decision to decompose further a domain's operating environment depends on the granularity level of its operations. Recall, large end-state architecture segments may not be as useful for the impending verification process.

Clustered Business Domains

It is gradually more apparent that business models and strategies drive the distribution of business domains. In other words, the business direction typically affects the way it operates and is structured and distributed. As we have learned so far, a federated business, for example, is formed this way to enable information sharing across large entities, such as production environments and organizations. A centralized domain structure, on the other hand, is more tightly coupled, enabling strong enforcement of policies.

The strategy by which an enterprise incurs revenues calls for changes to the organization's structure. Indeed, organizational profits are tied with many other factors that affect the distribution of business domains. Some are affiliated with the demands of the industry in which a business is operating. Consumer requirements are another important ingredient that drives the formation of a business. A business model must take all these key factors in consideration and carve out a strategy for survival. Unfortunately, not all enterprises have a clear direction and a plan for the future. Some even grow organically—expanding with no guiding master plan.

When it comes to organizational structure, the term "organic" means disarray. This scenario reflects the state of most organizations that do not maintain a clear business structure. The clustered business domain formation is conceived as an organically grown environment, in which a business domain group has mutual commerce interest and must share information for existence. The relationships formed among the domain group members resemble the mesh fabric pattern. Each of the domains maintains direct associations with its peers, a point-to-point style of communication.

When it comes to the end-state architecture decomposition, the clustered business domains formation introduces myriad challenges to the discovery of lines of business.

This convoluted way of doing business also renders an intricate design and distribution model that is hard to decipher and, obviously, decompose. With topology and application mapping tools, discussed in Chapters 5 and 6, it would be possible to uncover the distribution plot of the clustered environment.

Figure 10.6 depicts a book publishing organization with its affiliated business domains. As shown, each domain not only represents the services it offers, but also is established as an end-state architecture segment:

Architecture segment 1: book proposal review domain
Architecture segment 2: contract domain
Architecture segment 3: content development domain
Architecture segment 4: book production domain
Architecture segment 5: publication domain
Architecture segment 6: marketing and sales domain

Note that the book publishing organization structure is a tightly coupled, yet distributed formation. Because it resembles the mesh fabric pattern, the underpinning technology inherits the distribution attributes of the depicted cluster business domains.

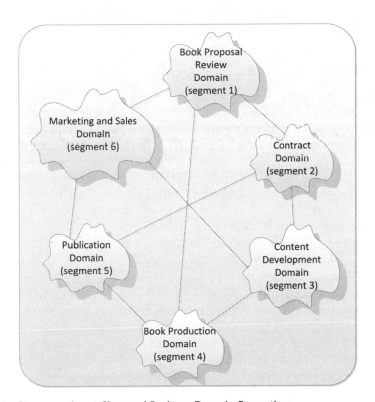

Figure 10.6   Decomposing a Clustered Business Domain Formation

Decomposing End-State Architecture into Volatile Business Segments

One of the most practical methods to decompose an end-state architecture is to identify areas defined as *volatile*. The term "volatile" pertains to segments in the architecture that are prone to business change. In other words, business changes prompt modifications to applications, components, middleware, and network infrastructure entities running in production. These entities are perceived as volatile because they are error-prone. And so are the production sections in which they operate.

These volatile spaces are easy to spot because monitoring and alerting systems are typically in place. However, it would not be an easy task to predict volatile business sections in an end-state architecture proposition if the design is merely on paper. How could then one forecast future alterations of software that has not yet been deployed? Engaging in a speculative guess would be counterproductive. The correct approach should then be to strike a fine balance between the "probable" and the "more likely" business volatility scenarios. It is more likely that in new design, construction, and deployment initiatives, changes to software and operating environment sections are known ahead of time.

This approach of architecture decomposition goes hand in hand with development, configuration, and integration projects launched to not only apply changes to an environment, but also to add and configure software entities. Again, a volatile architecture section is where it's likely more changes would be administered. And the areas that require changes are the interest of the end-state architecture decomposition practice.

Types of Volatilities in an End-State Architecture

Every modification to software or an integrated environment introduces potential errors. This makes them more vulnerable than any other entity that has not been modified. Most of us are aware that changes to software applications and components, for example, always take place during projects or regular maintenance of a run-time ecosystem. Moreover, before even starting with the construction of a product, it would be possible to reveal areas of volatility in an architecture blueprint. In both cases, either an operating production landscape or a mere design on paper, the volatility aspect should be investigated. The challenge would then be to locate these sensitive software assets and their potentially volatile related regions.

Business Drivers Contribute to Technological Volatility

We must understand that changes to organizational assets do not occur without trends in business strategies, visions, or missions. In fact, every shift in organizational thinking can trigger a large number of alterations to the way a firm conducts business. Any change in the market could initiate a number of product development and integration projects devised to win the competition. Any deviation from an ongoing stream of consumer demands could result in development of new concepts and generate a slew of project plans. Consequently, new business requirements spur new architecture endeavors.

The changes to the business galvanize organizational software development initiatives. The technological arm of an enterprise promotes changes to the way business solutions are executed. Acquisitions of superior technologies, such as middleware and hardware, make sections in a production environment volatile, too. There are endless permutations that could contribute to an unstable run-time ecosystem.

Volatile Enterprise Sources

Numerous volatile areas in an end-state architecture can be found. Therefore, in this section we refer to the most common ones. We must be aware, though, that there could always be unexpected areas prone to change which no one is able to predict. So let us have a look at Figure 10.7, which identifies enterprise asset sources that could be perceived as volatile. This illustration depicts two columns: crosscutting elements and enterprise assets. Under the former, we observe end-state architecture elements that are commonly used by all systems and applications in production:

Communication platforms These software or hardware entity groups may include messaging capabilities, intermediaries, and proxies that enable the transmission of information between systems and/or applications. Communications also pertain to software that enables or handles protocols for message exchange purposes.

Operations Under this category, we gather all production devices and production platforms, such as monitoring utilities, alerting and notification systems, and automated reporting.

Security Security platforms, such as identity and credential verification and authentication, are gathered in this group.

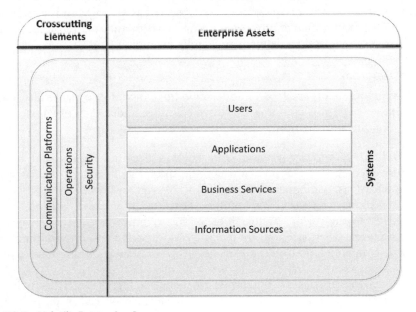

Figure 10.7   Volatile Enterprise Sources

The enterprise assets column, on the other hand, gathers common system elements that could be also observed as prone to change:

Users The users group identifies consuming entities, such as people, message request processes, consuming applications and components, or even business partners.

Applications These software implementations represent consumer platforms for services, such as banking applications, trading applications, car manufacturing applications, retail applications, and more.

Business services These software entities are typically distributed or federated components that execute business transactions on behalf of the applications.

Information sources Data sources, data warehouses, and third-party data providers are included in this prone to change group.

An Environment Volatility Model

End-state architecture may be composed of innumerable applications, software components, middleware products, and network infrastructure entities. It is common to apply changes to countless production areas during a large enterprise project. The array of modifications grows exponentially when substantial deployment and integration activities are also part of such a product development and launching initiative.

Therefore, there is a need for creating an *environment volatility model* that could shed light on the specific prone-to-change segments in end-state architecture. Sections in the grand design that are identified as likely to change, meaning volatile, should be candidate segments for architecture verification (refer to Chapters 12–15 to read more about the incremental software architecture verification process). So what about the slices of the architecture that have not been observed as volatile? In the context of a project or a business initiative, there is nothing to worry about because they may not even be a part of the product delivery and deployment plan.

Volatility Diagram

Let us have a look at Figure 10.8 to understand how to compose a volatility diagram. As shown, the diagram is comprised of three columns, under each of which we place the corresponding information:

1. *End-state architecture segments.* This column identifies the end-state architecture decomposed sections, in which the enterprise IT assets, such as systems, applications, components, and middleware products, reside.
2. *Crosscutting elements.* This column shows the common platforms that are shared by the various applications, middleware products, and network infrastructure elements. These are typically security products, provisioning servers, and communication mechanisms, such as messaging infrastructure, proxies, and gateways.
3. *Volatile enterprise assets.* The prone-to-change elements under this column are typically the applications that deliver business services, users, presentation layer facilities, data access layer, data sources, and more.

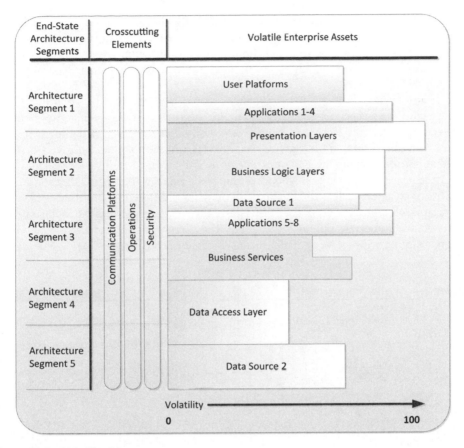

Figure 10.8   Volatility Diagram

Volatility Diagram Analysis

When the volatility diagram, depicted in Figure 10.8, becomes subject for analysis, there are two important columns to inspect: 1) The most left column named "end-state architecture segments," which includes the result of the end-state architecture decomposition effort. In this illustration, we observe five different segments. 2) The most right column named "volatile enterprise assets," which includes volatile production assets, prone to change, such as applications, components, services, and repositories.

Consider the relationship formed between these two columns:

1. End-state architecture segment 1 includes user platforms, applications 1–4, and some presentation layer components.
2. End-state architecture segment 2 contains some presentation layer components and business logic layers.
3. End-state architecture segment 3 is made up of data source 1, applications 5–8, and some business services.
4. End-state architecture segment 4 consists of some business services and some data access layer components.
5. End-state architecture segment 5 encompasses some data access layer components and data source 2.

This break down demonstrates that a software entity may not always reside in a single architecture segment. The decision to make some presentation layer components, for example, available in two different architecture segments depends on design decisions. Considerations such as component reuse may drive such decomposition boundaries.

An additional observation that must be noted is related to the volatility values of the volatile enterprise assets. For example, the presentation layer components in end-state architecture segments 1 and 2 are defined as extremely volatile (100 value on the volatility scale). This implies that special attention should be given to these implementations during the end-state verification process.

Another interesting aspect when it comes to measuring volatility is that some components of an asset, such as the business services, have different volatility values in two end-state architecture segments. In this case, the business services bar appears to be longer in architecture segment 4 than in 3. This determination typically depends on design assumptions that were made during the analysis process.

Note

1. Michael Bell, *Service-Oriented Modeling (SOA): Service Analysis, Design, and Architecture*, 2008, John Wiley & Sons, p. 203

CHAPTER 11

Environment Behavior Drives End-State Architecture Decomposition

Once again we explore how to decompose an end-state architecture in a different way. Doing this would best prepare us for pursuing the incremental software architecture verification process, elaborated on in Chapters 12 to 15. This process calls for verifying parts of the end-state architecture and then certifying the overall grand-scale design.

So far, we have learned a number of methods of end-state architecture decomposition. The main one is driven by breaking the grand enterprise design into structural formations, such as business and technical sub-architectures. We also studied how to slice an end-state architecture into segments by analyzing business structures, such as layers, tiers, clusters, and federations. In addition, identifying volatile business areas is another method for segmenting an end-state architecture.

Now it is time to study how to dissect an end-state architecture into areas of behavior. To accomplish this, functionality, processes, and activities of systems and their related assets, such as applications, components, and middleware should be identified.

All these behaviors together would reveal the overall direction and strategy of an end-state architecture. Most important however, promote the functional decomposition of an end-state architecture.

The traditional term "functional decomposition" is largely known as the practice of breaking down a complex process into simple and smaller activities. This pertains to any type of process, such as business or even technical ones. The chief idea is to take apart complex functionality to learn its underpinning activities. So what would be the purpose of such traditional decomposition? There are countless benefits of pursuing this practice. One is performed by application analysts to understand better the implementation goals, and most important, learn about the driving requirements. Architects and software developers, too, tend to employ functional decomposition to build loosely coupled and reusable software components. Indeed, the list of paybacks is long.

End-State Architecture Environment Behavior Decomposition

A multifaceted real-time environment that hosts systems and their related applications, supporting middleware, and network infrastructure entities would be more challenging to decompose. When it comes to breaking down an end-state architecture environment such as this, the traditional functional decomposition, as described in the introduction of this chapter, would be limited to slicing up processes of applications and software components.

But what about the end-state architecture environment itself? How would one break up the functionality of the grand design that encompasses systems and their related applications, middleware, and supporting middleware and network infrastructure products? Would it be possible to employ the traditional functional decomposition method to separate an end-state architecture behavior?

Indeed, the term "end-state architecture behavior" refers to a vital concept: *behavior of an architecture environment as a whole*. In this context, behavior refers to the *capability* of such computing landscape to offer solutions. Therefore, here behavior means *overall functionality*. Behavior means processes. Behavior means component activities. Behavior means actions taken by integrated off-the-shelf products to exchange messages with other software or hardware entities. The questions that follow can clarify more the meaning of environment behavior:

- How should an end-state architecture be decomposed into areas of behavior?
- Could behavior areas of a decomposed end-state architecture reveal an enterprise design strategy or expose design decisions?
- Could behavioral decomposition shed light on the driving business and technical requirements of an end-state architecture?
- What are the relationships between application processes and component activities?
- How does system functionality affect application processes?
- How should middleware product functionality be broken down?
- Could a group of functions represent business or technological capabilities?

Now it is clear that an end-state architecture environment behavioral decomposition could divulge imperative details about the architecture's justification to exist. Each segment of the grand architecture can tell a story about the driving business requirements. Each part of the design could shed light on the composition of systems and applications. A collaboration between the architecture segments could divulge the overall enterprise integration scheme. But beyond the interaction between the architecture elements, the behavior of the environment would be an essential aspect to discover. And the behavior of the environment as a whole depends on the decomposed architecture segments.

End-State Architecture Environment Behavior Levels

In the previous introduction, it was mentioned that an end-state architecture environment is multifaceted. This assertion is generally true since it depicts a complex production landscape whose design is difficult to decipher. Behavior decomposition of the environment comes in handy now because it enables managers, architects, developers, and analysts to see beyond the integration clutter. It helps business and IT professionals to grasp the vast deployment of myriad enterprise software and hardware assets. The decomposition endeavor also opens new perspectives in an environment that is hard to maintain and repair. To attain such benefits, we must first employ a method for environment behavior decomposition.

Environment Behavior Decomposition Model

Now, let us have a look at Figure 11.1 to understand the proposed approach by which an end-state architecture landscape behavior can be later decomposed. But even before slicing up an end-state architecture, let us look at the model to understand how assets in a production environment related to each other. This illustration depicts a hierarchical structure of three behavioral layers in an overall system environment: *system-level crosscutting assets behavior, application-level behavior, and component-level behavior*:

1. System-level crosscutting assets behavior. This top level of an environment behavior reflects the functionality and features of crosscutting products and implementations used by applications and components, such as middleware, proxies, security platforms, and network infrastructure entities.
2. Application-level behavior. Applications are positioned under the system-level crosscutting assets behavior layer in the environment behavior hierarchy. An application behavior is discovered by analyzing its processes. Breaking down an application into processes is the task of application-level behavior decomposition.
3. Component-level behavior. The lowest level in the environment behavior hierarchy consists of components. Breaking down a component into activities is the task of component-level behavior decomposition.

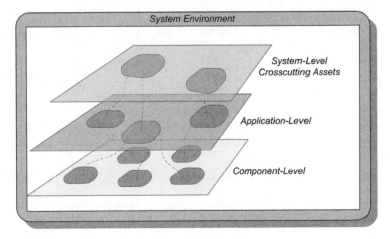

Figure 11.1   Environment Behavior Decomposition Model

The work of environment behavior decomposition should start with the lowest one in the hierarchy, the component level, next moving up to the application level, and finally concluding with the system-level crosscutting asset. It is important to note that each layer in the environment structure directly or indirectly depends on each other. Another way of perceiving the environment is by visualizing the influence of system-level crosscutting asset behavior on applications and lower-level components.

Cascading Behaviors in End-State Architecture Environment

The cascading effect of an end-state architecture environment behavior is therefore apparent. That is, any functional behavior that occurs on the system-level trickles down to the lower levels. This influence could be viewed in Figure 11.2. It is also clear that any information manipulated on the system-level could be potentially transmitted to the dependent applications and components. Data could also be disseminated and shared between all environment behavior layers. The collaboration between all three levels is highly dependable, therefore in many production environments tightly coupled. This is perhaps one of the chief reasons for failing systems, integration, and operations in production environments. The three architecture behavior layers have been increasingly getting thicker. Consequently, the dependencies between crosscutting system assets, applications, and components create constant integration and support challenges.

Upstream Environment-Level Behavior Influences

When decomposing an architecture into behavior areas, an intriguing aspect should be investigated: Does the lowest component level affect operations of the system level crosscutting assets? The resounding answer is "yes." This round-trip influence by the lowest components in the food chain has an immense impact on the behavior of the highest levels. This is not a mere theory. Source code glitches, for example, could potentially affect the performance of large systems. Moving up the behavior hierarchy, application bottlenecks and response time are other causes for system failures.

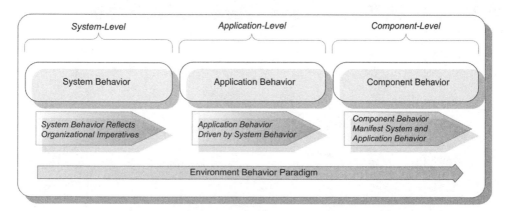

Figure 11.2   Cascading Effect of Environment Behavior

Understanding how behaviors of applications and components affect system-level performance and stability could be the key for loosening up a production environment.

The mindfulness of ill-designed applications carries powerful benefits for preventing deployment of broken systems.

Therefore, be aware of upstream environment-level behavior influences. Simply put, the devil is always in the details—big bad things typically happen because of accumulated small ones. Continuous deployments of software to a production environment increase the vulnerability across an ecosystem landscape. The more problems the lower behavior levels of the system accumulate, the more influence they have on the higher levels.

Attention should be paid to the balance between low behavior levels to high ones. Organizations should weigh the effect of environment behavior levels on each other. Especially ponder the influences of components and applications on systems crosscutting assets, such as middleware and network infrastructure. This analysis upshot would most likely be subjective and introduce different conclusions.

Consider the questions that follow to determine the influence of low behavior levels on higher ones:

- Could the collective behavior of a large number of component activities affect system and their related application behaviors?
- Could the joint behavior of applications influence the behavior of systems?
- Could a combined behavior of applications and components affect system behavior?

Component-Level Behavior Decomposition

Most business and IT practitioners understand what a software component is. In this chapter, we refer to the same industry standard component definition. A component is a piece of software, generally smaller than an application. It is recognized as the nucleus of every loosely coupled design and construction initiative. A Web service for example, is often referred to as a component since it typically offers a narrow range of activities. The chief design motivation for grounding a development initiative on components is to boost software reuse. Components also foster separation of business or technical concerns into smaller and nimbler units of functionality. Characteristically, a tightly coupled or monolithic application that is established upon libraries, not necessarily components, would offer fewer or no components in the least.

When looking at the big picture, depicted in Figure 11.1, a hierarchical behavior structure is revealed. A system as a whole may be composed of multiple applications, components, middleware, and network infrastructure elements. A loosely coupled application is typically made up of multiple components. Thus, in the hierarchical structure of an environment behavior, software component activities are positioned at the lower level.

But wait. This introduction implies that a component is a part of an application. This may not be the case in a distributed environment, in which software constructs are dispersed across a large production landscape. The notion that a component is only an integral part of an application is incorrect. In contrast, autonomous components could live independently in a production environment without being physically included in applications. That is, an independent component could be a part of system cross-cutting assets. A Web service, for example, is a component that could be deployed independently in any Web application server.

We start here with behavior-level component decomposition. This task calls for identifying the fine-grained functions executed by software components. These functions are named component activities.

The concept of component-level behavior decomposition would be easy to understand with an example.

Component-Level Behavior Decomposition Example

We continue then with a component-level behavior decomposition example that comes with Figure 11.3. This is a classic case of the traditional functional decomposition method, employed during software development to improve asset reuse and foster nimbleness. The illustration clearly shows a separation of concerns case for the investment research services group.

Note that the depicted functional decomposition task centers on component activities, not processes that are more affiliated to applications. An activity is a finer-grained function, finer than a process. In fact, a process encompasses one or more activities. The correlation between activities and processes is discussed in the

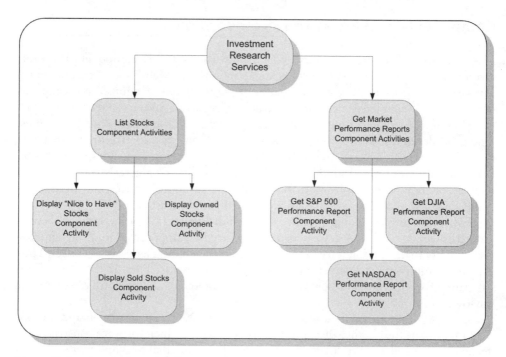

Figure 11.3   Component-Level Behavior Decomposition

upcoming Application-Level Behavior Decomposition section. But for now, let us continue to investigate the functional decomposition presented in Figure 11.3.

The hierarchical structure rendered by the functional decomposition of the investment research services group is broken apart into two chief component activity subgroups: list stocks component activities and get market performance reports component activities. Each of these subgroups yields three activities.

- List stocks component activities group:
  - Display "nice to have" stocks component activity
  - Display sold stocks component activity
  - Display owned stocks component activity
- Get market performance reports component activities group:
  - Get S&P 500 performance report component activity
  - Get NASDAQ performance report component activity
  - Get DJIA performance report component activity

Is It Now Time for Overall End-State Architecture Decomposition?

Could the functional decomposition of the component-level behavior pursued thus far yield useful end-state architecture segments. Would these sections of the design be valuable for the imminent end-state architecture verification process (discussed in Chapters 12–15)? Aren't these design segments too fine-grained?

The only honest answer to these questions would be, "let us wait." Do not rush to establish architecture segments right after the component-level behavior functional decomposition. It is probably too early. One must view the bigger picture and climb up the ladder of behavior levels to understand how it would be possible to slice up an environment based on behavior considerations.

Moreover, the example in Figure 11.3 does not represent a component-level behavior environment worth breaking up to create end-state architecture segments. It is simply too small of an environment, lacking functionality. It is merely an example to demonstrate functional decomposition of component activities. But even in the real computing world, the component-level behavior area may introduce such a dilemma. Components alone may not include enough business or technical functions to produce valuable end-state architecture segments.

Application-Level Behavior Decomposition

For the discussion in this section, let us look again at Figure 11.1. As shown, the application-level behavior layer is located under the system crosscutting asset layer and above the component layer. This intermediate position is set for any type of applications, either homegrown implementations or commercial off-the-self products (COTS). The term "application" is used to describe client-facing and back-end software that not only provides user interfaces, but also offers interaction capabilities with many types of services driven by business logic. There are numerous categories of applications in a variety of fields, such as financial, accounting, trading, gaming, and many more.

With the rapid evolution of advanced technologies, application distribution and deployment go far beyond a production environment. That is, an application could also be installed on a client desktop. Others are even downloaded to smartphones or other handheld devices. But even with remote deployments such as this, many distributed applications must be supported by middleware and/or network infrastructure.

For example, a home security application installed on a smartphone may require remote cloud storage to save the monitoring video clips. Other remotely distributed programs, such as social media applications, leverage cloud capacity to share images with friends and family on the Internet. These offered services must support dedicated infrastructure and repositories in a production environment to be able to accommodate customer demands.

For that reason, the application-level behavior decomposition must take into account all environment variables and permutations to establish a solid functional decomposition. The challenge would then be to understand the complex distribution of applications and study their relationship with users and the supporting infrastructure.

Application-Level Behavior Decomposition Example

For the application-level behavior decomposition, once again, use the functional decomposition approach to separate concerns and group capabilities. When it comes to separating application functionality, we no longer decompose the behavior into activities, as is pursued with component decomposition, discussed earlier. Here, an application is broken down into coarse-grained functions, referred to as processes. As mentioned previously, processes encompass one or more activities.

Figure 11.4 illustrates the functional decomposition of an application-level behavior. The trading application is broken down into two main processes: trade and get statements. Consider their related sub-processes in the list that follows:

- Trade process
  - Search symbols sub-process
  - Submit trade orders sub-process
- Get statements process
  - Get business account statements sub-process
  - Get individual account statements sub-process

A process could be broken into an infinite number of sub-processes. This would obviously increase the decomposition tree and deepen its structure. The practice of functional decomposition, though, calls for building concise hierarchies. Instead of creating a tree with a large number of levels, group related fine-grained processes (named here sub-processes) under a more generic process name. By doing this, the tree structure would only include the vital processes, without unnecessary details.

Another important functional decomposition aspect to note in Figure 11.4 is the inclusion of two application-related component activities: generate order confirmations and render statements. Although these activities belong to the component-level

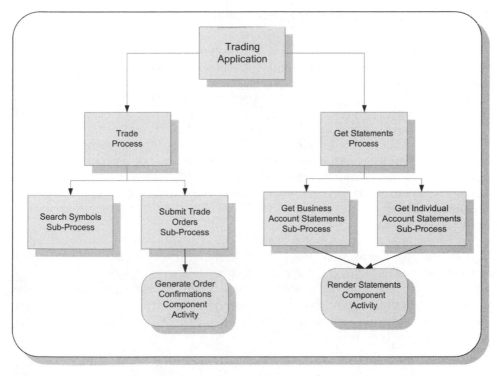

Figure 11.4   Application-Level Behavior Decomposition

behavior layer discussed earlier, they are depicted here to demonstrate the relationship with the application-level behavior layer.

Another vital aspect to remember is that components are the best candidates for reuse. In other words, a software component should offer generic interfaces to be utilized by external entities, such as applications or middleware products. The example provided in this illustration shows that the render statement component activity is indeed utilized by the two trading application processes: get business account statements and get individual account statements. The generate order confirmations component activity, on the other hand, is only used by the submit trade orders sub-process.

Is It Time Now for Overall End-State Architecture Decomposition?

After concluding with the functional decomposition of the component-level and application-level behaviors, it would be the proper time to start thinking about grouping activities and processes into logical business or technical capabilities. This does not mean that the end-state architecture segmentation should go full steam ahead. The entire environment behavior has not been uncovered and analyzed yet. A big piece of information is still missing, one that is elaborated on in the next section.

System-Level Behavior Decomposition

A system is one of the largest entities in a production environment. Thus, the analysis requires detail examination of its comprising elements. As stated throughout this book, a system encompasses many software and hardware products, each of which contributes business or technical capabilities. A system environment typically contains crosscutting products, software components, and applications that execute activities and processes.

A system crosscutting asset environment also contains supporting middleware. This may include an ESB, data access layers, gateways, application servers, data aggregators, search engines, business rules engines, software proxies, and many more. Moreover, production support entities include a wide range of security platforms and management utilities. For example, monitoring capabilities, asset management products, and performance-monitoring tools are only a few items from the production engineers' toolbox.

Network infrastructure products add to the system-level crosscutting arsenal of capabilities. Applications would not be able to trade information without message routing and load balancing devices. Without efficient and wise topology configurations, a network grid would introduce bottlenecks and performance degradation. Without proper network protocols, it would be impossible to serve wireless consumers. Without cloud infrastructure and virtual server and desktop capabilities, the world of computing would seem utterly limited.

What Is System Behavior Decomposition?

Consequently, the complex world of a system should be decomposed into functions, features, processes, and activities. The term "system," therefore, is analogous to an operating environment, an area in a production landscape, or perhaps even a segment of an end-state architecture. An intricate environment like this behaves in specific ways to provide solutions, offer services, and meet business goals. Now, it is time to analyze a *system environment behavior* through a larger perspective—the system view.

The work of system environment decomposition then calls for identifying areas of behaviors in its environment. To accomplish this attend to the three fundamental discovery tasks that one should pursue:

1. What functions and features the system-level crosscutting assets offer (as discussed these are the supporting middleware and network infrastructure)?
2. What are the provided application processes?
3. What activities the components provide?

Again, discovering system functionality, features, processes, and activities is the chief mission. By doing this, we would be able to understand the direction of the design and ascertain the underpinning system assets that drive the overall behavior.

System-Level Behavior Decomposition Example

Figure 11.5 depicts the decomposition of a system environment behavior breakdown. In this illustration the separation of concerns are visible by separating the system entities into groups of distinct services on different levels of granularity. It is important

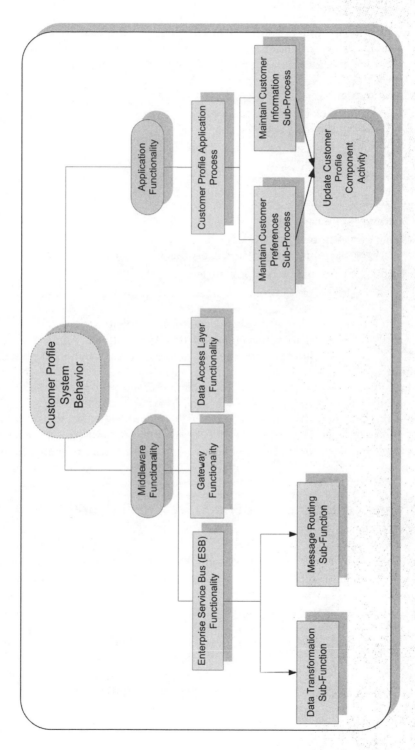

Figure 11.5   System-Level Behavior Decomposition

to note that the overall system-level behavior includes all the encompassed system assets. In our case, for demonstration purposes, Figure 11.5 depicts also the functional decomposition of application-level processes and component-level activities. These functional decompositions are shown earlier in the sections Application-Level Behavior Decomposition and Component-Level Behavior Decomposition.

■ Middleware Functionality (system-level crosscutting asset)
  • Enterprise service bus (ESB) functionality
    • Data transformation sub-function
    • Message routing sub-function
  • Gateway functionality
  • Data access layer functionality
■ Application functionality (application-level asset)
  • Customer profile application process
    • Maintain customer preferences sub-process
    • Maintain customer information sub-process
■ Component functionality (component-level asset)
  • Update customer profile component activity

Figure 11.5 makes it clear that the decomposition of a system environment behavior must contain all collaborating elements that offer solutions. Applications and components in this illustration are separated by employing the functional decomposition practice. Other system-level crosscutting assets—the middleware assets ESB, gateway, and the data access layer—are not decomposed into processes or activities. Instead, the analysis is centered on discovering their functionalities by studying the features they provide. As illustrated, the ESB functionality is further broken down into the two depicted capabilities: data transformation and message routing. Here, the specification of functionality explains what the ESB technical abilities and features are.

Environment Behavior Drives End-State Architecture Decomposition

So far the three levels of environment behavior have been functionally decomposed: component-level, application-level, and system-level crosscutting assets. On the component-level, software actions were broken down into fine-grained activities. These were small-scale operations, carried by components to accomplish narrow ranges of business and/or technical goals. Next, the functional decomposition continued with separating applications into processes. These are coarse-grained operations, typically devised to fire up a wider range of actions, such as sub-processes and/or component activities. We concluded then with separating the system-level environment into functionalities of applications, components, and middleware crosscutting products.

The three different functional decomposition initiatives not only uncovered the behavior of each level in a system or an area in an end-state architecture, but also revealed the direction of the overall enterprise design. It has become increasingly clear what the environment is designed to achieve and the means it employs to fulfill business and technical goals. It is important to recall that this exercise, though, is not about modeling business processes. Nor is the intention to map message paths. It is much simpler: Discover the functions of components, applications, and systems. Mainly, understand the behavior and decompose it.

During each of the previous sections, the question raised was whether we are ready to decompose the end-state architecture into segments even before the system-level functional breakdown. Were we? To some extent, though, the attempt to segment an environment only based on the discovered decomposed processes of applications would be a hasty decision. Do not rush to segment the end-state architecture before the entire process concludes. There would be instances, however, that application-level functional decomposition would suffice if a project or an end-state architecture is limited in scope. But enterprise-level initiative appeals for investigating larger functional behavior spaces.

This brings the discussion to the point where all is ready to begin with the end-state architecture decomposition. This upcoming slicing task is all about segmenting an enterprise architecture or a project design into sections, each of which should embody related functionalities, each of which represent a behavior. To do this, let us have a look at an example demonstrating this process.

Create an End-State Architecture Environment Behavior Diagram

In this section, the focus is on building a diagram that exemplifies the concept of end-state architecture environment behavior. Simply put, the goal is then to create an environment behavior diagram. This straightforward task would only require any flowchart software that allows the creation of a swim lane chart. Let us review Figure 11.6 to understand how the lanes should be arranged and what architecture elements each of them ought to contain.

We start with the top swim lane. This space is prepared for placing system-level crosscutting assets. Note that an end-state architecture may include multiple systems. Position in it all the functional decomposition artifacts that have been created for the system-level crosscutting assets. As depicted in Figure 11.6 these are middleware elements and cloud services. Note the three product groups: data integrator, message-oriented middleware, and cloud services. Each of these system-level supporting assets offers distinct services to support the behavior levels beneath, apparent as application and component swim lanes. The discussion about what each asset offers, functionality, and features will take place shortly. Let us first focus now on overall diagram structure.

The middle swim lane is dedicated to application processes. Simply place here the breakdown of application behaviors. In the example in Figure 11.6, there are three online applications, each of which offers a different line of product: books, men's grooming, and luggage. For each depicted line of business, there are also related processes, arranged in a tree structure, illustrating the applications' functional decomposition.

Lastly, the component-level behavior breakdown should be placed in the bottom swim lane. Most end-state architecture software components could be positioned there. There is no need, though, to drop in components that are insignificant to the overall design. Reusable or key business and/or technical components should

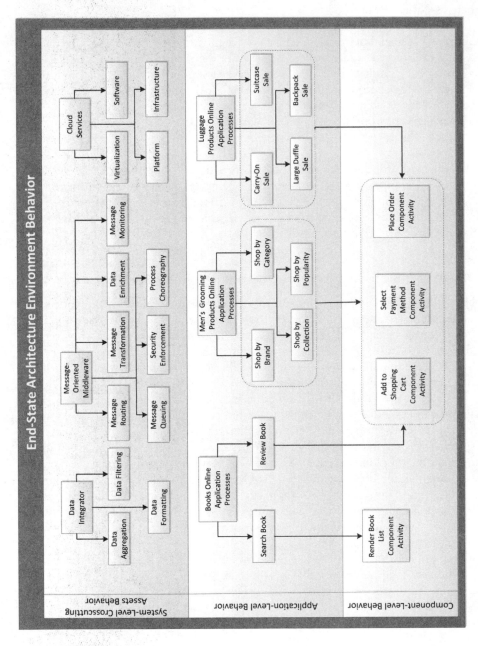

Figure 11.6 End-State Architecture Environment Behavior Diagram

be the best candidates for placement. Moreover, it is apparent that the depicted components in the bottom swim lane are also used by the three applications located in the application-level behavior swim lane. However, the component-level behavior swim lane may include stand-alone components operating autonomously, perhaps executed by the system-level crosscutting assets swim lane. In this example, however, there are no such components.

So here we go. We have all that is needed to start thinking about end-state architecture decomposition, a segmentation initiative based on the functional behavior of the environment.

End-State Architecture Environment Behavior Diagram Analysis

There is so much more to display in an end-state environment behavior diagram. Relationships between organizational software and hardware assets could be shown. There may be assets that belong to two or all of the diagram swim lanes. These are typically hybrid types of entities that embody the application process, and on the other hand, include middleware components. Think about the thick desktop application that contains all necessary business logic, yet it also includes a presentation layer and even protocol handling. Another hybrid implementation example would be a monolithic application that maintains its own data, and of course, executes business transactions. Hybrid, indeed.

The end-state architecture environment behavior diagram in Figure 11.6 is simplified. However, the concept of environment functional decomposition comes across clearly by showing the possible relationship between the three behavior layers. Looking at the behavior landscape of an end-state architecture for a project or an enterprise initiative is a fundamental requirement for design segmentation. Furthermore, the ability to create separate levels of behaviors to inspect the granularity of operations would be beneficial to the simplification of enterprise architecture. Understanding how each behavior layer affects its adjacent layer could foster a more loosely coupled environment. The dependency between enterprise software and hardware entities could be reduced, too.

The end-state architecture system-level crosscutting assets behavior illustrated in Figure 11.6 includes vital middleware and infrastructure functionalities to support the application-level and component-level behavior:

- Data integrator
  - Data aggregation
  - Data formatting
  - Data filtering
- Message-oriented middleware
  - Message routing
  - Message transformation
  - Data enrichment
  - Message monitoring
  - Message queuing
  - Security enforcement
  - Process choreography

- Cloud services
  - Virtualization
  - Software
  - Platform
  - Infrastructure

The application-level behavior space includes three online retail business processes:

- Books online application processes
  - Search book
  - Review book
- Men's grooming products online processes
  - Shop by brand
  - Shop by category
  - Shop by collection
  - Shop by popularity
- Luggage products online
  - Carry-on sale
  - Suitcase sale
  - Large duffle sale
  - Backpack sale

The component-level behavior contains the render book list component activity used only by the application process search book. The other three component activities—add to shopping cart, select payment method, and place order—are reused by the men's grooming products online and luggage products online application processes.

Finally, End-State Architecture Decomposition: A Segmentation Process

The decisive moment has arrived. It is subjective, though. Interpretations of the environment behavior diagram might yield myriad variations of end-state architecture segments. As easy as it sounds, there would not be full consensus about the design partitioning effort. However, the show must go on. It is mandatory to come up with architecture segments so the impending incremental software architecture verification can begin (see Chapters 12–15). Slicing an end-state architecture is a must for verifying if an architecture will work in production. Separating end-state architecture areas of behavior must conclude so developers could start proving that the design is sound and reliable.

There is nothing more to add before studying Figure 11.7. This illustration demonstrates the segmentation of the end-state architecture environment behavior diagram. As depicted, two design segments were encircled: end-state architecture 1 and end-state architecture 2. The two segments overlap in the component-behavior level swim lane. This was necessary because of the loosely coupled and nimble nature of the components—they simply offer a great deal of reuse.

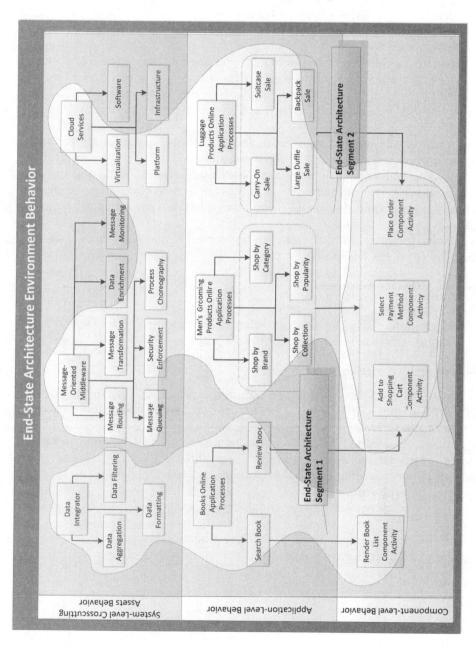

Figure 11.7 Decomposing an End-State Architecture into Segments

177

Consider the two enclosures that mark the behavior of the two end-state architecture segments:

End-state architecture segment 1   Data integrator middleware, books online application processes, render book list component activity, add to shopping cart component activity, select payment method component activity, and place order component activity

End-state architecture segment 2   Message-oriented middleware, cloud services, men's grooming products online application processes, luggage products online application processes, add to shopping cart component activity, select payment method component activity, and place order component activity

Any end-state architecture segmentation scenario should not be based on arbitrary decisions or strategies. This design breakdown must be driven by architecture direction and vision. This is also a good time to query the architects, demand explanation, and ask for clarifications. Obviously, the partition of the end-state architecture in Figure 11.7 does not give hints about the reasons behind the end-state architecture segmentation decisions.

Consider the questions that follow to understand the motives of the end-state architecture segmentation efforts:

End-state architecture segment 1

Why is the data integrator in the system-level crosscutting assets behavior swim lane affiliated with the books online application processes? Does the data integrator aggregate information for the application?

End-state architecture segment 2

Why is the data enrichment and message monitoring functionality (in the message-oriented middleware formation) excluded from this end-state architecture segment?

Similarly, why are the software and infrastructure services (in the cloud formation) excluded from this end-state architecture segment?

What is the contribution of the message-oriented middleware to end-state architecture segment 2?

By the same token, how do the cloud services facilitate end-state architecture segment 2?

Why are the men's grooming products online application processes and the luggage online application processes bundled in end-state architecture segment 2?

PART FOUR

End-State Architecture Verification

The process of end-state architecture verification comes last. After the architecture discovery, analysis, and decomposition activities have taken place, the verification process begins. This phase calls for a number of tasks devised to certify the enterprise grand-scale design. It is now time to substantiate the solidity of an end-state architecture. Without the verification process, no budgets should be allocated to support an unproven design.

When the verification process is launched to certify a computing environment that has been already operating in production, obviously there is no need for software development and integration activities. Certification tasks for an active environment like this ought to be conducted to spot troubling implementations and to correct them.

For new enterprise projects, however, an end-state architecture verification should include software development and integration of individual sections, pursued one at a time or even in parallel. Confirming that the software development efforts meet business and technical requirements is the ultimate proof that the design is reliable.

When pursuing the incremental software architecture approach, the traditional software development phase is no longer named construction; and the process of integration and delivery is no longer named transition. Here, they are part of the end-state architecture verification process.

Moreover, the incremental architecture method calls for limiting the scope of the source code construction to sections of the end-state architecture. In other words, the work of construction, deployment, and integration is dictated by the content of individual sections. This method mitigates the risks involved with launching large development projects.

Consider the three practices employed to validate and certify an end-state architecture. These are elaborated on in the chapters that follow:

1. *Design substantiation (Chapter 12).* These software development, deployment, and integration processes are devised to prove that each segment of the end-state architecture environment indeed operates as specified in business and technical requirements. (End-state architecture segments are established during the decomposition activities, discussed in Chapters 7–11.)
2. *End-state architecture stress testing (Chapters 13 and 14).* An end-state architecture environment is tested to discover breaking points in the overall design.
3. *Enterprise capacity planning (Chapter 15).* This process renders an enterprise resource utilization plan that mandates sizing an end-state architecture environment.

CHAPTER 12
Design Substantiation

Nothing proves more conclusively that an end-state architecture is indeed performing as expected than its sound implementation. If the design proposition were still an architecture blueprint, the task would be then to implement segments of the overall architecture to substantiate the founding planning and assumptions.

At this crucial junction in the incremental software architecture process, the charter is clear: *Prove it by implementing it.*

However, if the end-state architecture has been delivered, deployed, and now operates in production, then the task is different. Here, the mission would be to discover troubling segments of the end-state architecture, ascertain the root cause issues, and apply proper remedies. In some cases, though, it would be wise to retire a troubling system or an application if the efforts to avert a shutdown outweigh the benefits of rescue. This also goes for a failing environment, in which systems, applications, middleware, or network infrastructures do not meet business or technical requirements.

Either of these scenarios calls for action. In the former, when a software construction is about to take place to verify an architecture, a design substantiation effort must be pursued. For such an endeavor, continue though the sections that follow to learn about process of *design substantiation*. If the aim is to find troubling architecture segments or to save failing implementations, simply refer to Chapters 13 15. These chapters introduce stress testing and capacity planning methods for assessing the strength of the overall end-state architecture environment and capabilities to meet requirements.

Before moving on to the next section, now it is time to assert what the design substantiation is all about: *As part of the end-state architecture verification process, a software construction and integration efforts are launched to validate segments of the enterprise grand-scale design.*

A Shift from Software Development to Design Substantiation

No matter which software development methodology an organization embraces, in the context of the incremental software architecture, the traditional software development endeavor, as we know it, is not applicable. No one should launch mammoth development initiatives with no end in sight. No one should manage long-term projects without an unforeseeable destination. No one should be engaged in long-standing software construction projects without tangible and rapid achievements to show for the efforts. Moreover, no software construction should be launched without an end-state architecture proposition. Without a clear and detail design blueprint, budgets should not be allocated.

The likelihood that a long-lasting project changes its goals midstream is extremely high. A project scope creep could then take place. Specifically, the project timeline would extend due to a variety of reasons, such as poor management, and nebulous business and technical requirements. An ambiguous business model and affiliated strategies could also cause mismanaged product development and missed delivery deadlines.

On the other hand, the less time it takes for software construction, the sooner business goals can be achieved. Not only are short development durations more affordable to enterprise sponsors, the coordination between team members is manageable. Imminent successful outcomes bestow quick wins to hardworking software construction teams. Indeed, the window for success is narrow, even narrower with today's growing customer demands.

Therefore, say "NO" to the traditional software development phase driven by interminable requirements that are arduous to achieve. Say "NO" to a product construction initiative that is not driven by design requirements. In fact, the incremental software architecture practice calls for replacing the term "software development" with "design substantiation." This shift denotes a shift toward a more practical software construction charter: *insuring success of enterprise design*. No longer should developers pursue software development for the sake of testing experimental technologies. No longer should anyone chase personal agendas to prove questionable ideas.

Instead, design substantiation is a defined and clear goal to attain. It comes with a narrow purpose to fulfill—*developing software to achieve architecture goals with less emphasis on development goals*.

The Challenges with Waterfall, Iterative, and Incremental Software Development Approaches

Many would argue that an iterative software development is in essence an improved waterfall approach. There is some truth to this claim. As we delve into the details and understand what each method is about, it should become apparent that no matter how the product life cycle time is sliced to pursue various development practices, the progression through the project seems to be the same. Both call for sequential software development tasks that depend on each other. Both mandate a chronological progression through the development life cycle stages. And both require the evaluation of produced artifact at the end of each milestone.

A Sequential Flow of Software Development

To understand this comparison better, let us look at the fundamental building blocks of each approach. The waterfall method introduces a sequential flow of software development evolution. This process contains a number of stages that must be met in a strict order until the product life cycle concludes: requirements, design, implementation, testing, and finally maintenance. The linear progression though the life cycle activities is simple, structured, and easy to grasp. Changes to a product in midstream, however, would be hard to apply. Modification to business or technical requirements could lengthen the process of development and require revisions of already allocated budgets.

From a high-level view, the iterative method of software development is also a sequential method for constructing software. Indeed, it is linear because the progress through the product life cycle must meet similar milestone stages[1]: inception, elaboration, construction, and transition. However, the improvement over the water-fall approach is rooted in the idea of development iterations, each of which represents an incremental effort until requirements are met. For example, requirement-gathering activities repeat through each life cycle stage. Similarly, software construction starts at inception and lasts through the transition phase.

The iterative software development approach legitimizes business or technical changes that may occur during a product's life span. However, the complex nature of the iterations may introduce management and administration costs that are typically hard to recoup. The concept of software development iterations is not an easy idea to grasp, either. The confusion could even grow when multiple iterations are pursued simultaneously.

Often interchangeably referred to, incremental software development is akin to the iterative approach. Some would even argue that the iterative approach embodies the incremental one. Incremental sprints of software construction, in either successions or iterations, meet intermediate milestones until the ultimate aim of a development initiative is achieved.

Software Entropy

With all the acknowledged benefits of these concepts, the repeating cycles of soft-ware implementation could divert the focus from design requirements to taxing process coordination issues. In addition, there is no assurance that each construction increment indeed enhances its previous version. In some cases, adding layers of implementations during each life cycle stage only sidetracks the focus from the overall architecture strat-egy. This diversion, of course, could result in a failing product that does not meet business direction and requirements.

A software increment or iteration typically introduces changes and additions to its earlier version, an effort that increases its vulnerability and volatility. This software erosion effect agrees with the law of software entropy[2]: the more a system is altered or reformed, the greater the potential for chaos.

The Design Substantiation Promise

Conventionally, a proof-of-concepts is constructed to verify that a design would indeed work once its implementation is deployed to production. This is typically a small piece of software created to confirm architectural assumptions made during the design efforts. But such a narrow scale of implementation would merely verify the validity of a small computing landscape where an application or components operate. If a proof-of-concepts, however, is designed to validate a larger architecture space, then again the effort would seem more like a full-fledged software development initiative—not an intended proof-of-concepts.

Understandably, the design substantiation method, presented in this book, is not a proof-of-concepts. *It is a software construction and integration method devised to assist enterprise architects in proving that segments of an end-state architecture are solid and meet functional and nonfunctional requirements.*

In this context, functional requirements are affiliated to the behavior of an end-state architecture, as discussed in Chapter 11. The behavior involves the actions, processes, activities, and services of an environment with its hosted organizational assets. In contrast, nonfunctional requirements pertain to a set of run-time parameters that a system, application, or component must conform to. These may include performance, response time, availability, scalability, interoperability, disaster recovery, and many more.

Avoiding Design Debt

One of the most compelling reasons to pursue the design substantiation method is to circumvent design debt.[3] The term "design debt" pertains to software development circumstances where unfulfilled design requirements keep piling up because of project disorder or other implementation delays and disturbances. Unaccomplished prior design milestones are referred to as debts because the progression of software development always hinges on previous design or construction deliverables. For example, if a data schema has not been developed, a database could not be created, and thus no application would be able to retrieve information.

This simple design debt concept could be devastating to any software construction process: waterfall, incremental, iterative, or others. The more debts heap up, the harder it is to reverse the course of the software construction. This goes back to the subject of software entropy discussed in the previous section. A chaotic situation like this could derail a wide range of enterprise architecture implementations and impact business continuity.

To address this undesired condition, the design substantiation approach confines software construction and integration activities to small segments of an end-state architecture to dodge design debts. These areas of interest are tightly boxed and structured to restrict the scope of a software development initiative and to insure that all design requirements have been met. The most important benefit, though, is that the design is locked, or frozen, until the software construction is completed. Once the design substantiation is concluded, the segment is unlocked to enable design refinement. This is named design loop-back, during which architects go back to the drawing board to fine-tune their work. This approach calls for pacing the software construction and integration activities to design evolution. In simpler words: first design, then implementation, all within the narrow scope of an end-state architecture segment.

Parallel Design Substantiation

The need for verifying architecture assumptions and decisions that were made within the boundary of one segment is important for containing the scope of a software construction effort in a decomposed design area. However, the design substantiation process does not necessarily have to be a single-threaded effort. Parallel initiatives can take place simultaneously. In fact, a sequential, or one-at-a-time, design segment substantiation would be inefficient if an end-state architecture environment is vast. But even beyond the effectiveness argument, it would be essential to tackle multiple end-state architecture segments. This should be accomplished if there are vital architecture assumptions that must be verified involving more than one segment or if they are unaffiliated.

One of the leading justifications is to prove that the interaction between two highly dependent end-state architecture segments is indeed functioning as expected. For example, the dependency factor could be high if two applications located in two different segments exchange high-volume messages or if a software component in one segment retrieves large chunks of information from a repository position in a neighboring segment.

These scenarios fall under the category of integration verification, an aspect that largely involves multiple architecture segments. (Refer to Chapters 13–15 for a more elaborate discussion about the environment verification process through stress testing and capacity planning tasks.) Here, however, we should not be concerned about cross segments integration on a large scale. The design substantiation effort, therefore, should be narrowed to a single architecture segment; parallel substantiations should take place if the cause is justified, though.

Another reason to pursue the parallel design substantiation would be to avoid a lengthy product development effort. Therefore, multiple unrelated end-state architecture segments could be verified all at once. The term "unrelated" indicates that it would be possible to verify simultaneously end-state architecture segments that are not tightly coupled and have a low level of dependency. Again, the design substantiation should not step beyond the boundary of a single segment. In certain circumstances, however, neighboring end-state architecture segments should be substantiated.

Pursuing Architecture Substantiation by Cross-Functional Contracts

A product development initiative often requires a wide range of expertise to meet business and technical requirements. However, a development team that has been working in a slow-growing technical environment for a long time is typically unable to offer a variety of advanced solutions for rapid business growth and increasing customer demands. True, a team like this keeps gaining experience, and as time goes by, the range of its services increases significantly. Still, in many cases, even with the team's impressive learning progress, its overall capabilities to offer a broad and innovative set of skills for building products could fall short of expectations.

This brings us to one of the most common reasons for failing IT implementations: lack of skills to develop a product. (Refer to Chapter 3 for a more elaborate discussion.) Lack of skills typically means that the team is not sufficiently qualified at gathering requirements, lacks design capabilities, is incapable of developing source code, or is unable to perform product integration in production.

To address this burning issue, organizations assemble a temporary team that possesses a vast spectrum of knowledge in a particular subject relevant to a software construction project. This idea would require recruiting professionals from different departments or divisions, or even from other firms, who can contribute their multidisciplinary skills to specific product development and delivery initiatives.

Contracting is the act of such directed employment. This effort would create a self-directed group of solution providers that focus on achieving business or technical goals. Although the individuals drawn into such an effort typically introduce multiple, and out-of-the-box perspectives and solutions, the product building initiative must end with a sound consensus. Unfortunately, since projects of this nature do not allow a lengthy period for consensus building, decision-making must be pursued rapidly.

Cross-functional contracts are therefore essential to the design substantiation process to boost design verification capabilities of architecture segments that employ a variety of technologies. Obviously, these are not contracts in a legal sense. However, the recruited professions must be aware of a few fundamental agreement conditions:

- The term of employment would be between one and four weeks.
- The chief goal of the initiative would be to substantiate an end-state architecture segment.
- The work of design substantiation may include multiple end-state architecture segments. In this case the term of employment should be lengthened to accommodate parallel design substantiation efforts for multiple end-state architecture segments.
- Source code construction and integration must be performed to substantiate a design segment.
- Business and technological best practices should drive the substantiation effort.
- A contract could be renewed for other incremental software architecture efforts.

Roles

There is no room for administrative roles during the design substantiation process. The contracted personnel should bring to the table valuable business and technical skills that can complete the job of end-state architecture segment substantiation. Without specific management roles, the team should be self-directed, guided by leading individuals who understand the business direction and the empowered technologies. Furthermore, the contracted parties should maintain professional relationships, leveraging their required superb communication skills to accomplish the work that they are commissioned for.

Since the focus on deliverables is extremely high and the time frame particularly short, it should not be surprising to learn that the design substantiation effort requires a small team of subject matter experts. Nimble, motivated, and out-of-the-box thinkers are then required to offer tangible and creative business and technical solutions—all in the narrow scope of an end-state architecture segment substantiation. Moreover, the assignment that they were hired for may not necessarily last a long time. The architecture segment they were engaged to substantiate may not be a vast one either. However, the responsibility and accountability should lay at their feet, since the consequences of failure could be detrimental to the business. To understand the obligations each of the roles has during the segment substantiation process, refer to the RACI[4] chart (Table 12.1).

The sections that follow describe three roles for the design substantiation process. This does not mean that a team should include only three professionals expected to accomplish the work of verifying a design. That role could be assigned to multiple team members. For instance, a number of team participants could assume the role of software construction.

It is advisable, though, to restrict the size of the substantiation team to a bare minimum to reduce human resource overhead, limit unnecessary chatter, and increase work efficiency. With today's advanced technologies, modeling tools, integrated development environments (IDEs), and deployment and configuration software, the need for large teams is not necessary.

For example, a small end-state architecture segment, in which a number of software components and a repository trade messages, would perhaps require 4 to 6 team members. Then again, if a design segment contains middleware components, a couple of applications, and a repository, about 7 to 12 professionals would be needed for code development, integration, and redesign efforts. The rule of thumb then suggests that the end-state decomposition efforts (discussed in Chapters 7–11) should yield small segments to avoid a long-lasting substantiation process and reduce the head count in each design verification initiative.

Software Engineer

A software engineer possesses life cycle product development skills and is well versed in software design, construction, integration, and maintenance. These responsibilities are central to the design substantiation process. Software construction efforts are an essential ingredient for confirming that an end-state architecture segment would indeed operate flawlessly in production. Without the actual implementation, no one can predict the behavior of a system, application, middleware, or environment.

A wide range of software construction skills exists in today's industry. Many software engineers specialize in application design and development. Others dedicate their time to design and code systems to keep computers or electronic devices running, such as operating systems, drivers, or firmware. Web development is a different specialty that gained popularity during the past two decades. This list encompasses only a few proficiencies needed to design, develop, and maintain rapid growing technologies. Furthermore, the array of modeling languages, language platforms, utilities, and tools is almost infinite.

In the context of enterprise technologies and architecture, the skills required to develop and keep up a robust production environment range from simple script writing to complex integration of middleware and network infrastructure. The type of knowledge that an organization must acquire depends on a variety of factors, such as enterprise business model, architecture strategy, types of applications, and technologies. Some enterprises, for example, must maintain wireless infrastructure to meet consumers' demands. Others provide cloud services, such as applications and development platforms.

When assembling a team for the design substantiation effort, a software engineer must be adept at a wide array of technologies that an organization supports. A well-rounded skill set would not only be required to develop an end-state architecture segment, but also to deploy and integrate the implementation in production. Indeed, this process of verification would involve experienced personnel that excel in the field of the diverse software engineering.

Consider the activities that a software engineer would be commissioned to contribute to when contracted for a design substantiation effort:

- Application analysis and design
- End-state architecture segment analysis and design
- Software construction
- Unit testing
- Module testing
- Architecture segment testing
- Software deployment and integration

Observer Patron

It has become more common to involve business personnel in software development initiatives. A growing number of organizations include stakeholders to weigh in on software design, construction, and deployment and integration processes. The term "stakeholders" pertains to decision makers and business development specialists that bring to the table multiple perspectives and solution propositions. It is obligatory to involve stakeholders in a product development life cycle. It is not even a choice; it is a strategic necessity.

Who else could be included in the patron participant category? It depends on the type of technology and applications an end-state architecture segment contains. In most cases, when a business application is one of the design elements to be substantiated, business product managers must join the decision-making group. Others may be product sponsors and business owners concerned about the future of the organization. In addition, business strategists and high-level enterprise executives who shape the business model of an organization may also participate in design substantiation efforts. When the stakes are even higher, perhaps when an organization's existence hinges on a particular business and technological implementation, a CTO, CIO, or CEO may join strategic end-state architecture segment substantiations.

The list of observers may be long. However, they should not be managing a design substantiation effort. The role of an observer patron, therefore, is chiefly to be informed. Raising concerns about the software construction direction or its leading strategy is one of the observer's duties. Inserting a business perspective and voice into the process of software construction is another vital obligation of the observing patron. Finally, the observer's mission is to be mindful of the budget allocated to construct an end-state architecture segment and to verify it. An observer patron who holds the money for product development initiatives should participate in such endeavors to monitor the progress and raise concerns when the expense outruns the allocated budget.

Consider a list of duties that the observer patron should contribute to in certain capacities:

- Budget allocation and monitoring
- Inserting business perspectives into the design substantiation process
- Participating in design segment coordination and prioritization
- Architecture verification process involvement
- Design loop-back participation

Architecture Verification Principal

An architecture verification principal is primarily an experienced enterprise architect whose business knowledge and design and technical skills are well suited to address enterprise architecture concerns. The array of responsibilities of an enterprise architect chiefly includes strategic implementations that are in line with the business model and strategies of the organization. An enterprise architect is mostly focused on the big picture of an enterprise grand-scale design. This encompasses technological strategies, adoption of leading middleware and network infrastructure products, and overall integration of organizational assets in production. Enterprise architects also devise policies and foster software development and integration best practices.

When an enterprise initiative is planned, the enterprise architect provides road maps and end-state architecture propositions to the business and the IT communities. These deliverables are formed based on a deep knowledge of an organizational production environment and its deployed systems, applications, strategic components, middleware, and network infrastructure assets. This familiarity with enterprise software and hardware integration must also include an understanding of messaging platforms and infrastructure, data sources, data source providers, software intermediaries, and even network devices. As an adroit enterprise software designer, the enterprise architect must be able to integrate new technologies with legacy systems to increase organizational reuse, reduce expenditure, and increase asset consolidation.

The role of an architecture verification principal then is to guide and lead the software engineers through the process of the design substantiation. It is clearly not a managerial or an administrative role. The mission to verify an end-state architecture segment by constructing the code and integrating assets is utterly vital.

Consequently, the architecture verification principal must take the lead. The duties of such a role include coordination and prioritization of the substantiation work. The driving priorities are clearly business imperatives that require immediate attention. These typically pressing issues or organizational concerns must be tackled straightaway. On the other hand, architecture and technological urgencies should be prioritized, too. Both burning business and technological issues should be brought to the table and scheduled for implementation by the architecture verification principal.

Consider the chief occupation activities of the architecture verification principal:

- Lead the design substantiation efforts of end-state architecture segments
- Prioritize and coordinate work for design substantiation activities
- Verify architecture assumptions and design decisions by testing the constructed and integrated implementations
- Foster adherence to business and technical requirements
- Enforce design and software construction best practices
- Initiate design loop-back and take the lead on end-state architecture segment redesign activities

Events

As depicted in Figure 12.1, the design substantiation process calls for four events, each of which is explained in the sections that follow:

Architecture segment analysis and refinement This involves studying segment design requirements, prioritizing substantiation tasks, and fine-tuning segment scope.

Architecture segment construction and integration This event calls for software development and integrating the implementation in production.

Architecture segment validation and certification This calls for verifying if the software implementation meets design specifications.

Architecture segment design loop-back. This involves re-architecting a segment if design flaws have been discovered.

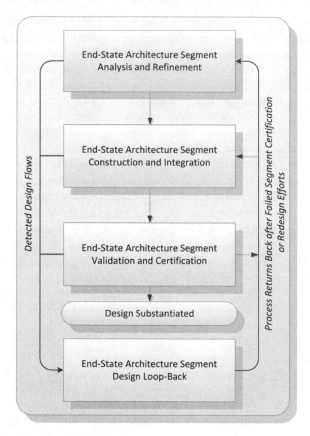

Figure 12.1   Design Substantiation Events

As is apparent, these events are not necessarily sequential. However, they must occur within the planned time frame for segment verification. We then begin with an analysis process to understand the design requirements for an end-state architecture segment. Remember, the study of an end-state architecture segment is necessary because it leads the software development efforts: again, first design, then development.

The software construction effort comes next. There is no time to spare. It must be concise and accomplished without leaving out any unfulfilled requirements to circumvent design debt. In simple words: no loose ends permitted. Moreover, discovery of design flaws should terminate development activities with the initiation of the design loop-back event as depicted in Figure 12.1.

The verification of the end-state architecture segment starts immediately after the software development initiative was concluded successfully. This validation process comes in handy to spot unfinished development or compliance issues with design specifications.

Then again, design errors detected during the validation and certification event more likely would start the segment redesign efforts, starting the design loop-back process.

Finally, after the segment redesign efforts, the process of substantiation may return to the analysis and refinement event or directly engage the development team in software construction. Returning to either of these events does not mean that the substantiation process promotes an iterative development approach. In most cases, this merely implies that after mending the design flaws design substantiation may start afresh.

The sections that follow discuss in details the activities of each design substantiation event.

End-State Architecture Segment Analysis and Refinement

Right after the design substantiation process is launched, the contracted team must be presented with the design requirements and specifications for the particular end-state architecture segment. This introduction is not only essential for understanding the direction and the decision making that led to the present end-state architecture segment, but also learning about the technical requirements. This may include analysis of the systems and their related applications, components, or middleware products involved. In addition, elaborating on how these assets must be integrated in production would shed light on message exchange routes and network configurations.

It also refers to the requirements of the organizational assets that must be constructed in the segment framework.

During the analysis and refinement event, there would also be an opportunity to spot errors in the end-state architecture segment design. This practice is not out of the ordinary. Drilling down into architecture details typically yields new approaches and perspectives, enhancing the original design. Consequently, improvements to the segment design could be applied immediately, thereby postponing the upcoming software construction efforts. In such a case, sending the architecture verification principal, the in-charge enterprise architect, back to the drawing board begins the design loop-back event, as described in the Segment Design Loop-Back section later in this chapter.

The segment analysis and refinement activities also call for tweaking the scope of the software construction work. In some cases, the range of an end-state architecture segment may be reduced because of feasibility concerns. That is, the designated team may require revision of an end-state architecture segment size to avert delivery delays. This segment boundary refinement is an essential process to adjust expectations and stay within budget constraints.

After understanding the overall scope of work, it would be a good time to prioritize the development activities and assess the efforts involved. Ordering the efforts that pertain to design substantiation may even include coordinating multiple segment verifications. This pertains to efforts that must be taken to verify more than one end-state architecture segment in case two or more segments are highly dependent or their design is assessed as tightly coupled.

This brings this discussion to the last important point. The segment design substantiation analysis also calls for understanding the environment beyond a single segment scope. An overall end-state architecture overview should be given to elaborate on how the grand-scale environment behaves and what chief middleware and network infrastructure are involved. This would shed light on the various messaging platforms and other commercial off-the-shelf products that must meet business and technical requirements.

To recapture these tasks, consider the chief end-state architecture segment analysis and refinement activities:

- Reviewing the overall end-state architecture environment and its deployed assets
- Refining the boundaries and scope of an end-state architecture segment
- Assessing the feasibility of an end-state architecture segment
- Prioritizing the verification process for a single or multiple design segments

End-State Architecture Segment Construction and Integration

Software construction duration depends on the size of an end-state architecture segment. Remember that determining the scale of segments takes place during the end-state architecture decomposition process (discussed in Chapters 7–11). The rule of thumb suggests that the smaller an architecture segment, the shorter the development process would be.

As mentioned throughout this chapter, avoiding unnecessary iterations or incremental software building would simplify the development process. This would also ease off the coordination activities needed to harmonize the design substantiation activities. Moreover, keep the development process short and strive to comply with architecture requirements and best practices. Indeed, software construction iterations are not recommended as they could only add to software entropy and amass design debts. The software construction process then should conclude when all design specifications are accomplished.

Remember, design efforts, either enhancements or an architecture overhaul, that take place while the software is being built only add to design debt that would be hard to repay. Therefore, while pursuing software development activities, the end-state architecture segment must be *design-locked*—no design initiative should take place while the construction is in progress.

And what about testing during the software development phase to insure the stability and accuracy of the implementation? A number of tests should be applied to validate the quality of the implementation:

Unit testing   This activity calls for scrutinizing the smallest units of source code, such as functions, procedures, and components. Software developers apply such testing to ensure flawless operation of small chunks of code. This process could be automated by unit-testing tools or performed manually. A test-driven approach requires creation of testing code that runs to detect expected results based on variable of input parameters.

Software module testing   A software module is a part of an executable or a program. It may encompass functions, procedures, and interfaces. Some consider a module as a collection of components, each of which executes a narrow range of technical and business requirements. Since a module may consist a number of components, automated tests driven by scripts should be executed to examine functional and nonfunctional aspects of the implementation.

Architecture segment testing   After a segment has been built to design specifications, it is time for a new type of tests. This round of testing is akin to module testing. The chief goal would be to test if the end-state architecture segment components function. Remember, at this stage we are not validating and certifying a segment. The certification is pursued in the next section, an event named End-State Architecture Validation and Certification. Here instead, the segment's various components are tested against their technical requirements. Again, automated testing could be applied to run the segment testing.

Combined segment testing   If the implementation requires testing of two or more related and highly dependent segments, the mission would be to expand the inspection of architecture capabilities. However, the combined segment testing is not about testing the entire end-state architecture environment. This, however, would be required later on during the incremental software architecture process. (Refer to Chapters 13 and 14 to read more about stress testing strategies.)

The work of asset integration in the scope of a single or multiple segments is also the duty of the development team. Software engineers, for that matter, are not only required to construct the code, but also to deploy, configure, and integrate their implementation. No matter what the software assets are, delivery and configuration plans must be devised to ease the transition of the implementation to production.

The software engineering team is also commissioned to participate in the segment validation and certification process described in the next section. Although they would not bear most of the responsibilities for the segment design validation, their presence is mandatory to help assess the design after it has been implemented.

The list that follows summarizes the chief activities required for the end-state architecture construction and integration event:

- Segment analysis
- Segment development
- Unit testing
- Module testing
- Segment testing
- Combined segment testing
- Segment deployment and integration
- Segment verification

End-State Architecture Segment Validation and Certification

This is one of the most crucial events of the segment design substantiation. The work that is required here is simple: *verifying if indeed the end-state architecture specifications are implemented*. In other words, a requirement at a time should be examined to verify if an actual implementation fulfills its goals. The ultimate validation, however, should prove that the architecture strategy, planning, and direction are embodied in the actual implementation. Ask the questions that follow to confirm if indeed the design is *solid and proven*:

- Do the segment's elements, such as systems, applications, or components operate as designed?
- Are these assets integrated properly?
- Has the design yielded a tangible and solid environment that can be trusted and easily maintained?
- Does the implemented end-state architecture segment sustain high-volume transactions?

- Does the end-state architecture segment satisfy functional requirements?
- Does the performance and availability of the end-state architecture segment meet nonfunctional requirements?

Remember, however, that here the chief concern is the validation of a single or a few segments—not verification of the entire end-state architecture. To be able to verify the whole end-state architecture environment, all segments must be validated and certified. This would be a step-by-step process, a thorough evolution crucial to the incremental software architecture endeavor.

The certification of the implementation and the verification of the design materialize with the final sign-off by the architecture verification principal and his team members: software engineers and observer patrons. When all parties are satisfied with the segment deliverables, the segment is declared "final."

It is important to understand that until the process of the certification is concluded, the design must be locked. The term "locked" implies that no design changes to the end-state architecture segment should take place. In other words, design activities should cease until this event occurs.

As shown in Figure 12.1, if the design segment has not been proven, meaning not certified, the process of substantiation goes back to the construction event for augmentations and modifications. As an alternative, if flaws were discovered in the design itself, the design loop-back would be the next step.

Consider the chief activities of the end-state architecture segment validation and certification:

- Validate design requirements against source code implementation
- Validate segment workload sustainability
- Validate segment integration
- Validate segment performance
- Validate segment compliance with functional and nonfunctional requirements
- Certify end-state architecture segment

Segment Design Loop-Back

The design loop-back event is all about going back to the design drawing board and enhancing the architecture of a segment. The architecture verification principal, an experienced enterprise architect, is accountable for this process. A number of enterprise architects, though, may collaborate on redesigning or improving the design of a segment if the scope of the work is large.

So why would an end-state architecture segment find its way back to the design stage? There are umpteen justifications. Consider the chief reasons that could be established in each design substantiation event:

- Findings during the end-state architecture segment analysis and refinement event:
  - Business and/or technical requirements are nebulous.
  - Business requirements and/or technical specifications are unfeasible. The source code construction effort would not be able to meet these imperatives.
  - Functional and/or nonfunctional requirements are unattainable.

- End-state architecture segment blueprint is unclear.
- The implementation scope of an end-state architecture segment is too large.
- Findings during the end-state architecture segment construction and integration:
    - Segment design specifications are unclear or ambiguous. Therefore, source code development could not be completed.
    - Incomplete design specifications halted the software construction.
    - Design specifications are too complex. The development efforts could not continue.
    - There is a need to simplify the design because of sudden budget constraints.
- Findings during the end-state architecture segment validation and certification:
    - A gap was found between design specifications and the actual implementation. The development effort did not meet technical, functional, or nonfunctional requirements.
    - There is a discrepancy between the design and the integration of the end-state architecture segment.
    - The source code fails because of complex design requirements.
    - The design did not accommodate high-volume transaction scenarios. The implementation buckles under network pressure.
    - The design failed to offer robust performance and availability capabilities. The implementation demonstrates slow response time.

Each of the above reasons for initiating a design loop-back must be tackled. An end-state architecture segment that does not meet design specifications demonstrates vulnerability that should not be disregarded. Even after the design loop-back process concludes, the process must go back to its previous stage.

For example, if architecture issues were discovered during the development phase, the software construction efforts should continue only after the design has been enhanced. If a segment has been completely redesigned, however, it would be prudent to restart the process of design substantiation by starting over with the end-state architecture segment analysis and refinement event. See again Figure 12.1 to observe the full process of the design substantiation.

RACI Chart

Now it is time to have a look at the level of involvement of each design substantiation role. To accomplish this, let us inspect Table 12.1. The business and IT industries recognize this role and task breakdown as an RACI chart. (The acronym stands for responsible, accountable, consulted, and informed.) These degrees of participation in an initiative indicate the commitment level of each contracted team member. Some would be fully committed and shoulder the responsibility for the success of a particular task. Others would be held accountable for any activity failure to which they are assigned. Moreover, certain team members would only join the team for consultation purposes while the remaining ones are only informed about occurring activities.

This range of involvement should be indicated in the contract that the team members sign. The leading roles would be assigned to individuals who are accountable for its success (in Table 12.1 the letter "A" indicates accountability). Furthermore, the

Table 12.1 RACI Chart for the Design Substitution Process

Substantiation Task	Software Engineer	Observer Patron	Architecture Verification Principal (Enterprise Architect)
Budget Allocation	I	A	R
Inserting business Perspective	I	A	R
Segment Analysis	R	I	A
Application Analysis and Design	A	I	R
Segment Prioritization and Scoping	I	A	R
Software Construction	A	I	R
Unit Testing	A	I	I
Module Testing	A	I	I
Architecture Segment Testing	R	I	A
Combined Segment Testing	R	I	A
Segment Construction Coordination	I	C	A
Architecture Segment Verification	R	C	A
Best Practices Enforcement	C	I	A
Design Loop-Back Initiation	I	C	A

second commanding role would be for those who are marked as responsible (with the letter "R").

Take the time now to review Table 12.1 and understand in-depth the three chief roles for the design substantiation process. Obviously, the column titled "Substantiation Task" identifies the all-important tasks to accomplish. The next three adjacent columns, "Software Engineer," "Observer Patron," and "Architecture Verification Principal," are the roles that take part in this segment verification endeavor. The last thing to recall before delving into the table is the letters that identify the level of involvement of each individual on the team:

- "R"—Responsible
- "A"—Accountable
- "C"—Consulted
- "I"—Informed

Notes

1. Rational Unified Process (RUP) calls for these four life cycle stages: http://searchsoftwarequality.techtarget.com/definition/Rational-Unified-Process
2. Ivar Jacobson, *Object Oriented Software Engineering: A Use Case Driven Approach*, 1992, Addison-Wesley Professional, p. 134
3. Girish Suryanarayana, Ganesh Samarthyam, Tushar Sharma, *Refactoring for Software Design Smells: Managing Technical Debt*, 2014, Morgan Kaufmann
4. http://racichart.org/

CHAPTER 13

Introduction to End-State Architecture Stress Testing

A kin to *stress tests* performed on financial institutions to prevent monetary collapse during economic crises, examinations are required to ensure the firmness and solidity of an end-state architecture. Ironically, these instances seem identical: A failing production environment may lead to a financial disaster and the demise of an organization.

Stress testing should then be pursued to verify if an end-state architecture environment could indeed sustain intense message exchange load over an abnormally long time. The result of such scrutiny should indicate if an environment is stable under extreme transaction circumstances. It should also demonstrate business and technical capabilities to provide solutions without reaching breaking points. If any of the pressure points buckle under the extreme conditions of the stress testing, the environment obviously fails to prove industrial-strength that is required to withstand treacherous business and technological conditions.

It is not surprising that now we are no longer discussing the endurance and solidity of an end-state architecture segment. This is discussed in detail in Chapter 12. Now the environment's firmness and performance is our chief concern. But end-state architecture stress testing is not only about performance. The investigation in this chapter is centered on the capability of an architecture landscape to respond to changes in commerce trends, to modifications of consumer preferences and demands, to alterations of business models and strategies, and to changes in technological direction.

All these fluctuations in business and technological environments must be responded with mighty and keen enterprise architecture. This should be a nimble design that is ready for change. This should be a dynamic end-state architecture environment smart enough to learn business behaviors and technological trends. This should be a grand-scale enterprise design devised by regional communities of experts that understand the nature of local business. This should be an organizational architecture capable of embracing rapid changes of global economies.

So far, end-state architecture segments have been substantiated and certified. Now it is time to connect the dots, to look at the grand design as a whole and assess its fitness. Therefore, the focus is on the stress testing mission, an undertaking that could discover architecture flaws, implementation errors, or even inadequate middleware or network infrastructure supporting environments.

This chapter and the one that follows, therefore, introduce vital focus points required for accomplishing an effective end-state architecture stress testing:

- Three types of strains that could be inflicted on end-state architecture elements: structural, behavioral, and volatile pressures (discussed in the sections that follow)
- End-state architecture pressure points (Chapter 14)
- Failure conditions of end-state architecture pressure points (Chapter 14)
- Three leading stress testing methods: recovery discovery, breaking point discovery, and durability discovery (Chapter 14)

Scales of Environment Pressures

A production environment is analogous to a city's electrical grid. When all goes well, the supply of power to homes and businesses is steady, reliable, and continuous. Throughout the year, citizens can enjoy the uninterrupted flow of energy with no worries about major fluctuations or outages of services. The blind trust in technology and particularly in the system that provides power to millions of consumers is rather peculiar. Not only do we tend to charge almost every device we own just about every day, but our daily duties rely profoundly on unlimited distribution of energy to the places we work and live. Humans developed this dependency during the second industrial revolution and continue to enjoy the trends in technology today.

But to make an electrical grid reliable and solid there must be a supporting infrastructure, a network that delivers electricity from suppliers to consumers. Furthermore, technological developments facilitate the transmission of power over long geographical distances, spanning cities, regions, states, and even continents. Not everything is rosy in the Garden of Eden, though. Even with the mighty technological capabilities societies possess, there are myriad things that can go wrong. Even with the reassuring promises of power suppliers and utility companies, the prospect of a major electrical grid collapse is still high.

And this brings the discussion to our own backyard. In the information age we currently live in, a production environment is empowered by a network that links software and hardware to provide organizational solutions. Unlike ancient societies, we tend to deliver services in a digital format. Digital streams of information, known as messages, flow from one server to another and are manipulated by systems and applications. And just like with a city's electrical grid, some areas on a computer production network are more congested than others.

The term "congested" pertains to sections on a network where message transmission slows down or halts. A congested area in production is caused by a variety of environment pressures. For example, a clotted network region could be a symptom of busy network circuits, overwhelmed by a heavy load of messages transmitted under insufficient bandwidth conditions. In this scenario, the heavy load of travelling information is considered to be pressure.

In other instances, congestion may be caused by slow servers, sluggish systems and applications response time, protocol transmission errors, and even by latency of network devices. Here again, all the reasons for congestion are thought of as environment pressures.

Consider another example: Congestion could be caused by inefficient configuration of routers that halt flow of information in a particular network segment.

The term "pressure" is then easy to define: *Any strain, squeeze, or burden on any organizational asset that causes network congestion is regarded as a pressured environment.*

What Is a Pressured Architecture Area?

The previous section centered on the term "environment pressures," but not much on pressured architecture areas. We learned that congested areas on a network could be caused by a wide range of pressures, all of which result in latency of message flows. Subsequently, when pressure builds up, messages can no longer travel between consumers and their related services. The consequences of such mishaps may be devastating to an organization that relies on a network to promote the business. Any discontinuation of services typically results in loss of revenue and unproductive time spent mending network capacity and performance issues.

Environment pressures are common in any production landscape. Mounting network pressures do not necessarily have to trigger outages, bring down systems, and cause financial havoc. Stabilizing vibrant computer ecosystems requires superb planning, suitable architectures, appropriate implementations, and proper maintenance. In this chapter, though, we focus more on pressured architecture areas and how they can be identified to pursue an effective overall stress test of end-state architecture.

So now let us discuss what a pressured architecture area is. In simple words, *any underperforming environment affected by a design direction, decision, or flaw is regarded as a pressured architecture area.*

This short definition divulges the impetus behind conducting an end-state architecture stress test. The mission then is not only to identify areas in the end-state architecture that are predisposed to performance failures, but also launch a redesign effort to mend architecture errors. This implies that architecture errors are the chief causes of strains in a production environment.

In other words, *burdened architecture areas are always caused by bad design qualities—nothing else.*

Moreover, in the world of computing, there could be numerous reasons for mounting pressures in architecture areas. The most common ones are due to increasing consumer demands. This translates to high business transaction volumes. But this is not the only cause of a network gridlock. Let us not forget that efficient software architecture of systems, applications, and components must take capacity limitations into consideration. That is, resource utilization in a given production environment must be a vital parameter that is not neglected. (To learn more about enterprise capacity planning, refer to Chapter 15.) This accentuates the need for avoiding software design flaws that contribute to network backlog and message exchange delays.

Types of Architectural Pressures

Now, let us have a look at Figure 13.1 to understand what types of architecture area pressures should be observed when performing stress testing. As depicted, business and technical environments typically introduce three types of network pressures that

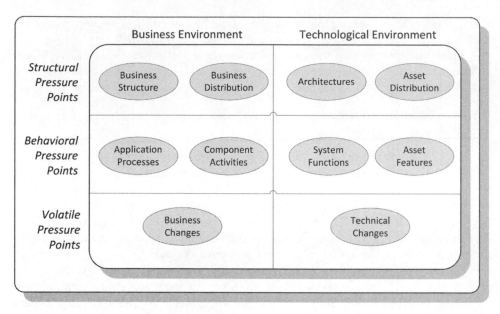

Figure 13.1   Types of Architectural Pressures

should be mitigated to avert business and technological disasters. These pressures may occur independently, two at a time, or all at once:

1. *Architecture structural pressures.* Certain attributes of architecture structures, such as monolithic, mesh, federated, and centralized, could cause stressed network conditions. The manner by which software and hardware assets are distributed across the enterprise could also form pressure disorders in a production environment.
2. *Behavioral pressures.* In many circumstances, system and related application functionality, processes, and activities can introduce areas of network congestion. Behavioral aspects then should be inspected to understand their impact on message exchange performance and system availability.
3. *Architecture volatile pressures.* Architecture segments prone to change are referred to as volatile pressure points. In other words, locations on a network of software and hardware that undergo change should be the subject of any investigation into network pressure abnormalities.

Timing Architecture Pressures

Any pressure formed in an architecture environment is neither steady nor linear. It all depends on a wide range of concurrent events occurring on a network. Pressures may start and then halt in short successions, or build up until message routes are completely clotted. The unstable nature of information flaw pressures, therefore, must be observed and measured during periods of time during which their causes are discovered and analyzed. Tracing behaviors of pressured architecture areas, though, calls for

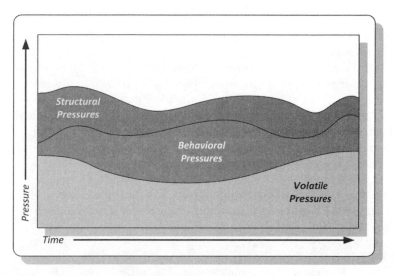

Figure 13.2   Timing Architecture Pressures

employing monitoring and workload detection tools. By doing this, one can ascertain pressure sources and the risks they pose to the environment.

An effective visualization that demonstrates the application of pressures during time is depicted in Figure 13.2. Note that the presented area graph contains three types of pressures in an architecture environment: structural pressures, behavioral pressures, and volatile pressures. These are measured based on a pressure buildup scale over increasing time values. Moreover, as discussed in the previous section, different types of message exchange pressures may occur independently or simultaneously. In this illustration, the three pressures take place at the same time.

As is apparent, in this end-state architecture environment the structural pressure is the highest among the three. Behavioral pressure is high too. Last, the volatile pressures are the lowest on the presented pressure scale. Such an architecture landscape represents a high degree of operational risks that call for an immediate alleviation of message exchange pressures.

Architecture Structural Pressures

It is not hard to imagine a building in an urban area collapsing under a structural pressure. Every expert in the construction business would claim that such calamity is more likely to occur because of a variety of internal and/or external events or condition changes. These may include architecture errors, weak foundations, overwhelming loads, earthquakes, or even weather disasters.

Undoubtedly, design faults are one of the main reasons for crumbling building structures. One pressure occurrence typically triggers another. Consequently, accumulating pressure events could bring down a huge construction site, an event that few would be comfortable even thinking about. To reduce the peril of a collapsing building, *architects must alleviate risks by fine-tuning the pressures applied to weaker points in their design*. In other words, they must anticipate which sections of the building would be most affected by sudden or persistent internal and external pressures and apply proper preventive measures.

Building architecture and software architecture have much in common. In a production environment, a myriad of organizational software and hardware assets collaborate to enable business transactions and provide enterprise solutions. Pressures on software entities such as applications and components are everyday reality. Pressures on systems constantly occur. And pressures on network devices and other infrastructure facilities are common. The questions that we should be asking are about the fitness of an end-state architecture structure:

- Can such a design withstand internal and external pressures?
- What are the criteria for discovering architecture structural pressures?
- What type of structural pressures should we focus on the most?

In the sections that follow, we propose two types of structural influences that are worth investigating when performing end-state architecture stress testing: technical architecture structural pressures and business structural pressures.

Discovering Architecture Structural Pressures

Think about an architecture structure as a formation that encompasses business and/or technical solutions. The structure, logical or physical, identifies visual properties of a design integrated on a network. That is, the manner by which architecture is layered, tiered, or distributed in a production environment, or even beyond an enterprise boundary, is regarded as structure. Moreover, the arrangement of architecture elements on a network and the connecting message routes reveals a great deal of information about an architecture's direction or capability. For example, if an architecture calls for promoting federation between two organizations to enable information sharing, the structural signature must be familiar to business and IT professionals.

The term "structural signature" pertains to the visual presentation of an architecture and its components. The structural signature of a federated architecture, for example, is easy to spot. Just picture a long pipe (happens to be an ESB), through which messages flow in and out, delivering information to subscribed consumers. Consumers in this context could be any application, users, and/or components. Since a federated architecture is typically devised to enable interoperability between two computing environments, the imaginary long pipe would reside between the two distinct organizational landscapes.

Another structural signature example depicts an N-tier architecture where each tier is assigned a different responsibility. In this case, the tiers seem to be loosely coupled, separated, and distributed across a production environment.

Learning from the mentioned architecture structure signature examples, we conclude that two visual aspects can easily help identify an architecture structure:

1. The fabric patterns on which an architecture is founded upon. This refers to the arrangement of an architecture's elements on a network and the message routes that link them. (Refer to fabric patterns in Chapter 4.)

2. The type of architecture. Here we refer to the four enterprise sub-architecture classes and their attributes that can affect a production ecosystem (discussed in Chapter 7: monolithic, mesh, federated, and centralized).

Indeed, the arrangement of architecture elements on a network and the way they are associated to each other are commonly known to cause message exchange pressures on a network. The responsibility of architects then is to ensure that the distribution style of assets in a production environment prevents communication collapse. This practice of integration is utterly fundamental to the performance of systems and applications. Every integration effort should be meticulously planned.

And the concept of structural pressures must be a key ingredient in architecture decisions.

Examples of bad integration strategies are widely covered in this book. One example can exemplify how lack of knowledge and erroneous integration strategy could cause systems in production to fail: overemployment of software intermediaries. The practice of inserting unnecessary message mediators between consumers and services could not only slow down entire network sections, but also delay message response time. An architecture structure like this must be revamped to lift pointless pressures formed by incorrect design decisions.

Alleviating structural pressures in a particular area of a design is not always straightforward. In fact, when it comes to integration issues, there are always multiple reasons for a failing deployment. Not only one unsuitable architecture structure can introduce dangerous pressures in an integrated computing environment. Joint structures of diverse sub-architectures also may be the root cause of a faltering implementation. These compounded pressure forces could lead to devastating production environment events and obviously discontinuation of business operations.

A Case Study Breakdown

We must start here with a case study, an example that illustrates an end-state architecture that includes a number of production fabric patterns and sub-architectures. But before we discuss how these structures induce environment pressures, let us break down the architecture environment shown in Figure 13.3. Once you see it, it may bring a smile to your face because it resembles so many production environments that organizations strive to maintain. Furthermore, this depiction is an informal presentation of a distributed environment, seemingly loosely coupled and federated.

An ESB, shown in its very center, promotes the federation between two organizations. To apprehend the ownership scopes of the presented end-state architecture, have a look at Figure 13.4, in which the boundaries of the two departments 1 and 2 are apparent. By now, however, let us focus on breaking down this architecture into elements so further discussions could refer to them.

After performing a quick analysis of Figure 13.3, consider a list of the end-state architecture elements:

- Applications 1 to 4
- Business services 1 to 4
- Applications 5 to 8
- Service locator middleware that connects applications 1 to 4 and business services 1 to 4

204

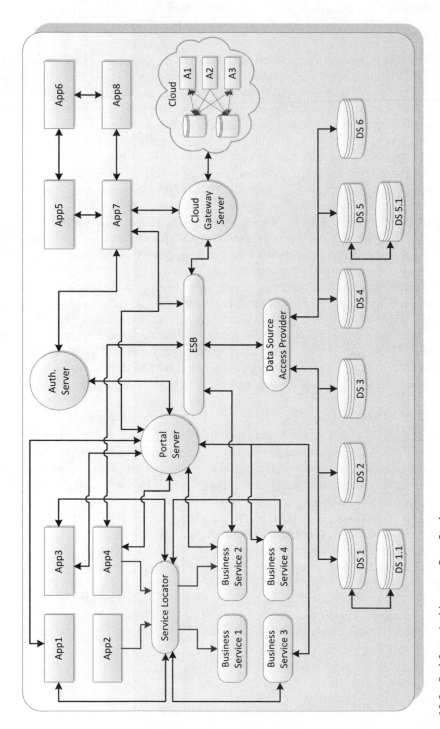

Figure 13.3   End-State Architecture Case Study

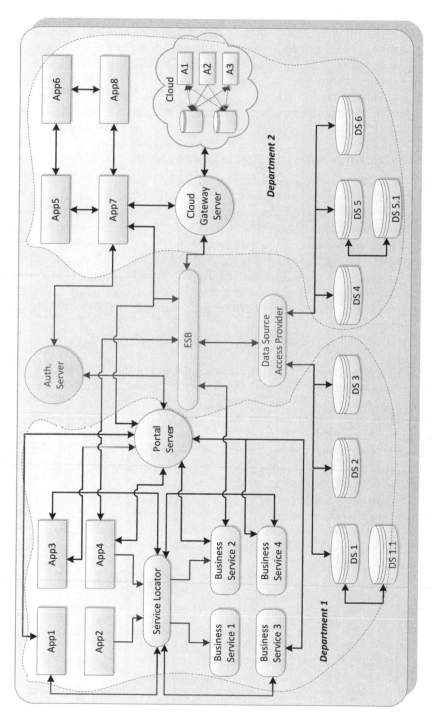

Figure 13.4   End-State Architecture Ownership

- Portal server that offers presentation layer services to applications 1, 3 and 4, and business services 2, 3, and 4
- Central ESB middleware that connects application 4, business service 2, data source access provider, cloud gateway server, application 7, and portal server
- Data source access provider middleware that is linked to the ESB and shields eight data sources: DS 1 to DS 6, DS 1.1, and DS 5.1.
- Cloud gateway middleware that enables access to the cloud and is linked to the ESB and application 7
- Authentication server that authorizes consumers, linked to the portal server and application 7

Discovering Fabric Patterns in an End-State Architecture to Identify Pressure Areas

Now is a good time to refresh the memory with the fabric patterns discussed in Chapter 4. Mapping out end-state architecture fabric patterns can uncover the manner by which organizational assets are distributed and the relationships they establish on a network. This discovery will pinpoint the architecture pressure areas we ought to ascertain, discussed in the next section.

As mentioned, a production fabric is composed of nodes and their connecting message routes. A logical view of a fabric pattern diagram then illustrates a clear view of asset integration. The most important aspect that comes across is the structural composition of an environment, a formation that can assist discovering potential pressures on architecture areas.

Here is an outline for each fabric pattern discussed in Chapter 4:

Community fabric pattern   This arrangement of entities on a network, identified by nodes, depicts a distributed and point-to-point architecture structure. In such an environment, entities such as applications, components, middleware products, and others communicate directly with each other.

Community center fabric pattern   Nodes such as applications, components, and other assets are arranged in a centralized structure similar to a star formation, in which a central hub is deployed to serve its surrounding consuming entities. This resembles the hub-and-spokes architecture pattern.

Message transport fabric pattern   The message transport formation is a production fabric pattern that employs bus technologies to transmit information from consumers and services. This style of distribution is mostly employed to ease interoperability challenges, foster the information sharing, and promote architecture expansion and federation.

Family fabric pattern   This is a hierarchical arrangement of nodes connected by a message path and arranged in a tree-like formation, in which a parent node exchanges information with its offspring. Siblings in the tree can also trade messages.

Circular message route fabric pattern   Messages flow from one node to another, forming a circular pattern of message exchange. The last node always transmits the information to the originating node.

Chained message route fabric pattern   A linear transmission of message style originates at the initiating node and concludes with the last node in the row.

Bridge and crossroad fabric pattern   These patterns identify intermediary nodes that intercept messages and route them to end point nodes. These styles are typically employed to expand an enterprise architecture and achieve a higher degree of loose coupling formations.

Compound fabric pattern   A combination of two or more of the fabric patterns on this list.

To clarify the point made about how a fabric pattern can help discover a pressured part of architecture, let us analyze Figure 13.5 and review the encircled areas of the presented end-state architecture. Here, we discover a number of fabric patterns in an enterprise grand design. To simplify the illustration, a node in a production fabric could represent a server, an application, a component, or even a data source:

- *Community center fabric pattern 1* includes the service locator middleware (a hub), applications 1 to 4, and business services 1 to 4.
- *Community center fabric pattern 2* includes the portal server (hub). Its subscribing consumers are not encircled for clarity reasons: application 1, 3 and 4, business services 2 and 3, authentication server, application 7, and ESB.
- *Community center fabric pattern 3* includes the ESB (hub). Here, too, its subscribing consumers are not encircled for clarity reasons: application 4, business service 2, portal server, application 7, data source access provider middleware, and cloud gateway server.
- *Compound fabric pattern* includes two distinct fabric patterns:
  - *Family fabric pattern* is composed of data source access provider and its subordinate offspring: DS 1 to DS 6 and DS 1.1 and DS 5.1.
  - *Chained message fabric pattern* is made up of data sources DS 1 to DS 6.
- *Bridge fabric pattern* is composed of the intermediary middleware cloud gateway server and its three consumers: ESB, application 7, and the cloud.
- *Community fabric pattern* includes all cloud elements.
- *Circular fabric pattern* is made up of applications 5 to 8.

Fabric Patterns Lead to Discovery of Pressured Architecture Areas

The decisive moment has arrived. Now we are ready to identify areas in the end-state architecture that are pressure-prone. This is a significant accomplishment since we are about to pinpoint structural sections that must be given special attention during the end-state architecture stress testing. Not all the discovered end-state architecture fabric patterns are pressure-prone, though. Some would rarely pose danger to a production system because of their structural composition. A few in particular must be examined to ensure that the integration pattern they offer would not be misused, a fact that may increase the risks of mounting architecture structural pressures.

Architects, integrators, operation engineers, and developers must be aware of the pressure-prone fabric patterns that are about to be discussed in the sections that follow. Therefore, we pruned the list of the fabric patterns that were discovered in Figure 13.5 to pressure-prone structural areas in the end-state architecture. These newly three circled areas of pressure are illustrated in Figure 13.6: pressure area 1, pressure area 2, and pressure area 3.

Note that these pressure areas do not include all fabric patters discovered in the previous section. These are target areas of concerns for the impending end-state architecture stress testing efforts. Moreover, as depicted in Figure 13.6, a pressure area

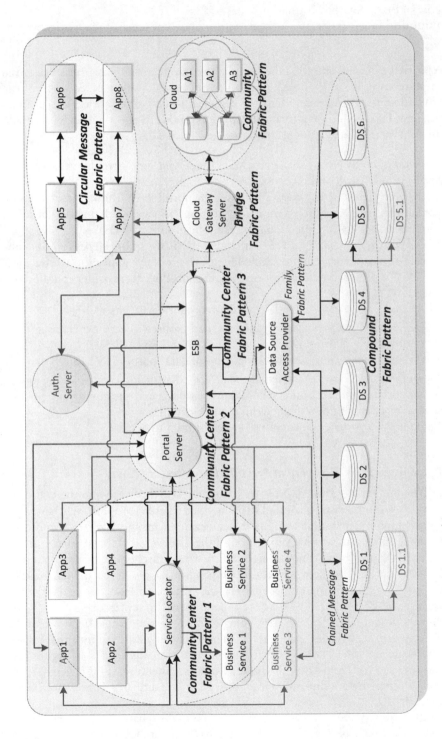

Figure 13.5   Fabric Patterns in End-State Architecture

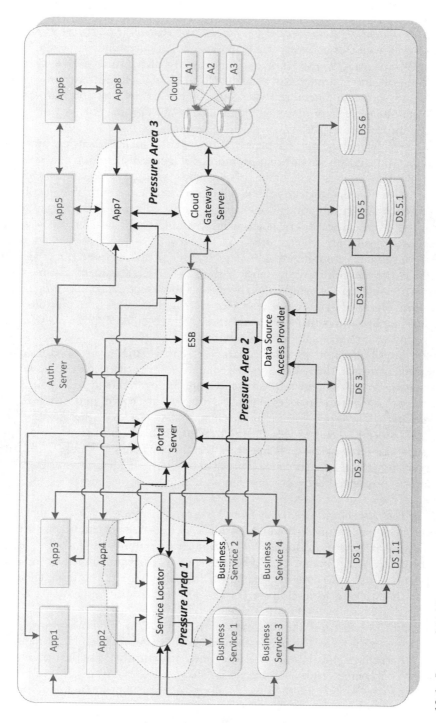

Figure 13.6   Pressured Architecture Areas

identifies a boundary in an end-state architecture that may not necessarily include a single fabric pattern, just as it comes across in pressure areas 2 and 3.

Be Aware of Potential Community Center Fabric Pattern Structural Pressures
Discussed throughout this book, especially in Chapter 4, the community center fabric pattern depicts an area in a production environment in which entities such as applications and components are arranged in a star-like formation. Such a pattern, also known as the hub-and-spokes architecture style, could be one of the most pressure-prone spots in an end-state architecture landscape. In fact, in most production environments multiple community center patterns could be detected.

This node arrangement style happens to be more convenient rather than practical or efficient. An integration scheme that promotes a star-like distribution of assets like this, where a central hub serves a number of consumers, is utterly risky. In many cases, organizations discover that the central hub buckles under the pressure of high volume transactions once the consumption of consumers increases. Even with the most powerful horizontal or vertical scalability mechanisms, the hub is still considered as a single point of failure in end-state architecture.

And in our example too, Figure 13.6 depicts three pressure-prone areas, each of which includes the community center fabric pattern. It is noticeable that pressure area 1 carries high-pressure network traffic risks because of the structural composition of the fabric pattern. The hub, in this case the service locator, devised to search for business services, links eight entities that may be disposed to high-volume message exchange pressures: application 1 to 4 and business service 1 to 4.

Pressure area 1, therefore, should be marked as sensitive to pressure and thus must be stress tested to reduce the risk of network congestion. An architecture stress test in this case may discover low network bandwidth capacity or even sluggish application implementation that must be corrected to work properly in a community center fabric pattern formation. The service locator hub itself may be subject for further examination to find out if indeed it must be redesigned to fulfill the role of a broker.

The same concerns go for pressure areas 2 and 3, depicted in Figure 13.6. The portal server and ESB in pressure area 2 are also providing mediation services. Each of these hubs is positioned between considerable amounts of consumers.

Be Aware of Potential Family Fabric Pattern Structural Pressures   The family fabric formation is another example that could introduce architecture structural pressures in a production environment. To understand how such a condition might occur, let us review pressure area 2 in Figure 13.6. The data source access provider is a candidate for investigation since it is a parent node in the family fabric structure. The six children nodes in this hierarchical formation are DS 1 to DS 6. In addition, the offspring DS 1.1 and DS 5.1 are located on the lower tree level.

In hierarchical structures like this, most of the network traffic flows through the top-level parent in the tree. The parent then routes messages to its children nodes. It resembles the arrangement of the community center structure because the data source access provider, in our example, acts like a hub. However, one must acknowledge that the parent, the data source access provider, along with its subordinate nodes form a distinct formation of a tree.

The family fabric pattern in pressure area 2, therefore, is another candidate for examination during the end-state architecture stress testing. Any tree formation like this, especially the top-level parent node, is sensitive to structural pressures. The children nodes, databases, applications, components, or whatever entities they may be are less exposed to pressure risk because they are shielded from the environment by the parent.

Be Aware of Bridge and Crossroad Fabric Pattern Structure Pressures   The cloud gateway server located in pressure area 3, as shown in Figure 13.6, is not linked to too many consumers. Why then would such an entity be considered pressure-prone? In this illustration, the cloud gateway server represents a bridge fabric pattern, a message broker that is typically assigned data transformation and protocol conversion to enable interoperability.

The assumption is that such an intermediary would be required to accommodate high-volume transactions because it is positioned behind the ESB and in front of a cloud. A structural pressure on the cloud gateway server may be overwhelming because of its data transformation and manipulation duties. In fact, servers that handle any kind of information processing, especially when transforming data from one format to another, experience performance slowdown. Growing message exchange volumes exchanged between the ESB and cloud may become a bottleneck concern when a cloud gateway is positioned in between the two entities.

Let us now look at the bridge and crossroad fabric structure from a different perspective. It becomes increasingly clear that software intermediaries, such as the bridge and crossroad brokers, increase the distance between a service and its related consumers. Mediation services like this enable an expansion of an existing architecture, although spreading out architecture elements typically promotes loose coupling, a positive integration practice. Some would even argue that spreading out architecture elements could alleviate structural pressures. On the other hand, though, increasing distances between consuming parties such as applications or components and service providers such as middleware products may contribute to message trading performance degradation. This trade-off must be examined to assess the consequences of each design stand.

Joint Architectural Pressures

Not all structural pressures originate from one source. Joint structural pressures coming from different formations on a network could be devastating to a production environment. The compound force of transactions exchanged between groups of entities on a network can significantly slow down business operations. What then would be the source of increasing pressures on an end-state architecture environment? Joint consumers, no matter what systems or applications they interact with, are a force that can increase pressure on network areas. The rising information consumption by software and hardware entities and the acceleration of data requests from repositories are other aspects that only add pressure to an already strained production landscape.

Sub-Architectures Structural Pressures   But the most powerful pressures on a network don't come only from individuals or groups of consumers seeking services. Indeed, these could increase to extreme volumes of messages and put a big strain on applications, components, middleware products, or network infrastructure. But joint structural pressures of two or more sub-architectures in an enterprise-computing environment should not be disregarded.

A collaborative strain on an environment inflicted by sub-architecture structures could cover large distances in a distributed environment. Pressures applied by sub-architecture burden production software and hardware entities.

The enormous compounded weights of such sub-architecture formations, therefore, could affect organizational operations and cross enterprise business activities.

Most organizations that support sizeable production environments have experienced cascading system shutdowns caused by sub-architecture structural pressures. That is, dependencies of sub-architecture on another typically lead to a chain reaction that is hard to halt. This is akin to a collapsing electric grid that results in a wide area of power shortages.

To understand how such compounding forces could affect a computing environment, let us inspect Figure 13.7. In this illustration, three powerful sub-architectures offer services to a large-scale environment, in which applications, business services, and data sources exchange messages. Our discovery process yielded three sub-architectures:

1. A *centralized sub-architecture* that includes a service locator (hub), consuming applications 1 to 4, and business services 1 to 4
2. A *federated sub-architecture* (only the entry point to this architecture is apparent for clarity reasons); the whole architecture includes other linked distributed entities: cloud gateway service, the data source provider, application 4, business service 2, application 7, and portal server. It is utterly true that such deployment may be considered as a star formation, in this example however, we chose a different view of the architecture, a federated formation. Architects, therefore, should shy away from devising such an ambiguous design and avoid employing an ESB as a central hub.
3. A *mesh sub-architecture* in the cloud formation

Structural pressures could affect any area in the end-state architecture squeezed between sub-architectures. This strain may include areas that are internal or external to a sub-architecture. To understand this idea, let us have a look again at Figure 13.7.

- Although the portal server is a part of the federated sub-architecture, it is pressured by its location between the centralized sub-architecture and the federated sub-architecture itself.
- In the same fashion, the cloud gateway server (a part of the federated sub-architecture) is clasped between the federated sub-architecture itself and the cloud. The combined message exchange forces from both sides would apply pressure on the cloud gateway.

Joint Pressures of Business Structures Strained production areas are caused not only by technical architectural structures. The notion that every network tailback is to be blamed on the way network devices are configured or on the quality of a design is not entirely accurate. Business aspects are also important factors that may generate pressure areas in a production ecosystem. The dominance of business domain activities and the manner in which a business is structured could affect network stability. As discussed in Chapter 10, the structural formations of business layers and tiers can immensely contribute to pressure areas in end-state architecture. In addition, federated, centralized, and clustered distributed business structures across the enterprise typically form stressed architecture sections that must be carefully

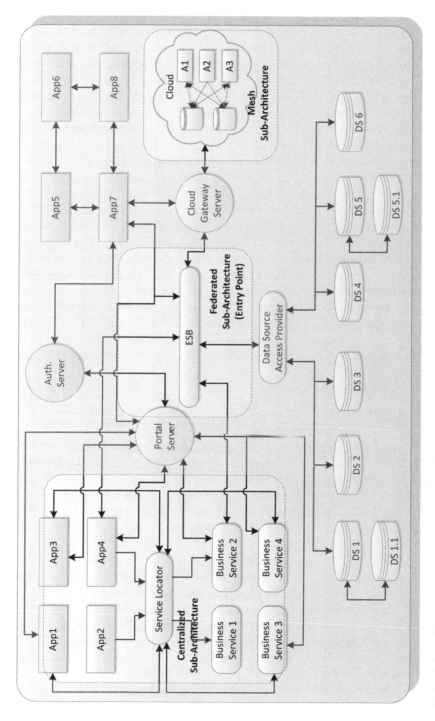

Figure 13.7   Sub-Architectures Introduce Structural Pressures

inspected, too. Therefore, both technological and business bearings must be studied to understand how they can affect the balance of operation pressures in real-time environments.

There is nothing more powerful than structural pressures of two or more business structures. This scenario represents two or more business organizations that collaborate to offer enterprise solutions. The term "organization" may include business partners, lines of business, business domains, divisions, departments, and more. The pressure that mounts in between these two large entities may not be sustainable by the pressed areas. No matter what elements of the architecture are located in between, the squeeze may be so overwhelming that the area may buckle under the pressure of the surrounding organizations. Sections of a production environment, therefore, that offer business interoperability should be an important checkpoint for the end-state stress testing efforts. In many cases, an ESB, gateway, proxy server, and intermediary middleware enable such message exchange capabilities between organizations.

Figure 13.4 exemplifies this joint venture. Department 1 and department 2 collaborate on information sharing. The former supports application 1 to 4, business services 1 to 4, service locator, a portal server, DS 1 to DS 3, and DS 1.1. The latter, on the other hand, includes applications 5 to 8, cloud gateway, cloud, DS 4 to 6 and DS 5.1.

In this scenario, the authentication server, the ESB, and the data source access provider middleware are pressure-prone. Indeed, any proxy middleware inserted between large institutions like this must be scaled enough. The establishment of disaster recovery facilities would then be needed to offer high availability capabilities. Strengthening the computing power of this pressured environment would enable the organization to share information without production downtime and business interruptions.

Behavioral Pressures

The topic of end-state architecture behavioral decomposition is largely discussed in Chapter 11. The chief goal was to break up a grand-scale design into functions, processes, and activities to simplify the architecture. Next, in Chapter 12, the mission was to prove that these decomposed segments of the end-state architecture perform as designed. To accomplish this, software construction and integration are performed as a part of the design substantiation process. During the course of this effort, redesign activities should be pursued if flaws are discovered.

In this chapter, the discussion centers on the preparations for the end-state architecture stress testing. Here, we are commissioned to discover delicate locations in the design, pressure-prone areas that should be scrutinized during the stress testing efforts. Architecture structural pressures on a real-time environment are introduced first, elaborating on a range of design formations and their influences on performance, transaction stability, message exchange efficiency, and business continuity.

Now it is time to inspect behavioral pressures in a production environment. So what is a system, an application, or a component behavior? Again, this is largely discussed in Chapter 11. The actions taken to deliver business or technical solutions are named behaviors. A behavior could also be thought of as functionality, processes, or activities. Any behavior of an application or a middleware product, for example, invokes a message request or response. This exchange of information on the network introduces pressures in certain capacities. Some are negligible strains that do not cause any harm to an environment. Other behavior pressures may be so intense that no software or hardware entity in production could withstand them. Behaviors of entities such as these could induce pressures that we must be concerned about during the end-state architecture stress testing.

As described in the sections that follow, when analyzing potential damaging behavioral pressures in the end-state architecture, the focus should be on the integration scheme. Specifically, some integration models are more agile then others, elastic enough to bend under extreme behavioral pressures, yet rarely break. Others would not be flexible enough and collapse in a short time. An integrated environment should be adaptable and be able to endure long network stress conditions inflicted by powerful behaviors.

Cascading Effects of Behavioral Pressures

Let us inspect Figure 13.8 to understand how behaviors could apply pressures on different architecture levels in production. As discussed throughout this book, a crowded production environment, overpopulated with a myriad of systems, applications, middleware, and network infrastructure products, is multifaceted. In other words, it is too complex to decipher and understand.

To alleviate the pain of such analysis, in Chapter 11, it is proposed to decompose a production ecosystem into three layers of behavior: system behavior, application behavior, and component behavior. Logical isolation of each layer would not only clarify a complex integration environment, but also would shed light on how each layer communicates with the others. Discovering the relationship between the layers would also reveal how one layer's behavior affects the other.

Obviously, Figure 13.8 is a simplified system within a production environment, provided merely to demonstrate the concept of behavioral pressure. A real production diagram such as this may include tens or even hundreds of production entities.

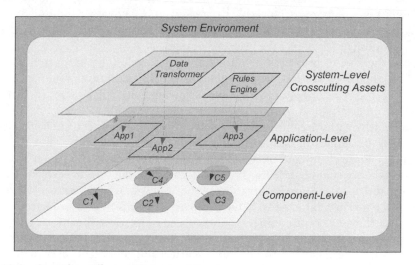

Figure 13.8   Cascading Effects of Behavioral Pressures

For the time being, let us focus on the effect of behavioral pressures. The analysis of this illustration renders a number of observations that are easy to spot:

- In this case study, the system-level crosscutting assets behavior includes two middleware components: data transformer and rules engine. The former is devised to convert information from one format to another. The latter is also a middleware product that executes business processes, typically triggered by business logic driven by organizational policies on behalf of an application.
- The application-level consists of three business applications: app1 to app3.
- Beneath, the lower level is dedicated for components. These may include internal or autonomous software implementations.

It is easy to understand that behavioral pressures inflicted by one level could affect the other. In this section, we discuss downstream pressures—that is, pressures originating on the higher behavior levels, cascading down to the lower levels. It is common to find production landscapes where transactional pressures emanating from a system could affect application operations. This implies that the top level in the behavioral scale could easily apply pressure on the one beneath. A data transformer, as depicted in Figure 13.8, located on the system-level crosscutting assets, potentially could feed applications app1 and app2 with a hefty load of information, applying unsustainable pressures that must be investigated to avert failed integration. To avoid such pressure risks, an application must be designed well enough to withstand pressures originated at the system level—in our case, strain caused by the data transformer.

Moving a notch down to the application-level behavior, any application located on this layer could apply overwhelming message load pressures on the component level to the extent that a component could collapse during operations. A slow server that hosts such a component may be the reason for the mounting pressures transmitted by an application. Insufficient memory or CPU resource may be other causes for the increasing sluggishness of a component. Furthermore, a component may be found pressure-prone, if its reusability factor is low. In other words, the more reusable a component is, the more invulnerable to pressure it is. Whatever the source of pressure might be, a comprehensive analysis during the end-state architecture stress testing should be conducted to detect the pressure source.

Could the risk of pressures be mitigated by good design approaches and practices? This rhetoric question provides the answer. Indeed, an architecture strategy must reduce the risks of cascading pressures flowing from the system level, through the application level, down to the component level.

Finally, other pressure-prone production entities that connect a behavior level to another may be under the risk of destructing pressures. To understand this point, look again at Figure 13.8 and imagine that a software intermediary, such as a proxy, was deployed between the data transformer (located on the system-level crosscutting asset layer) and app1 and app2 (operating on the application behavior level.) We name such an intermediary "glue proxy." Glue proxies are sensitive to pressure, too, not only because they intercept messages, but they also must route the information to the proper end-point. In fact, it is common to find countless proxies in a production environment. Some are deployed to enhance security, and others are even deployed to augment data.

Upstream Effects of Behavioral Pressures

It is easy to understand why pressures from the lower-level behavioral scale have an immense impact on the higher ones. Let us now inspect Figure 13.9 and trace message-originating entities in production that have the potential to instigate pressures that flow upstream on the behavioral scale.

We start with the component level. Ironically, a component characteristically offers a small range of solutions and provides a narrow choice of services. Notwithstanding their small implementation scope, and at times, compact size, their impact on the application behavior level could be detrimental to a production environment. Ill-advised integration practices are typically the cause for environment inducing pressures that emanate from one or a collection of components. There are umpteen examples that could explain such phenomena. It all depends on the particular responsibility of such component. A software component that handles file uploads that must be submitted to the application level may introduce extreme message exchange pressures on an application. In Figure 13.9, that component may be C1 and the application is app2.

Another scenario: A collection of intense processing components could increase pressure on a single application, just as components C1, C2, and C3 apply pressure on application app2. This upstream behavioral burden is caused by the compound power of multiple components, applying collaborative stresses on an application. If the latter could not withstand the message transmission strain, the architecture must be revised. Some solutions mitigate the risk of end-state architecture environment collapse such as this by scheduling uploads of data or intense processing activities at off-peak hours.

Now we are moving up on the behavioral scale: Application-level pressures on the system level are even more powerful. Since an application could be composed of multiple modules, components, layers, or tiers, their compound power of transactions could tip the balance of operations toward chaos. The risk is even higher when a number of processing-intense applications collaborate to offer a business or technical solution that could not be attained because of system-level crosscutting product limitations.

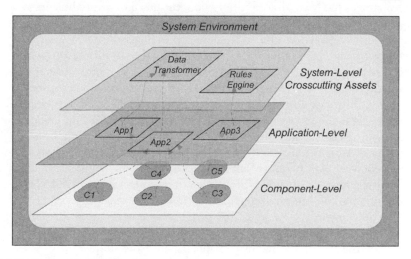

Figure 13.9   Upstream Behavioral Pressures

This is so common in a production environment that engineers set their first analysis priorities to inspect if middleware and/or network infrastructure could indeed offer adequate services. Mounting pressures of entities on the application level could introduce serious challenges to system-level crosscutting elements. In Figure 13.9, the potential pressure induced by applications app1 and app2 operating on the application-level possibly could inflict unsustainable pressures on the data transformer on the system-level crosscutting behavior layer. In fact, data transformer products offered by vendors have immeasurably improved. Nowadays, hardware rather than software products handle powerful data transformation duties.

The same goes for any middleware product deployed for enterprise reuse. Business rules engines, message orchestration servers, and even language translators are only a few examples.

Induced Pressures by Volatile Architecture Areas

Changes to a production environment are the riskiest efforts applied to organizational assets. Whatever they may be, once modifications to software are made, deployments and configurations are altered, and middleware integration is revised, the peril of introducing volatile areas in production is high. The concept of volatility (caused by business change) is introduced in Chapter 10 to facilitate the decomposition of an end-state architecture into segments. Each discovered segment represents an isolated area that must be proved to be performing flawlessly in production.

This process of end-state architecture verification continues now. Here again, volatile pressures are naturally found in change-prone areas where modifications to software and hardware take place. So what exactly is a volatile pressure? *The condition of an architecture element after it has undergone a change may strain its related environment.* Specifically, any kind of production entity—a system, application, or component—may induce pressure on an operating environment if it has been modified.

The concept of change is easily understood. Most of the modifications to a production environment are indeed areas of interest to the end-state architecture stress testing. Whatever has been altered should be scrutinized to insure business continuity. This brings us to the discussion of the business imperative changes that trigger alterations to technical direction and strategies. But perhaps the most interesting aspect of a business change is its aftermath. The upshot of a morphing business could be observed across an enterprise. This touches a wide range of organizational aspects such as business model, mission, culture, and, of course, technological direction.

So how is the general idea of a business change related to the end-state architecture stress testing? The most important aspect to remember is that business changes trigger technological changes. And any technological trend clearly affects the way we design systems. An end-state architecture proposition, therefore, is a direct reflection of business changes. Any product that requires automation would also necessitate the beginning of a life cycle, during which software architecture, software construction, and configuration and integration efforts would be necessary. A product life cycle, therefore, would introduce changes to a production environment. This may include alterations to configuration, integration, and distribution of software. And as mentioned earlier, these changes are now inspected to avoid unnecessary pressures that could bring down areas in a production landscape.

Volatile Business Pressures

So business change may be the chief cause for almost every risky pressure in an end-state architecture. Ironically, business changes introduce opportunities. And this is the right time to begin analyzing an end-state architecture environment to discover changes that correlate with volatile business areas in production. We call them business areas because this perspective of production environment focuses on fundamental imperatives such as ownership, lines of business boundaries, domains, and revenue incurring regions.

Perhaps one of the most discouraging aspects of analyzing the efficiency of a production environment is that in many cases it is treated as a cost center, not as an ecosystem that is funded to offer solutions and ultimately bring in revenue. When production has a negative impact on an organization's revenue, long-term services to consumers are hard to justify—there is an incentive to discontinue offerings even before they are proven profitable.

In the context of this section, a production environment must be thought of as a profitability center that fulfills business goals, not as an experimental marketing tool to promote tactical and short-term initiatives. The business strategy, therefore, must drive the architecture of a production landscape. End-state architecture stress testing, though, calls for slicing and dicing a run-time environment like this into areas that are prone to change. In other words, detect volatile business pressures to insure business continuity.

Another point must be clarified before moving on to the next section: how a volatile business area in production is the source of message exchange and network pressures. The list that follows specifies a number of business areas that may induce pressures on production entities and network traffic:

- Software modifications that contain response-time hindering errors
- Software replacements that introduce performance bottlenecks
- Inadequate capacity to run a new ESB product that supports business operations
- An altered asset integration in production that cannot accommodate increasing customer requests

A Model for Business Change

It is becoming increasingly obvious that a change in business, whatever it may be, is always visible in a production environment. As stated previously, the focus should be on volatile parts of an end-state architecture that are predisposed to risk. Any change in production that is related to business initiatives should be stress tested. Any shift in business thinking and concepts results in production environment modifications, enhancements, revamping, augmentation, or rolling back activities. This correlation then is easy to comprehend.

To be able to map changes in business to areas of business in production, a model for business change is introduced here. But before presenting this alignment approach, be aware that unfortunately ownership of systems or applications in production is not always strongly affiliated with business owners. Ownership of software entities, such as these, is sometimes forgotten, setting the responsibility for their operation on the shoulders of production engineers. In many cases, the ties between the business organization and their products in production are weak. Use this model, therefore, to understand how business changes correlate directly to business areas in production.

Now it is time to study Figure 13.10 and analyze its content. Let us break down the model for business change into three columns as presented in this illustration:

Business change   Any change in business management, structure, alteration to business strategies, policies, customer requirements, business partners, services and products, and staff or organizational expertise is typically reflected in business-related areas in production.

Common volatility factors   This column represents prevailing aspects related to enterprise business change: It is always about the consumers, services, and organizational revenue.

Volatile business areas in production   These areas in production correlate to the change in business indicated in the business change column. These locations do not necessarily pinpoint the exact physical spots in the end-state architecture. Instead, they point to potential prone-to-change software assets.

Mapping Business Change to Volatile Business Areas

Let us look again at Figure 13.10 to understand the correlation between the business changes and the related business areas in production. The breakdown clearly shows

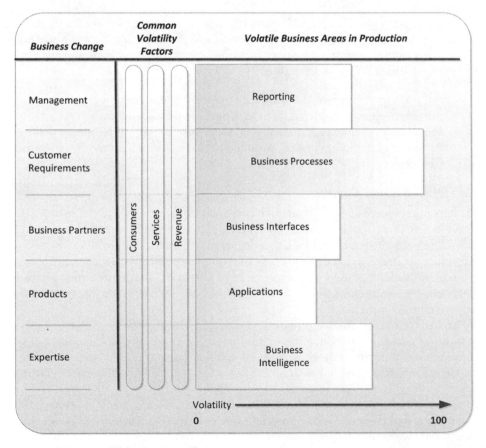

Figure 13.10   A Model for Business Change

how the alteration of a business aspect points to pressure-prone areas in end-state architecture. We thus describe the correlation between the content under the column named "business change" to the items under the column titled "volatile business areas in production."

Management   These business-oriented places in production are associated with software assets that offer reporting capabilities dispatching information about organizational performance, revenue, and even marketing efforts.

Customer requests   New customer necessities always call for changes to business processes in production. These business functions are typically executed by business applications and components. Business logic could also be spotted in business rules engines or even invoked by ESB orchestration capabilities.

Business partners   Software adapters and interfaces are vital to the externalization of functionality of applications. Web service interfaces, for example, are exposed to the outside world to enable business partners, such as suppliers and collaborating organizations, to invoke remote business services.

Products   Any demand for business functionality change by an organization to existing products prompts modifications to business applications and their related components in production. Areas in production, therefore, that are affected by a shift in business priorities or product planning introduce changes to related applications. Applications in this context pertain to business logic that must be altered to meet new or modified business requirements.

Expertise   Changes to business knowledge, such as medical materials or healthcare information that benefit consumers, are related to business production areas where intellectual property is being stored.

Business Volatility Triggers Technical Volatility

It is clear by now that almost every change in business-related operations could affect technical aspects in production. In simple words: *Business volatility elicits technical volatility*. This correlation is discussed in the last two sections. Here, however, we drill a tad down into the actual world of production technologies to observe the direct implication of such volatilities. As discussed earlier, these changes to actual production assets may prompt unwanted pressures that could cause business discontinuity.

Figure 13.11 then represents the correlation between business changes to technologies and architectural features in production ("business changes" and "volatile architecture areas in production" columns, respectively.) Note that the volatility scale ranges from 0 to 100. This is a mere volatility assessment that ultimately prods pressure strengths in prone-to-change business areas.

Management   Changes to organizational management, strategies, and policies are associated with reporting, technical and business monitoring platforms, and provisioning capabilities in production. Such business changes would then require alterations to production facilities that provide up-to-date information to management for assessing the state of business affairs and progress.

Customer requirements   New customer demands should be met with changes to technological capabilities. The modifications to production entities that contain business processes, functional alterations, and even additions to existing implementations could include a wide range of applications and components.

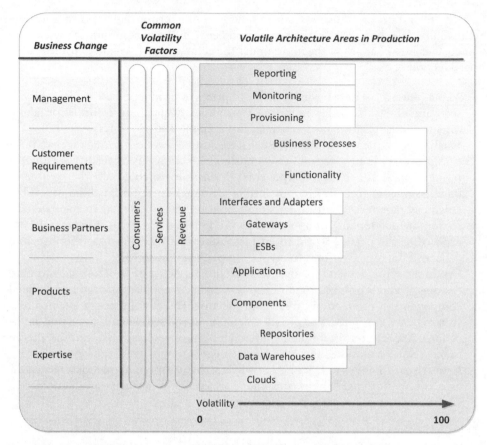

Figure 13.11   Correlations between Business Volatility and Technical Volatility

Business partners   Maintaining solid relationships with business partners such as suppliers and other collaborating organizations would necessitate accessibility mechanisms to allow information sharing. The technical measurements, therefore, are extended with the additions of adapters and interfaces to existing legacy systems or monolithic applications. The employment of an ESB is typically an efficient method to insure tight relationships with business partners.

Products   A shift of organizational strategy and mission is typically accompanied by launching a new line of products or modifying existing implementations. Business applications and components in production are the primary target for changes. Alterations to business applications usually prompt new integration initiatives and adaption of middleware products.

Expertise   Any change to business means to incur revenue calls for developing new organizational expertise and increase of the enterprise knowledge pool. To persist, such intellectual property technological capabilities must accommodate preservation of such information in repositories. There are many ways to store organizational knowledge. The most common are databases, data warehouses, and even clouds.

CHAPTER 14

End-State Architecture Stress Testing Driven by Pressure Points

Here we are again, continuing the discussion about the preparation for the end-state architecture stress testing. The methods of discovering pressure sources in an integrated production environment have been covered so far. By now it is clear that pressure-prone areas in an end-state architecture could be caused by a wide range of software and hardware conditions that simply clot or congest network sections. The analogy to a city power grid is indeed a good example that explains the phenomena of a computing environment slowdown or complete shutdown. Unfortunately, organizations are too familiar with such circumstances that only add chaos to existing production environments and threaten business profitability.

Discovering pressure-prone areas in end-state architecture (discussed in Chapter 13), either as a proposition on paper or already operating in a production environment, is a good start. As discussed, the analysis renders sections that could potentially harm business transactions on a network. This effort narrows down the vast production spaces into interest areas for the end-state stress testing initiative.

But the end-state architecture stress testing could not pinpoint the exact locations on a network or focus on a software entity if merely a trouble-prone area is called out. We need to do better than this.

The Justification for Inserting Pressure Points

The mission would then be to drill down into a pressure-prone area and mark one or more pressure points. By discovering pressure points, the end-state architecture stress testing effort would focus on particular production entities or specific network aspects that may be the source of pressure. This simple idea of targeting specific end-state architecture elements and avoiding trivial areas that are believed to be harmless to production is a valuable proposition.

Remember, inserting pressure points in an end-state architecture does not mean that the environment as a whole is marked as subject for stress testing. That is not the case. Pressure points are just intersections. They should be regarded as targeted spots for the stress testing efforts. The higher perspective then should reveal an end-state architecture environment that includes multiple pressure points. Collaborative pressure points on such a grand-scale design would uncover how strained the end-state architecture is and if its environment would be able to meet design specifications.

Therefore, ask these questions to confirm if the overall end-state architecture environment would indeed meet technical requirements:

- Will the collaborative pressure points affect systems and applications performance?
- Have too many pressure points been discovered in the end-state architecture?
- Where are the majority of the pressure points located? Are they pointing to systems? Applications? Components?
- Are there too many pressure points marking troubling spots on the network, suggesting insufficient network bandwidth?
- Do the majority of the pressure points suggest that asset integration would introduce performance risks?
- Do the pressure points call for further investigation into the mounting strain on organizational data sources?
- Are security measurements in end-state architecture causing applications to slow down?

Inserting Pressure Points in an End-State Architecture

It is clear that inserting pressure points into an end-state architecture should be applied in the already defined pressure-prone areas. This means that every discovered pressure point should be established within the boundaries of potentially strained areas in the end-state architecture. These stressed ranges are largely discussed in Chapter 13.

The end-state architecture stress testing effort then may start right after the pressure points have been located. The process of positioning a stress point in the grand scale design is simple. However, there could be many reasons for placing pressure points in particular strained spots. Some are affiliated with concerns about application response time and message exchange performance. Other reasons may be related to insufficient network bandwidth capacity. Moreover, a pressure point could focus one's attention on implementation errors that could form communication bottlenecks. Obviously, integration of assets in production may yield pressure points that must be given attention, too. The list of reasons is typically long. A meticulous analysis should determine the weight of a pressure point in the overall end-state architecture.

Focus on the Chief Stress Testing Mission: End-State Architecture Verification

Architecture structural, behavioral, or volatility reasons could inflict risky pressures in production. However, no matter what the reasons are behind positioning a pressure point on an end-state architecture map, we still need to focus on the fundamental motivation for conducting stress testing. The chief justification is rooted deep in the incremental architecture verification process. Proving that an end-state architecture would actually perform in production would be required to certify the environment's fitness.

Therefore, *inserting pressure points at potential transaction breaking points is the current mission.*

There is one more architecture verification aspect to focus on before moving on to an example demonstrating the insertion of pressure points. Recall that two leading types of pressures exist: internal and external. The former suggests that the pressure emanates from internal components of an application or a system. The latter, on the other hand, is related more to environment influences, in which architecture elements are linked to each other and collaborate to achieve a business goal. One would argue that internal pressures are the cause for external pressures. For example, a glitch in a software component could harm the communications with an external entity such as an ESB. This justifies the claim that both pressures, internal and external, are highly dependent. However, there may be instances where internal pressure would not necessarily prompt external ones.

End-State Architecture Pressure Points Use Case Study

Now it is time to turn the attention to Figure 14.1 to inspect the pressure points inserted in the end-state architecture pressure prone areas. Note that these areas are defined first in Figure 13.6. Obviously, these pressure points are fictional. They mark strained areas in the design merely to present a schematic concept. In addition, the rendered pressure points, P1 to P4, represent points of interest for the end-state architecture stress testing.

Let us break down Figure 14.1 into the discovered pressure points to understand why each was inserted in these particular locations:

- *Pressure point P1.* Positioned on the service locator in pressure area 1
- *Pressure point P2.* Located on the portal server in pressure area 2
- *Pressure point P3.* Placed on the data source access provider in pressure area 2
- *Pressure point P4.* Sited on the message route that connects the gateway server and the cloud

Pressure points are affiliated to concerns. These are typically architecture junctions representing points of strain on network infrastructure, hardware, message routes, and software implementations. As discussed throughout this chapter and largely in Chapter 13, one must be aware that the chief types of pressure-inducing sources are architectural structures, software behaviors, and volatile regions. Therefore, consider the reasons behind positioning these pressure points in the end-state architecture, as depicted in 14.1:

Structural Pressure points P1 (in pressure area 1) and P2 (in pressure area 2) are placed in the center of two centralized sub-architectures. P1 is positioned on the service locator, a hub that offers common services in a hub-and-spokes architecture formation. The reason is obvious: Hubs are typically sensitive to environmental pressures that are generated by their subscribing consumers. P2 was positioned on the portal server for the same exact reason. It is regarded as a point of concern for the stability of the architecture because of its potential to intercept the messages of more consumers. Another aspect to be concerned about is that P2's central position in the star-like structure may buckle under in the face of bombardment of oversized message loads.

Behavioral Pressure point P3 is placed on the data source access provider, a middleware product located in pressure area 2. In enterprise production environments, data access services offer a wide range of functionalities, all of which are

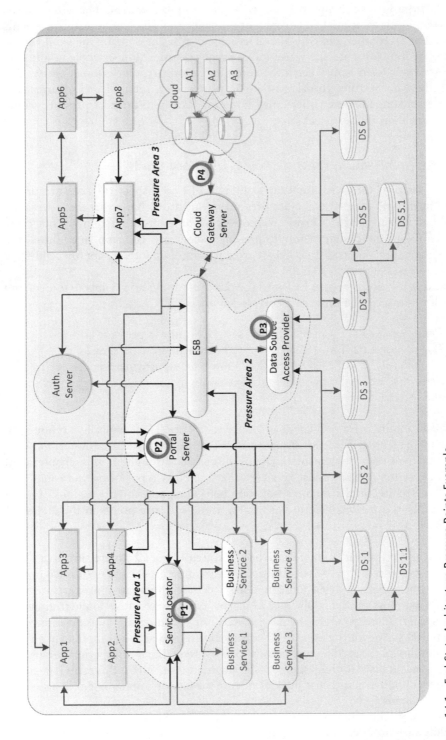

Figure 14.1   End-State Architecture Pressure Points Example

designed to shield repositories and data providers from the rest of the organization. Among such capabilities are CRUD (create, read, update, and delete) and other security features to protect the information. This behavioral aspect of the data source access provider may be subject to architecture pressures because of the demands of unanticipated or planned consumers.

Volatile   In our case study, pressure point P4 in pressure area 3 is positioned because of volatility concerns due to recent changes to the cloud interfaces. Note that P4 points to the message route connecting the cloud gateway server and the cloud. This would be a point of interest to the end-state architecture stress testing. Modifications applied to the cloud entry point may affect a large community of users and processes trying to access services. Placing such a prone-to-change spot in a strategic location is mandatory.

Methods of End-State Architecture Stress Testing

The establishment of pressure points in an end-state architecture is a major milestone. The discovery of these strained locations paves the road to a structured stress testing effort that must only focus on predefined troubling and risky spots in a production landscape. Pinpointing performance concerns in precise network locations would simplify the methods by which we are about to assess an end-state architecture fitness.

The process of end-state architecture stress testing must start with an analysis, during which the environment is studied thoroughly. The end-state architecture vision and mission are clear. And the integration of systems and their internal assets, such as applications, middleware products, and network infrastructure is understood.

The discovered pressure points must be prioritized next. Some may be regarded as negligible spots of interest to the stress testing. Others may be recognized as critical. Once the pressure points have been identified, a detailed stress test plan should be carved out, offering engineers a meticulous stress testing road map. The stress testing plan should also include the approaches taken to accomplish the examination of the end-state architecture environment. (Stress testing methods are discussed in the Stress Test Approaches section later in this chapter.) Moreover, the employment of specialized tools is fundamental to every stress-testing initiative. The selection of such tools must be conducted to be able to meet stress test plan requirements.

Establish Pressure Point Failure Conditions

There are no industry pressure point risk standards for organizations. What is defined as a pressure risk in one institute could not be applied to another. Setting a threshold for entering the zone of risk when pressures are applied on end-state architecture elements such as network, systems, or applications is indeed subjective to an enterprise. Only an organization, though, is able to define for itself the risk conditions that should be avoided. These specifications should be documented in a nonfunctional requirement paper.

In this section we then offer only certain quantifiable aspects that are affiliated with risks of pressure on organizational assets. This proposition includes a risk model for breaking points in an end-state architecture. The term "breaking point" pertains to the exact starting time at which an implementation, such as a system or its affiliated components, or applications, may buckle or underperform under the weight applied to a pressure point. Although the intention here is not to define measurable aspects of a pressure risk, the aim is to establish ranges of risks, a model that could be applied to an end-state architecture stress testing effort.

A Risk Model for Breaking Points

To view the range of risks associated with pressures applied on a pressure point in an end-state architecture, let us examine Figure 14.2. As is apparent, this risk model illustrates three distinct ranges of pressure risks that could be traced over time:

1. Low pressure risk
2. Medium pressure risk
3. High pressure risk

These risk scopes on the area chart set three boundaries for pressure levels. For each of them, an organization should specify the actual ranges in a nonfunctional requirements document. Clearly, the low pressure risk level identifies a range that would not raise breaking point concerns. As shown, the volatile pressure source, illustrated here as an example, is measured within this range. The behavioral and structural pressure sources, though, pose higher risks to the environment.

The medium pressure risk level, on the other hand, indicates that a risk that is carried by a stress on pressure points should be still acceptable to an organization. To some institutions, the term "medium" rings a warning bell, a cautionary reminder that mounting pressures on end-state architecture elements could cross the borderline into the high-risk level. Precautionary measures are typically applied to restrain the pressure risk to the low-level range. Therefore, finding the structural and behavioral

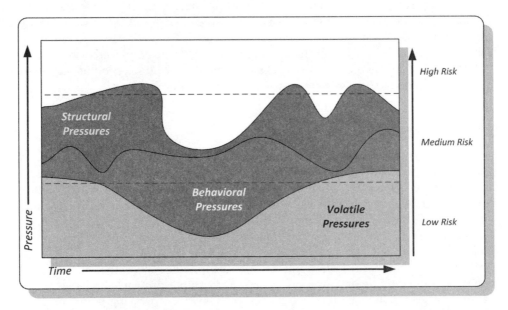

Figure 14.2   Breaking Points Risk Model

type of pressures, as depicted in Figure 14.2, in the medium-risk category should be an uncomfortable end-state architecture performance proposition.

The structural sources of pressures, as depicted in Figure 14.2, break through the higher end of the medium-risk scope into the high-risk range. No organization should accept pressure risks that fall under the high-risk category. An end-state architecture that contains architecture pressure points classified as high-risk should not be sponsored or supported. There is no defense for deploying or maintaining end-state architecture when parts of it are known to be extremely vulnerable to environmental pressures.

Consequences of Pressure Risk Levels

With every risk defined in the breaking points model, there are consequences that an organization should be prepared for. An environment with no risk at all is an idyllic ecosystem that can rarely be found. Even the lowest pressure risk level could still wreak havoc on production. To understand the costs of pressure point failures, let us classify them into three main categories:

1. *Low risk pressure.* The consequences of such risks are typically related to unstable and unpredictable performance of software entities. At this risk level, systems and/or application performance do not necessarily halt. Erratic functionality behavior with pauses could be observed.
2. *Medium risk pressure.* At this risk level, performance degradation and sluggish message exchange could affect a number of dependent software entities. The integration between architecture elements is at risk, of which all connected software entities suffer from slow response time and information exchange delays.
3. *High risk pressure.* This risk level typically results in total system halt, severely congested network, and shutdown of business applications.

Stress Test Approaches

The stress testing may start now. Before we start we must know, however, what methods should be employed to run stress tests for the end-state architecture. Some fundamental aspects must be remembered when accomplishing these fitness tests:

- An end-state architecture stress test should be driven by a detailed plan that specifies time frames, message load, preconditions, and assumptions and predictions about the outcome.
- The chief goal of an end-state architecture stress test is to verify if its corresponding *environment* is elastic, steady, durable, and sustainable. The grand scale design must be proven and certified.
- An end-state architecture stress test must employ tools with message injection capabilities. The term "message injection" refers to what is known as load testing, during which streams of data are directed toward a software entity, a server, or a network infrastructure asset to test its stability and capacity. Posting generated messages through message exchange routes in a variety of frequencies and strengths would enable control and monitoring on released pressures toward pressure points.

- The targets of an end-state architecture stress test must be predefined pressure points that are rendered by analyses of architectural structures, environment behaviors, and volatile breaking points.
- The simulated pressure should be measured by messages per second. A message size should be benchmarked equally across an end-state architecture to maintain standard pressures.
- The three methods of end-state architecture stress testing, as described in the sections that follow, should be performed to meet the certification requirements.

Recovery Discovery

The recovery discovery method for stress testing is depicted in the self-explanatory Figure 14.3. Time over pressure is the ratio that depicts how the test should be conducted. Specifically, simulated messages should be released into the network toward pressure points in three sequential bursts or more. As depicted in the illustration, each burst in the succession applies stronger pressure than the previous one. Moreover, between each pressure eruption, a pause should take place to measure the aftermath. This recess should give the opportunity to inspect the reaction to the applied pressure on various architecture elements, such as systems, applications, or components.

This method of stress testing measures the state of recovery from different strengths of pressure bursts. The ultimate goal would then be to discover the time it takes for an architecture element to revert to its normal state. For example, an application running in a virtual machine typically operates under normal conditions if the garbage collector is not suppressed and able to reclaim unused memory space without slowing down the implementation. Again, this approach of stress testing would allow measuring the time lapse between the end of a pressure burst and the beginning of operation recovery.

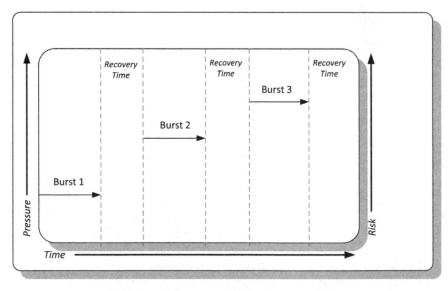

Figure 14.3   Recovery Discovery Stress Testing Method

Another aspect that should be tested is if the communication between pressure points and their environment has recovered. If architecture elements resume operation with normal message exchange rate within an acceptable time frame, the recovery process is considered successful. This test would verify if the integration between production assets meets design specifications.

Ask the questions that follow to confirm if indeed the recovery discovery stress testing on an end-state architecture concluded successfully:

- Did the pressure points on architecture elements, such as components, applications, and middleware products resume normal operation during message burst breaks?
- Was the resumption of operation within an acceptable timeframe?
- Did the message exchange between production environment entities recover?
- Was any pressure point shut down after or during pressure bursts?

Breaking Points Discovery

The breaking points discovery stress testing method is devised to accomplish one vital sustainability challenge driven by a principal question: Would an end-state architecture pressure point halt normal operation during a continuous and increasing pressure? That is, a stress test fails if a pressure point halts its activities during a steep climb in a strengthening pressure, as depicted in Figure 14.4. This simple concept of applying increasing pressure on an architecture element, such as message routes, middleware, or applications reveals if end-state architecture would indeed perform flawlessly in production.

Unlike the recovery discovery, discussed in the previous section, the breaking points discovery approach calls for continuous pressure that halts only when a breaking

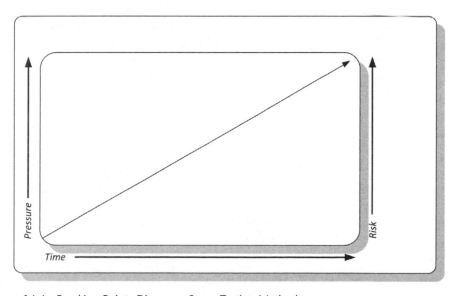

Figure 14.4   Breaking Points Discovery Stress Testing Method

point in the architecture is discovered. It is advised to raise the pressure level applied to pressure points beyond the specification for sustainability in the nonfunctional requirements. For example, if such requirement calls for a pressure point to process 1,000 messages per second, then the breaking point discovery stress test should double the pressure to 2,000 messages per second. Again, the stress test should not end there if a breaking point has not been discovered. The pressure must be increased even beyond the parameters in a stress test plan.

The rule of thumb therefore suggests that after the an end-state architecture stress testing the discovered breaking points should be cleared by mending the mounting pressure conditions. That is, the end-state architecture should not include any breaking points discovered above the allowable sustainability parameter (measured in messages per second) in the nonfunctional requirements document. This is one of the most important stipulations of the end-state architecture verification process. Therefore, no end-state architecture should be further funded or supported in production until all unacceptable breaking points are cleared away. Removing breaking points in such a grand-scale design should be accomplished by testing again the decomposed architecture segments and correcting critical design flaws by pursuing again the design substantiation process (discussed in Chapter 12).

Ask the questions that follow to insure that the breaking point discovery stress test was completed successfully:

- Have any breaking points been discovered during the stress test?
- What was the pressure intensity when a breaking point was discovered?
- Was the breaking point ascertained beyond the acceptable pressure indicated in the nonfunctional sustainability requirements?
- What is the organization's allowable breaking point pressure (in messages per seconds)?

Durability Discovery

Durability is one of the most fundamental requirements of the end-state architecture verification process. An architecture environment must be proven solid and maintain normal operation during different periods of the day. For example, an application would be required to operate under higher pressures, naturally occurring during message exchange peak time. The ultimate test to confirm stability and business continuity is to conduct the durability discovery, as illustrated in Figure 14.5.

Testing operations continuously during different periods of the day and under a variety of pressure strengths could uncover end-state architecture flaws. This simple test is worthwhile. It could expose environmental design defects that were hard to catch during the design substantiation process (discussed in Chapter 12).

Remember, unlike with the breaking point discovery stress test, during which it is expected to encounter shutdown of architecture elements, the durability discovery process is all about testing the fitness of an end-state architecture during normal and peak hours. Obviously, any design flaw discovery that fails in an architecture environment should only encourage efforts to correct it.

Once again, durability parameters in the nonfunctional requirements document must indicate the allowable pressure (messages per second) that an architecture element must sustain. Again, the durability parameters should pertain to different times of the day. A benchmark should be set for slow, busy, and peak times.

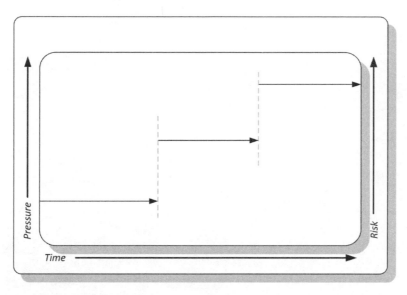

Figure 14.5   Durability Discovery Stress Testing Method

Ask the questions that follow to insure that the durability discovery stress test is successful:

- What were the durability parameter values (messages per second) in the nonfunctional requirements?
- Did the durability discovery stress test results surpass the durability parameters?
- Did any of the end-state architecture environment elements halt during the stress test?
- Did any of the end-state architecture elements slow down during the stress test?
- During which period of the day did a pressure point buckle under the persistent pressure of message exchange?

CHAPTER 15

Enterprise Capacity Planning for End-State Architecture

Nothing is static when it comes to a vibrant production ecosystem. Capacity planning for an end-state architecture that includes systems, applications, and any other entity in production is all about sizing. What does sizing mean? When an end-state architecture proposition is made or has already been deployed to production, the prevailing engineering obligation is to allocate enough computing resources for current and future entity consumption.

Ask these capacity-related questions to determine if end-state architecture elements such as components, applications, and/or systems will indeed operate flawlessly with current production capacity:

- Will the network bandwidth meet current message exchange volumes?
- Will the database storage allow for an increase in information persistence?
- Do the servers contain enough disk space for input/output (I/O) operations?
- Do the servers include enough memory to enable rapid computing?
- Are the servers' CPUs powerful enough to process data?

These associated capacity questions emphasize the current resource consumption needs for individual end-state architecture elements. Capacity planning is also about sizing software and hardware to assure solid business execution in the future. Over time, systems and their related applications are bound to grow beyond their original size. Repositories always expand beyond their initial state. More consumers subscribe to business services, and network traffic increases as time goes by. This production expansion calls for allocating additional resources such as hardware and software to enable the increase in computing demand.

When it comes to end-state architecture consumption needs, the term "*enterprise capacity planning*" is about not only properly sizing a server or insuring that network bandwidth is sufficient for running a system or application. It is chiefly about *sizing a computing environment*. The strategy is not only about sustaining the needs of a confined area on a network. The end-state architecture as a whole must be evaluated, analyzed, and modeled to meet the current and future growth of the business.

Moreover, it must be noted that unlike the *application capacity planning* discussed in Chapter 5, this chapter focuses on an *enterprise-level environment*. The title enterprise capacity planning process, therefore, takes a broader view to determine if the sum of all resources allocated to an end-state architecture software and hardware entities in

Figure 15.1   Enterprise Capacity Planning Chief Activities

production are indeed sufficient to insure faultless operation. Delivering a capacity plan for a single application, for example, would not necessarily address resource utilization concerns of an entire end-state architecture environment. Similarly, computing resources for a middleware product would certainly not satisfy utilization demands of an entire end-state architecture landscape.

And what about budgets? Unmistakably, the bottom line is always about the budgets allocated to enable the growing scope of enterprise assets. In the language of enterprise capacity planning, *sizing* is a fundamental requirement to satisfy current and future expansion of business services. It is a strategic imperative that should not be ignored. The end-state architecture verification process, therefore, must assure that not only the current enterprise computing resource capacity is met, but also that future growth and design elasticity is taken into account.

The sections that follow lay out a plan for enterprise capacity planning activities. This simple process is devised to size an environment for an end-state architecture. The collaborative consumption of end-state architecture elements should be satisfied in a production ecosystem. Figure 15.1 illustrates a schematic capacity planning life cycle during which five chief activities should be accomplished:

1. *End-state architecture artifact studies.* An end-state architecture environment, deployment, configuration, and integration of software and hardware entities should be studied to help carve out an enterprise capacity plan.
2. *Data collection.* This activity calls for collecting workload data from the end-state architecture pressure points.
3. *Data analysis.* Analyzing the obtained data from the end-state architecture pressure points would reveal fundamental consumption capabilities of production entities.
4. *Data Modeling* The collected data from the end-state architecture pressure points would assist with the creation of current and future performance models.
5. *Environment sizing..* The final capacity planning activity requires sizing an environment for an end-state architecture.

End-State Architecture Artifact Studies

The work of capacity planning starts here. The more we know about an end-state architecture strategy, direction, and requirements, the better a plan for resource utilization will be. The more we understand how a grand-scale enterprise design is devised to obtain business goals, the more conclusive a resource consumption plan will be.

The more familiar we are with an end-state architecture integration scheme, the better the plan for future consumption growth will be.

It would be difficult to discover resource utilization needs for an architecture, as indicated in a nonfunctional requirement document, if the design is not understood. The end-state architecture artifact studies then must start with an investigation of the grand-scale enterprise design proposition.

Study Business and Technical Requirements

To broaden the knowledge about an end-state architecture, consider the documentation needed for the preliminary review. While delving in the list of artifacts that follow, study the motivation behind the delivery of an end-state architecture proposition. Understand business requirements and technical specifications. If the end-state architecture has been already deployed to production, conduct enterprise capacity activities to detect underperforming or failing implementations.

Business motivation   The business problem domain document explains the threats to the enterprise and consequences if the concerns are not addressed.

Business imperatives   The business requirements document represents chief business necessities and suggested solutions.

Nonfunctional parameters.   The nonfunctional requirements document indicates various operational criteria, such as application and system response time, system availability, consumption requirements, and more.

Grand-scale enterprise design   End-state architecture artifacts provide enterprise strategies, direction, and grand-scale design for asset integration, product utilization, messaging platforms, system and application collaboration, and more.

Technical specifications   The technical specifications document of the end-state architecture includes implementation details for development, deployment, configuration, message routing, systems and application collaboration, and more.

Study Outcomes of the End-State Architecture Discovery and Analysis, Decomposition, and Stress Testing

Recall that the incremental software architecture practice approach calls for accomplishing end-state architecture discovery and analysis activities. End-state architecture decomposition is also required to breakdown the design into manageable and understandable areas to enable an efficient design verification process. In addition, as a part of the verification activities, stress testing is necessary to measure the end-state architecture fitness and solidity.

Here we are required, therefore, to review the outcome of these endeavors provided in the list that follows.

System fabric patterns   The discoveries of system fabric patterns in the end-state architecture should be studied carefully to understand the integration scheme of assets in production and their relationship. Refer to Chapter 4 to read more about the employment of fabric patterns.

Application discovery and analysis   Application-level discovery activities are discussed in Chapters 5 and 6. Subscribe to the methods that can assist locating applications on a network by employing mapping tools. Understand the applications' architectures. Identify dependencies of applications on entities of a production environment. Discover application performance and consumption metrics. Application-level capacity planning should be studied, too.

Mapping application topology   Learn about application logical and physical topology mapping introduced in Chapter 6. Study more about discovering application dependencies.

End-state architecture decomposition   Study the structural, behavioral, and volatile decomposition of an end-state architecture. These approaches can be found in Chapters 7–11.

Pressure points   Identify the end-state architecture pressure points. This topic is discussed in junction with environment stress testing in Chapters 13 and 14.

Data Collection

Now we are facing one of the most important tasks that must be accomplished to conduct any enterprise capacity planning goal: *data collection*. Why should data be collected? What would be the purpose of the data gathering effort? From where should the data be aggregated? And what type of data is required? To answer these questions, remember that no capacity planning initiative can be conducted without sample data. Having access to data aggregated from multiple locations would clearly enable us to assess the consumption of troubling spots in the enterprise end-state architecture environment.

Collect Data from End-State Architecture Pressure Points

The data collected from pressure points located in different locations in an end-state architecture will be analyzed later to determine if it is adequate for further modeling efforts. These data analysis and modeling activities are discussed later in the sections Data Analysis and Enterprise Capacity Planning Modeling.

Moreover, gathering data from pressure points does not imply that the capacity planning efforts are confined to isolated areas in the end-state architecture. Quite the opposite—the pressure points that are typically dispersed across a production environment are prospective breaking point indicators. These are concerning spots that point to software implementations and hardware. For example, a pressure point could be placed on a specific system or application location or point to middleware or network infrastructure. Consequently, the collective data gathered from the potential breaking point indicators should draw attention to an end-state architecture state of fitness.

One could argue that data should not be collected only from weak or troubling points in the end-state architecture. Why not gather data from the most vital production assets and then come up with an overall enterprise capacity plan? The answer is rooted in the promise of the enterprise capacity planning practice. More so, it is one of the most fundamental aspects of the end-state architecture verification: The incremental software architecture calls for verifying if an architecture would indeed operate flawlessly in production. Therefore, the plan of attack should target the weaker spots of an end-state architecture—namely, the pressure points that could potentially buckle under the strain of intense message exchange.

What Data Metrics Should Be Collected?

More is better would be the answer to this question. The traditional and still valuable data metric collection system calls for gathering a wide range of information from deployed software and hardware entities. This includes software and hardware, and network-related data metrics collected from multiple sources. Although the traditional data metric collection method requires gathering information from individual entities that do not necessarily represent the overall state of an end-state architecture fitness, it is vital to our enterprise capacity planning efforts. Focus, though, the collection effort on the five fundamental data metrics in the list that follows:

1. CPU utilization
2. Disk space capacity
3. Memory utilization
4. Database storage capacity
5. Network bandwidth

Finally, there is another point to clarify. We typically gather data from existing implementations that have already been deployed. But what about enterprise capacity planning efforts for an end-state architecture proposition? Where should the data come from? In the sections that follow, we discuss both circumstances: instrumentation and data generation.

Instrumentation Technologies

So now it is time to collect data from pressure points. Remember that this effort should not focus on a single pressure point. We must gather data from multiple pressure points, representative of weak points in an end-state architecture. This is not a manual effort. Specialized instrumentation tools designed to gather data from deployed environments should only accomplish this task. There is a variety of platforms on the market capable of monitoring hardware capabilities and software implementations. They offer a wide range of functionality, such as measuring performance, assessing memory utilization, and gathering data metrics continuously.

There are a few methods to trace performance and collect information from a deployed software entity and its network environment. The most common approach is introduced by the agent technology (a branch of the application performance management, or APM,[1] practice used in many production facilities. This intrusive method calls for compiling a program with instrumentation code and deploying the implementation to production.

The benefits for doing this are vast since now engineers can trace software capabilities and detect performance errors using instrumentation-monitoring presentation utilities. However, the cost could be high. In many cases, such an intrusive technology could also slow down the performance of systems, applications, and even their environment. Ironically, software execution latency is one of the major reasons that prompt engineers in the first place to use instrumentation. To mitigate this issue and save management, installation, and configuration costs, some instrumentation products offer agentless technologies that avoid the intrusion of source code—that is, no agents to install. Instead, the desired data metrics are collected from the operating system and other products that are already present on a server.

Finally, use instrumentation technologies to collect data metrics from end-state architecture pressure points. The collected information may range from minutes to even years. Therefore, store this gathered information in a repository for impending data modeling and trending tasks, discussed in this chapter's section on Enterprise Capacity Planning Modeling. Historic data such as this would be critical to predicting future consumption of resources and help the organization size the end-state architecture environment.

Data Generation Technologies

Where do data metrics come from if an end-state architecture proposition has not been yet implemented and deployed? How can it be confirmed that such a design on paper not fail once delivered to production? When the stakes are high, releasing an end-state architecture to a run-time landscape without a capacity plan would be utterly risky. Not having a plan for sizing an environment and predicting computing resource consumption could be detrimental to the business.

If data does not exist to base capacity assumptions on, the rule of thumb suggests generating it. Indeed, organizations employ a number of methods to make up data metrics that can be used for capacity planning data analysis and modeling. The production of artificial data could be achieved by employing a wide range of data generating products, software simulation platforms, and data analysis programs.

Data generators are commonly used for software testing during the development life cycle. They make up data based on several methods,[2] such as the random and intelligent data algorithms. Feeding a data generator with preliminary required parameters could affect the outcome. Some generators even allow setting numeric ranges for the created data, while others call for formulating a model by which outputs can be shaped.

Using simulation platforms is a known practice for testing a software entity that has not been deployed and integrated in production. Some simulation products employ models to determine the behavior of a nonexisting system. This requires considerable effort to set up the initial data and provide design parameters to generate a hypothetical model. In return, the model would then generate subsequent data that can be used for a wide range of testing and capacity planning.

Use any data generating available model that meets an end-state architecture requirements. Again, without such information, a capacity plan cannot be created.

Data Analysis

After the data metrics have been collected, the work of analysis begins. The term "data analysis" in the context of capacity planning simply implies to understand it, augment it, purify it, and prepare it for the impending resource consumption modeling activities. Moreover, the range of the data analysis activities may also include detecting information inconsistencies and discovering shifts in resource utilization volumes. These important tasks must be performed in advance of the data modeling and resource sizing. The bottom line: Capacity planning should not base its recommendations on raw data. Artificially generated data should be delivered in proper formats for capacity-planning modeling.

Understanding Collected Data

Understanding the gathered data for capacity planning is one of the most challenging efforts. There is a wide range of questions that an analyst must ask when reviewing these sets of data. The prevailing question is related to the meaning of the data. In other words, how could such gathered information from a pressure point in the end-state architecture be used to predict future breaking points?

Another common concern is to understand the format of the data that has been collected. Binary formats are hard to decipher. However, not all data appears scrambled. Some are character strings; others are XML, JSON, and many more. Data could also be delivered in industry-recognized format. One example is the ACORD[3] XML standard specific to the insurance business.

Not all data analysis efforts include information interpretation tasks. They also call for preparing the data for capacity planning modeling. This implies that the collected data is not always ready to be processed by modeling tools in their initial format. Some capacity planning modeling tools may not accept anything else other than character strings. In this case, gathered data that is wrapped in a markup language, such as XML, would necessitate pruning, cleaning, and simplification.

Data Gap Analysis

Another data analysis task would be to fill in time gaps because of interruptions during data collection. Reasons for pauses in data retrieval may vary. In some instances, a server may halt its operation. In others, the data collector agent may not be active for a while. Failure to collect continuous data could easily skew capacity planning modeling outcomes.

For example, if a model averages out CPU utilization values for two weeks with no values collected for four days, the average usage would appear much lower than it is supposed to. Consequently, gaps in data gathering must be compensated by filling in the missing information based on calculated assumptions. The other option would be to recollect the data from the end-state architecture pressure point to obtain a full set of values for the desired time range. If the recollection of data effort may produce the same result set, one may consider the employment of data generators to fill in the missing information gaps.

Data Trend Analysis

Data analysis attention should be given to collected values that seem off track. For example, if network utilization volumes appear to be too high or too low, a warning bell should go off. This data discovery is obviously compared to previous data collection efforts from the same end-state architecture pressure points. Such *changing patterns of data volumes* should be investigated carefully to determine if an error occurred during the data gathering process.

If the shift in resource consumption is indeed accurate, further analysis should investigate such a trend. The upshot of such examination may show a number of reasons for the irregular resource utilization. Some may be due to changes in consumers' usage. A few may show different utilization rates during weather seasons. Others may indicate an unstable business environment. Modifications to middleware or hardware could also be the cause of inconsistent data capacities.

Data Quality Analysis

Another aspect of this analysis process is to screen the gathered data for meaningful values for the upcoming capacity planning modeling efforts. The term "meaningful" suggests that the collected data may not always offer valuable information. For example, an organization may prefer to collect the percentage value of CPU utilization in lieu of other information that may be never used, such as number of cycles a processor performs in a second. Furthermore, disk I/O (input/output) writing rates or block size of disk flushing is another kind of information that may not be that useful for an enterprise-level capacity planning. These performance details should not be the focus of a resource utilization strategy for an end-state architecture.

The data quality analysis should also center on data integrity. This concern is widely construed and understood in many ways. In the framework of capacity planning, insuring data integrity means that during the process of collection from pressure points the information stays intact. That is, the data must not undergo any changes during the retrieval process. Missing fields or information loss are other integrity issues that should be closely watched. For example, if the percentage value for memory utilization were absent, no one would be able to draw a clear picture of current resource consumption and future utilization. A missing metric name, such as "data storage utilization" may leave the related information dangling without any suitable use.

Furthermore, collected data that later is stored in a database must be formatted and properly linked to its components. In other words, capacity planning chunks of data must maintain database affiliation that define their relational links. For example, a table that contains fields such as "Collection ID," "Metric ID," "Time Stamp," and "Pressure Point ID" should be linked to a second table that stores the actual values for such data collection activity. The fields in the additional table could be "Collection ID" and "Value." Without proper relational links, valuable data may be lost.

Insure that the collected data from pressure points is carefully reviewed, the content is useful, and the information stays intact. Use tools to analyze the integrity, the completeness, and the overall quality of the data. Obtaining data as intended should be the rule that guides the data analysis process.

Enterprise Capacity Planning Modeling

There is a double purpose for the enterprise capacity planning modeling for an end-state architecture: *reporting current baseline and forecasting resource utilization for an environment.* Clearly, the quality of the collected data, discussed in the previous section, plays a vital role in presenting an accurate state of fitness for an end-state architecture. Any information inconsistency, data integrity errors, or missing fields could skew the rendered data models. When using generated data sets, because of the inability to gather data from a deployed environment, the risk of modeling errors is greater. Artificial data is typically based on assumptions, not facts on the ground. In some instances, the inputs used to generate data are pure conjectures that may not yield reliable resource utilization predictions.

Setting Up an Enterprise Capacity Planning Model

Simply put, an enterprise capacity planning model is a scenario that is used to represent the resource utilization of collected data metrics. There is nothing complicated about such a model as it illustrates the consumption of certain computing resources over time. This depiction could be thought of as a snapshot of an existing or predictable end-state architecture fitness. When delving into the simple model example illustrated in Figure 15.2, it will become clear that the presented scenario does not necessarily depict the overall consumption of an entire end-state architecture environment. This compound capacity planning modeling approach is discussed in the next section.

Meanwhile, let us look at the fundamental building blocks of the illustrated enterprise capacity planning model and understand how to build one. Once the model skeleton is understood, it is possible to construct an enterprise end-state

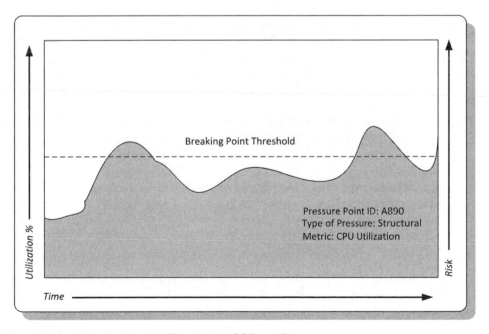

Figure 15.2   A Simple Capacity Planning Model Example

architecture scenario that contains multiple pressure points and metrics. Consider this model breakdown:

Utilization percentage   This axis indicates the resource consumption percentage of a particular data metric for a specific end-state architecture pressure point. It also represents the type of architectural strain applied on a pressure point. Note that in the depicted example, the utilization percentage indicates that an architecture structural pressure tests the fitness of pressure point A890.

Time   The collected data period is an important factor in this model. The time since the data gathering began until the collection was concluded represents the model time range. Organizations tend to collect data during weeks, months, and even years. The capacity planning model, therefore, should indicate the range of time to convey a clear modeling perspective.

Risk   In this illustration, it is apparent that the higher the utilization percentage is for a data metric, the greater the risk for reaching a pressure point performance on the verge of collapse. Lower risks, however, are observed when the resource consumption is low.

Breaking point threshold   An organization should set a break point brink that identifies the consumption risk level that should not be crossed, taking into consideration the current or future production environment capabilities. The break point threshold indicates the level at which an end-state architecture could not handle such a high utilization rate of any of its pressure points.

In addition, as illustrated in Figure 15.2, the enterprise capacity planning model skeleton identifies specific measurement parameters that should be targeted:

Pressure point ID   This identifies a pressure point in an end-state architecture by an assigned identification number. In this example, the arbitrary value is A890.

Type of pressure   There are three types of pressure that could strain a pressure point in an end-state architecture. These are discussed in Chapter 13: structural, behavioral, and volatile. In the represented example, the pressure is defined as structural.

Metric   The data metric that was collected from a pressure point should also be indicated. In this example, CPU utilization identifies this metric.

Compound Enterprise Capacity Planning Modeling for End-State Architecture

The simple enterprise capacity planning model discussed in the previous section can yield numerous permutations, each of which could represent a different view into an end-state architecture. This is what enterprise architecture fitness is all about—multiple perspectives that elaborate on the grand-scale design capability. An organization, therefore, could be free to decide how to examine the overall resource consumption of an end-state architecture. The more inspected versions of such a compound model, the more reliable the verification process will be. Moreover, this validation process comes down to one and only one goal: finding the breaking points of pressure points for a given data metric. The leading cause of such pressure should be indicated, too. As mentioned in the previous section, these are architecture structure, behavioral, and volatile reasons.

With not much time to spare, let us have a look at three compound enterprise capacity planning modeling scenarios, each of which represents a different view in an end-state architecture state of fitness. We start with a simple view, one that provides a narrower scope of an architecture environment. Then we offer a more complex perspective, increasing the scope of the inspected architecture space.

Single Pressure Point, Single Type of Pressure, Multiple Data Metrics

Let us have a look straightaway at Figure 15.3 to understand the presented capacity planning model example. There is nothing intricate about the presented scenario. As shown, this resource utilization view centers on a specific location in the end-state architecture, tagged as A890. In addition, the cause of pressure is identified as behavioral. Moreover, network utilization, data utilization, and CPU utilization are the data metrics collected for this pressure point.

It could be argued that a capacity planning model like this is narrow and does not encompass enough utilization information to determine if the entire end-state architecture is under risky pressure. This assertion is entirely correct. Indeed, the limited scope of such a perspective would not provide a wide range view that could reveal the perils related to such an end-state architecture environment. However, such a pinpointing method could focus on strategic spots in the enterprise architecture, an approach that could shed light on the resource consumption related to central areas. The most common example that comes to mind would be to employ such a utilization inspection pinpointing approach if the end-state architecture includes hub-and-spokes

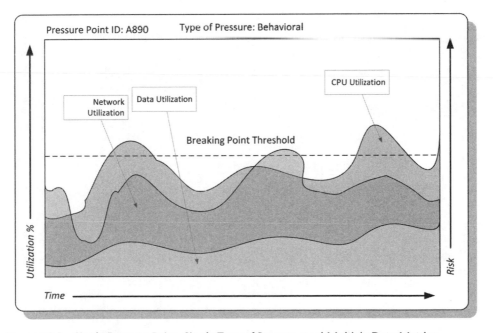

Figure 15.3   Single Pressure Point, Single Type of Pressure, and Multiple Data Metrics

sub-architecture styles. The pressure point, therefore, should be placed on the hub component to assess its utilization rates.

Multiple Pressure Points, Single Type of Pressure, Single Data Metric

To increase the scope of the enterprise capacity planning modeling view, Figure 15.4 represents a scenario in which the data collection is expanded, including three different pressure points in the end-state architecture environment. These are tagged as pressure point IDs 111, 222, and 333. Obviously, engineers may decide to include many more pressure points to cover a wider range of troubling spots in the end-state architecture. Undoubtedly, increase of pressure points in a capacity-planning model would bring about a more reliable and accurate incremental software architecture verification process.

In Figure 15.4, the capacity planning model is focused on prone-to-change spots in an end-state architecture. These are volatile-defined pressure points that may be responsible for failing implementations caused by lack of computing resources after a change had been applied to the environment. In this case, however, the inspection of resource consumption is narrow. The illustration suggests that only network utilization is compared to the same metric in the other pressure points. The choice to limit the capacity planning model to a single data metric is helpful when a network is suspected to be lacking bandwidth.

Note that the breaking point threshold in Figure 15.4 was crossed over by the two pressure points: 222 and 333. Immediate attention should be given to the increasing risk of depleting network resource consumption. An end-state architecture that possesses pressure points that lack sufficient computing resources should not be sponsored until such deficiencies are mended.

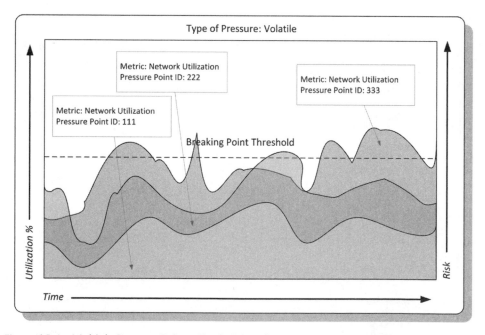

Figure 15.4   Multiple Pressure Points, Single Type of Pressure, Single Data Metric

Multiple Pressure Points, Multiple Types of Pressures, Multiple Data Metrics

The most complex, yet powerful, enterprise capacity model includes multiple pressure points, multiple types of pressures, and multiple data metrics. This is the broadest view that could be created when inspecting capacity utilization of an end-state architecture. In fact, the multifaceted perspective not only can include different troubling points in a design, but also provide reasons for the strains on different pressure point. In addition, the multiple data metrics only add to the diversity of resource consumption investigation parameters. Is this a good thing?

Let us have a look now at Figure 15.5 to understand the complexity of such a broad capacity utilization view. The three pressure points 111, 222, and 333 are investigated for three different metrics respectively: data utilization, network utilization, and disk utilization. Moreover, three architectural aspects cause the pressures on these points correspondingly: structural, behavioral, and volatile.

Indeed, this complex model requires studies to understand how each parameter is related to the other. This should be accomplished based on the context of the investigated end-state architecture environment. According to the scenario presented in Figure 15.5, there may be a correlation between data utilization, network utilization, and disk utilization. The model does not explain such a relationship, unless the engineer involved adds remakes to explain why such a model is created and elaborates on the relationship between the three metrics. Likewise, there must be some sort of association between the depicted types of pressures. Again, in the context of the overall design, there must be affiliations that prompt the creation of such an enterprise capacity planning model.

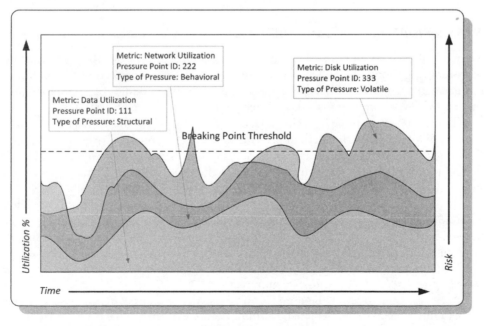

Figure 15.5   Multiple Pressure Points, Multiple Types of Pressure, Multiple Data Metrics

An Enterprise Capacity Plan for an End-State Architecture

The business organization, the development community, operation engineers, and stakeholders are waiting impatiently for the end-state architecture capacity plan. Without such a plan, the end-state architecture could not be verified and certified. Without a clear capacity plan, budgets will not be allocated to support an unproven grand-scale design. Without resource sizing guidance, the end-state architecture will not be deployed to production. Without a capacity plan that assesses future environment sizing, the implementation will not be approved. If the end-state architecture, though, already operates in production, without a capacity plan to size its computing resources, it is doomed to fail.

A Capacity Plan Is All about Sizing Resource Consumption Capabilities

The resource utilization-sizing artifact is the actual capacity plan for an end-state architecture. It is not a recommendation. Nor is it just a diagram created for pointing out the need for sizing a computing environment. Resource capacity sizing, therefore, must be sponsored to carry out the increase in technological capabilities. The sizing effort would enable the growth of an end-state architecture in a production environment.

Contribution to the architecture elasticity is one of the most important aspects of the capacity plan. The ability to strengthen the performance power of computing resources would enable the increase of consumers' transactions, ultimately resulting in growth of organizational revenue.

In the next section, we then propose a model for resource utilization sizing, describing a method for delivering a clear and compact capacity plan that could be implemented rapidly to fulfill end-state architecture environment consumption goals.

A Model for Sizing Resource Utilization

Remember that no one likes to read long documents to find out the proper sizing of computing resources. Extensive and tedious end-state architecture consumption requirements would not simplify the process of sizing either. Budget personnel, too, are eager to know one thing only—how much would the resource utilization sizing cost.

Therefore, the approach for the capacity utilization plan in this book is straightforward. A diagram drives the method of sizing an end-state architecture environment by showing the percentage of the required increase in utilization. This would also satisfy budget requirements by indicating how much to increase funds for resource utilization sizing of an end-state architecture.

Another crucial point to note is that this model for capacity utilization sizing is based on the data metrics collection from end-state architecture pressure points. Service level agreements (SLAs) and nonfunctional requirements (NFRs) should only provide preliminary estimates for performance and resource consumption. Unfortunately, in many cases SLAs and NFRs never represented the actual resource consumption needs for an end-state architecture.

Now it is time to review Figure 15.6 and grasp the concept of the enterprise capacity plan introduced in the depicted diagram. Before explaining this plan, consider the

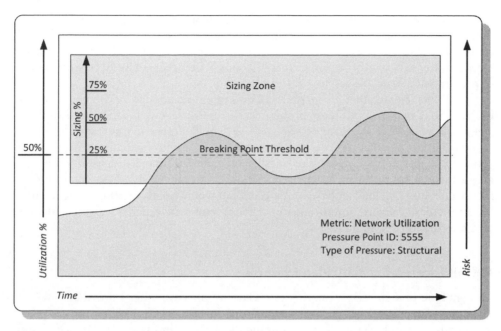

Figure 15.6   Capacity Utilization Sizing Model

breakdown of its elements, some of which already have been discussed previously in the section on Setting Up an Enterprise Capacity Planning Model. It is clear that the capacity utilization sizing is based on this model.

Utilization percentage   This indicates the resource consumption percentage of a particular data metric for a specific end-state architecture pressure point.
Time.   This is the range of time of the data collection period.
Risk   This is the risk associated with the increase in utilization.
Breaking point threshold   It is believed that beyond this line, an end-state architecture could not handle such a high utilization rate of any of its pressure points.
Sizing zone   If resource consumption utilization reaches this area in the graph, the capacity plan mandates sizing the consumption capabilities for the related data metric. Note that this zone also includes a sizing scale, named "Sizing %," measured in percentage and ranging from 0 to 100.

As illustrated in Figure 15.6, the capacity plan model also identifies parameters that should be targeted:

Pressure point ID   Pressure point identification
Type of pressure   Types of strains applied on a pressure point, structural, behavior, or volatile.
Metric   The data metric that was collected from a pressure point

This capacity sizing model is easy to understand. Note in the diagram that the utilization percentage for the network throughput, where the pressure point 5555 is located, reaches levels well above 50 percent. Accordingly, it is apparent in the sizing zone that the network throughput capability should be increased by 50 percent because of architecture structural issues.

It is ever clearer that an increase in resource utilization would render a capacity plan that instructs production engineers to boost resource capacity capabilities. *The sizing zone, therefore, is our capacity plan.* A plan like this could not and should not mandate anything other than a percentage increase in resource expansion. Budget allocations and dollar amounts are the sole responsibility of financial organizations. And an increase in software and hardware capabilities sits on the shoulders of production engineers. Thus, an indicated percentage amount would clearly communicate the need for an increase in consumption capability for an end-state architecture for a pressure point, as depicted in Figure 15.6.

A Multifaceted Capacity Plan Example

To conclude this chapter, a multifaceted capacity plan example is provided. We take an additional look at a capacity plan model that incorporates multiple pressure points in an end-state architecture. Let us examine the diagram in Figure 15.7, in which four data metrics are tested for utilization: memory utilization at pressure point 9004, data utilization at pressure point 8001, CPU utilization at pressure point 7007, and network utilization at pressure point 6009.

This compound pressure point utilization diagram spans four weeks during which structural, behavioral, and volatile pressures show different levels of consumption. As is apparent, the capacity plan does not require increasing the utilization capacity for network utilization at pressure point 6009. This would not be mandatory since the utilization for this pressure point seems to be below the diagram's sizing zone.

However, the CPU utilization at pressure point 7007 exceeds the sizing zone's lower edge. Such a resource consumption level would require an increase in CPU capacity of about 10 percent. Likewise, the pressure point 8001 calls for an increase in data storage since its highest utilization level exceeds the 50 percent mark in the sizing zone. Finally, the highest sizing request would be for memory capacity at pressure point 9004. The capacity plan mandates to increase the server's memory by about 75 percent, as depicted in the diagram's sizing zone.

The resource consumption and sizing analysis in Figure 15.7 suggests that an end-state architecture environment can be assessed for overall resource consumption. To insure that the grand-scale design would indeed function flawlessly in production, all its pressure points that operate under unacceptable capacity conditions should be sized according to the capacity plan. Additional end-state architecture capacity assessments should be performed to verify if indeed the resource capacity requirements for all included pressure points have been satisfied.

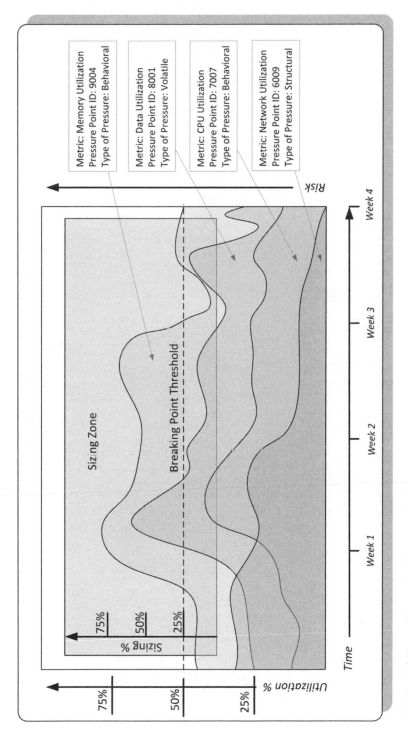

Figure 15.7 Multifaceted Capacity Plan Example

Notes

1. Michael J. Sydor, *APM Best Practices: Realizing Application Performance Management*, 2010, Apress, p. 21
2. Changjie Tang, Charles X. Ling, Xiaofang Zhou, *Advanced Data Mining and Applications: 4th International Conference, ADMA 2008, Chengdu, China, October 8-10, 2008, Proceedings*, 2008, Springer Science & Business Media, p. 403
3. https://www.acord.org/Pages/default.aspx

INDEX

A

acceptance testing, 32
account management services, 104, 106, 110–112, 117
account reporting services, 104, 106, 108–110, 116, 117
activities
  in design substantiation, 184
  as pressure points, 214
  vs. processes, 166, 168
  in system-level behavioral decomposition, 170–172
Air Force system failure example, 14–15
application(s)
  changes to, 156, 158
  definition of, 55
  physical distribution of, 68
application capacity planning, 61, 235, 236
application dependencies
  cataloging, 77–81
  mapping, 70–71
  patterns of, 76–77
  in sub-architectures, 110
  and system failure, 24
  types of, 72–76
application discovery
  architecture, 58–61
  asset management, 64–66
  and capacity planning, 237–238
  continuous, 56
  function of, 55, 67
  identity, 57–58, 78
  network infrastructure, 63–64
  performance/resource utilization, 61–63
  and system failure detection, 24
  tools for, 56–57
application-level behavioral decomposition, 163–165, 167–169, 172, 173
application-level design, 86, 87–88, 90–91
application-level pressure points, 215–218, 224
application life cycle management (ALM), 65
application mapping
  of dependencies, 24, 70–77
  function of, 67, 68
  of topology, 67–70, 238
application performance management (APM), 239
architecture
  application, 58–61
  capabilities of, 120, 122–128

elasticity of, 71, 248
enterprise (*see* enterprise architecture)
grand-scale (*see* grand-scale architecture)
architecture decomposition
  business-driven, 9, 145–160
  and capacity planning, 237, 238
  classification in, 91–102, 203
  defined, 5
  functional (behavioral), 161–178, 214
  grand-scale, 116–117, 138–144
  sub-architectures in, 103–114, 120
  technical analysis in (*see* technical analysis)
architecture decoupling scale, 91–94, 101, 109–114, 133, 137
architecture design
  application-level, 86, 87-88, 90-91
  vs. development, 3, 6
design flaws, 189, 190, 191, 194, 199, 232
end-state, 2-3
  enterprise-level, 86-87, 88-91
  to reduce pressure risk, 216
  unfulfilled requirements of (debt), 184
  verification of, 176–178, 194–195
  See also design substantiation
architecture distribution scale, 91–94, 101, 109–114, 133, 137
architecture expansion
  and chained message route fabric pattern, 50
  and compound fabric patterns, 52
  and federated architecture type, 89
  and system failure, 26–27, 28
architecture heterogeneity, 85
architecture patterns, 24, 28
architecture segmentation
  analysis/refinement, 189, 191–192
  construction/integration, 189, 192–193
  design loop-back, 189, 191, 194–195
  testing, 192–193
  validation/certification, 189, 193–194
architecture structure, 202–203
architecture verification
  authentication tasks in, 9
  and capacity planning, 236, 238
  and decomposition process, 149, 176
  design substantiation in, 181–196
  function of, 5–6, 179–180
  in incremental approach, 8–9, 83
  and software modeling/simulation, 7
  and stress testing, 224–225

architecture verification principal, 188–189, 194
asset(s)
    crosscutting, 163–165, 170, 172, 173, 215, 217
    distribution of, 24, 28, 200
    integration of, 203, 215, 224
    reuse of, 125, 126, 166
    volatility of, 159
asset management, 64–66, 77–81
authentication server, 127, 142
autonomy, 61

B
balance scorecard, 70
bandwidth
    and capacity planning, 235, 239
    and network congestion, 198
    in network infrastructure discovery, 63
    and pressure points, 224
behavioral (functional) decomposition
    application-level, 167–169
    cascading behaviors in, 164
    component-level, 165–167
    diagram for, 173–176
    model for, 163–165
    purpose of, 161–162, 172–173
    results of, 176–178
    system-level, 170–172
behavioral pressure points, 200, 214–218, 225–226,
        228, 244
best practices
    and change initiatives, 7–8
    to drive design substantiation, 186
bill pay application, 104, 106, 112–114, 116
blocking, 73
bottom-up architecture evolution, 8
breaking points, 227–229, 238–239, 241,
        244–247, 249
breaking points discovery stress testing, 231–232
bridge fabric patterns, 50–51, 52, 53, 77, 206,
        207, 211
broker-based architecture, 90, 123
budgets
    and architecture verification, 179
    and capacity planning, 32, 62, 236, 248, 250
    and design substantiation, 188
    and enterprise architecture design, 2, 3, 181
    and system failures, 14, 19, 20, 29, 30
    and system reuse, 26
bus architecture, 89
business analysis
    for sub-architecture discovery, 103–117
    for tracing architecture evolution, 117–118
business continuity
    and application dependency discovery, 71
    and asset management, 64
    and circular message route fabric pattern, 48
    ensuring, 33

    and pressure points, 214, 218,
        219, 232
business discovery, 102
business documentation, 237
business domains (lines)
    contextual, 146
    definition of, 146
    as pressure points, 212–214
    structural, 146–156
business federation, 44
business granularity, 149, 151, 154
business impact analysis, 20
business layer
    in application architecture, 59
    in application mapping, 69
    structural decomposition of, 151
business-level system failures, 17, 19–21
business logic layer, 60, 61, 76, 159
business model
    and architecture discovery/analysis process, 37
    and business-driven architecture decomposition,
        145, 154
    perpetual transaction cycles in, 47
    and system failure, 21
business ownership
    in architecture decomposition, 145
    and business change, 219
business process models, 37
business services
    sub-architectures supporting, 103, 104–105
    volatility of, 158, 159, 160
business solutions
    and application architecture type, 60
    and application discovery, 55
    and system fabric discovery, 39
business strategy
    and architecture discovery/analysis, 37, 58
    and architecture evolution, 118, 219
    and business domain distribution, 154
    sub-architecture execution of, 104
    and technical analysis, 141
business tiers, 149–151
business transactions
    circular, 46–47, 49
    discovery process, 24
    linear, 49
    mapping routes of, 67, 74
    stability of, 214
    tracing, to discover sub-architectures, 103–104,
        107
business view, 145
business volatility, 218–222
bus technologies, 43, 44

C
capacity planning
    architecture, 61–63, 235, 236
    enterprise, 9, 32, 235, 236, 248–251

function of, 199, 235–236, 248
  methodology for, 236–242
  modeling in, 241, 242–247
  in verification process, 180
capacity predictive modeling, 62
capacity utilization testing, 63
centralized architecture, 91–93, 97–99, 108, 109,
    115–118, 131, 136, 140, 142, 212
centralized business domain, 151–153
central processing unit (CPU), 32, 62, 80, 216, 235,
    239, 250
chained message route fabric pattern, 48–50, 77,
    135–136, 206, 207
change
  in architecture segments (volatility), 200
  in business segments (volatility), 156–160
  organizational, 7–9
  in production environments, 218–222
change management, 24
circular business transactions, 46–47, 49
circular message route fabric pattern, 46–48, 77,
    206, 207
client-server application architecture, 61
cloud computing, 125–126, 173, 222, 227
clustered business domain, 154–155, 212
combined segment testing, 193
common utilities, 60
communication platforms, volatility of, 157
communication protocols, 58
community center fabric pattern, 41–43, 77, 97,
    131, 135–136, 206, 207, 210
community fabric pattern, 40–41, 52, 77, 96,
    206, 207
component(s)
  definition of, 165
  reuse of, 169, 176, 216
component-level behavioral decomposition,
    163–167, 172, 173–174
component-level pressure points, 215–217, 224
compound fabric patterns, 51–53,
    77, 207
computing environment, size of, 235
configuration management
  and application discovery, 65
  and system failure detection, 24, 33
consumer(s)
  in application architecture diagram, 59, 60
  enterprise connection to, 58
consumer demand
  and architecture pressure, 199
  and business volatility pressure, 221
  performance data collected on, 242
consumer segmentation analysis, 20, 37
continuous application discovery, 56, 68
conversation, 72, 73
crosscutting layer, 59
cross-functional contracts, 185–195

crossroad fabric patterns, 50–51, 52, 53, 77,
    206–207, 211
CRUD (create, read, update, delete), 75, 79,
    124, 227
customer data integration (CDI), 127

D
data abstraction, 124
data access layer (DAL), 27, 32, 51, 59, 61, 75, 79,
    124, 142, 159, 172
data aggregator, 127–128, 142
data analysis, in capacity planning, 62, 240–242
data cataloging, 79–80
data collection, for capacity planning, 237,
    238–240
data collection technologies, 239–240
data exchange format, 80
data generation technologies, 240
data integrity, 242
data link layer, 80
data mining engine, 128
data source providers, 60, 210, 225–227
data storage
  caches, 75
  in capacity planning, 235, 239, 250
  warehouses, 69, 74, 79, 222
decentralized organizations, 1, 8
decomposition. See architecture decomposition
defect tracking, 65
delta analysis of applications, 56
design. See architecture design
design flaws, 189, 190, 191, 194, 199, 232
design patterns, 89
design substantiation
  cross-functional contracts in, 185–186
  function of, 181–185, 214
  process for, 189–195
  team members for, 186–189, 195–196
  in verification process, 9, 180
disaster recovery (DR) mechanisms, 28, 214
disk space, 80, 235, 239
distributed architecture, 51, 61, 72, 89, 135–136,
    165–166
durability discovery stress testing, 232–233

E
end-users
  acceptance testing by, 32
  as volatile business domain, 158
enterprise architecture
  artifact studies for, 236–238
  capacity planning for (see capacity planning)
  decomposition of (see architecture
    decomposition)
  design flaws in, 189, 190, 191, 194, 199, 232
  design of (see architecture design)
  design substantiation for (see design
    substantiation)

enterprise architecture (*Continued*)
  diagrams for, 3–4, 36
  evolution of, 8, 118, 143–144
  monolithic, 8, 58, 71, 76, 91–95, 165
  patterns for, 89–90
  perspectives of, 86–91, 145
  pressure points in (*see* pressure points)
  segmentation of, 176–178, 184–185, 189–195
  technical analysis case study, 120–122
  unified business categorization of, 114–117
  verification of (*see* architecture verification)
  volatility in, 156–160
enterprise architecture discovery/analysis process
  application discovery in, 55–66
  function of, 35–36
  prerequisites for, 36–37
  scenarios for, 36
  system fabric patterns in, 39–53
enterprise architecture-level system failures, 17,
    23–29
enterprise-level design, 86–87, 88–91
enterprise-level separation of concerns, 124
enterprise service bus (ESB)
  and application dependencies, 75, 77
  and architecture expansion, 27
  and cloud computing, 125
  in federated architecture, 99, 100, 203
  function of, 3
  as pressure point, 214
  in system-level behavioral decomposition, 172
  in technical analysis, 123–124
  See also ESB chaining
environment
  behavior of, 162
  definition of, 84
  pressure sources in, 199, 223
  See also production environment
environment behavior decomposition model,
    163–164, 175
environment volatility model, 158–160
ESB chaining, 124, 126, 131–132
external application dependencies, 74–76

F
fabric patterns. *See* system fabric
failure (of systems). *See* system failure
family fabric pattern, 44–46, 77, 206, 207,
    210–211
features, in system-level behavioral decomposition,
    170
federated architecture, 89, 91–93, 99–101, 108,
    115, 117, 118, 124, 129–131, 136, 140, 142,
    202, 212
federated business domain, 153–154
Ford Motor Co. system failure example, 15
forecast application performance, 63
functional decomposition. *See* behavioral
    decomposition

functionality externalization, 76
functions, in system-level behavioral
    decomposition, 170

G
gateways
  and architecture expansion, 27
  as architecture type, 90
  in federated architecture, 99
  function of, 75
  as pressure point, 214
  in system-level behavioral decomposition, 172
  in technical analysis, 126–127
glue proxies, 216
grand-scale architecture
  appropriateness of, 197
  and capacity planning, 237, 244, 250
  classification and decomposition, 116–117,
    138–144, 162
  design substantiation analysis, 191
  pressure points in, 224, 232
  See also enterprise architecture
granularity, 61

H
hardware
  budgeting for, 62
  capacity planning for, 235
  cataloging of, 77
  in technology analysis, 123
  in topology map, 67
high-availability (HA) testing, 63
hub-and-spokes architecture, 25–26, 90, 97, 108,
    131, 135–136, 142, 210, 225, 245–246

I
identity server, 125, 142
incremental software architecture approach
  and architecture decomposition, 83, 148
  and capacity planning, 237
  and discovery process, 55
  function of, 2, 3, 8
  process steps, 9
  verification process in, 179
  vs. software modeling/simulation, 7
information technology (IT)
  executive accountability in, 18
  risk assessment role of, 20
  volatility of, 158
infrastructure. *See* network infrastructure
infrastructure as service (IaS), 126
integrated development environment
    (IDE), 30, 31
integration
  of assets, 203, 215, 224
  of systems, 24, 28, 33
integration testing, 31–32
integration verification, 185

interfaces, in application architecture, 60
intermediary installations
  in broker-based architectures, 90
  excessive, 27, 28, 123, 203
  function of, 75
  as pressure points, 211, 214, 218
intermediary nodes, 50–51
internal application dependencies, 76
International Standards Organization (ISO), 80
interoperability
  and application dependencies, 71
  and architecture expansion, 27
  and ESBs, 123
  and federated architecture, 100–101, 129–131, 202
  and gateway architecture, 90, 99, 126
  and message transport fabric pattern, 44
  and pressure points, 214
  and system failure, 24, 29
iterative software development, 182–183

K
key performance indicators (KPIs), 69
keystone architecture structure classification and decomposition diagram, 91–102
  in sub-architecture classification, 108–114, 129, 132–133, 136–137

L
legacy systems, 112, 189
linear business transactions, 49
load testing, 229
logical application dependencies, 70
loose coupling, 60, 68, 71, 75, 83, 89, 96, 99, 110, 165, 175

M
management-level system failures, 17, 18–19
market segmentation analysis, 19, 37
memory utilization, 62, 80, 216, 235, 239, 250
mesh architecture, 40, 77, 91–93, 95–97, 108, 110–112, 115, 117, 118, 142
message augmentation, 51
message injection, 229
message paths
  and application dependencies, 75
  and architecture structure, 202
  and architecture type, 89–90
  congestion of, 198, 199, 224
  mapping routes of, 67
  stress testing of, 197, 229, 231, 232–233
  in sub-architecture discovery, 104
  in system-level behavioral decomposition, 172
  in technical profiling, 128
  types of, 39–53
message transport fabric pattern, 43–44, 51, 52, 77, 206

messaging infrastructure, 60
Micro-Organizations, 1, 2
microservices, 8
middleware
  application dependency on, 75–76
  in application discovery process, 56
  budgeting for, 62
  cataloging of, 77, 80–81
  as pressure point, 218
  in system-level behavioral decomposition, 170, 172, 173
  in technical analysis, 119, 123
  in topology map, 67
mobile applications, 57
model-view-controller application architecture (MVC), 61, 88
money transfer application, 105, 106, 112–114, 116
monolithic architecture, 8, 58, 71, 76, 91–95, 108, 112–116, 118, 142, 165

N
network infrastructure
  application dependency on, 75–76
  in application discovery process, 56, 63–64
  budgeting for, 62
  congestion in, 24, 25, 40, 165, 198, 199, 211, 223, 224, 229
  in system-level behavioral decomposition, 170
  in technical analysis, 119, 123
  in topology map, 67
  upgrades to, 33, 34
network layer, 80
network nodes
  and application dependency patterns, 77
  in bridge fabric pattern, 50–51, 52, 53
  in chained message route fabric pattern, 48–50
  in circular message route fabric pattern, 46–48
  in community center fabric pattern, 41–43
  in community fabric pattern, 40–41, 43, 52
  in compound fabric patterns, 51–53
  in crossroads fabric pattern, 50–51, 52, 53
  in family fabric pattern, 44–46
  in message transport fabric pattern, 43–44, 52
network performance/availability, 24
network topology
  mesh in, 40
  vs. network fabric, 39
  and system failure detection, 24
nonfunctional requirements (NFR) document, 62, 237, 248
N-tier application architecture, 61, 68–69, 88, 202

O
observer patron, in design substantiation, 188, 194
off-the-shelf applications, 57, 167
one-way message exchange, 73
open-source products, 8

open systems interconnection, 80
operation-level system failures, 17, 33–34
operations, volatility of, 157
organizational change, 7–9
    See also business volatility
organizational culture, 29
organizational structure, 1, 8, 154
    See also business domains
orphan nodes, 41, 42, 51

P
pattern matching, 128
performance measurement
    for applications, 61
    and application topology mapping, 69
    and capacity planning, 63
    and stress testing, 197
    technologies for, 239–240
physical application dependencies, 70, 238
physical layer, 80
platform as service (PaS), 126
point-to-point architecture, 25, 52, 77, 90, 96,
        110–112, 136, 142
power blackout (2003), 16, 29
presentation layer, 59, 60, 61, 159
pressure points
    behavioral, 200, 214–218, 225–226, 228
    data collection from, 236, 238–240, 241,
        244–250
    environmental vs. architectural, 198–201
    failure conditions for, 227–229
    inserting, 223–227
    joint, 203, 211–214
    and stress testing, 197
    structural, 200, 201–214, 224, 225, 228–229
    volatility, 200, 218–222, 225, 227, 228
private application dependencies, 72–73
processes
    vs. activities, 166, 168
    in design substantiation, 184
    as pressure points, 214
    in system-level behavioral decomposition,
        170–172
product description, 37
product development, 19–20
production
    and continuous application discovery, 56
    and ensuring business continuity, 33
production environment
    mapping application integration in, 67, 68
    multiple systems in, 10, 11–12
    pressure points in, 198–199, 202–203, 211, 214,
        215–216
    as profitability center, 219
product life cycle
    and business volatility, 218
    and system failure, 13, 23

product segmentation analysis, 20, 37
proxies, 75, 79, 90, 99, 214, 216
public application dependencies, 73–74

Q
quality of services (QoS), 70

R
RACI chart, 186, 195–196
recovery discovery stress testing, 230–231
release management (RM), 65–66
    documents, 34
request-response, 72
response time
    application, 70, 75
    and excessive message mediators, 203
    system, 25, 34
    and system-level behavior, 164
return on investment (ROI), 145
reusability, 61
rich Internet application (RIA), 57, 76
risk management
    and architecture discovery/analysis process,
        37
    and pressure points, 227–229, 244
    and system failure, 20
routers
    application dependency on, 75
    configurations, 39, 44
    and network congestion, 199
    as network infrastructure, 170

S
security breaches, 34
security platform, 60, 63, 157, 170, 224
segmentation analysis, 19–20
service applications, 57
service layer, 60
service-level agreements (SLAs)
    and application capacity, 61
    and architecture capacity, 248
    and end-state architecture design, 2
    KPIs for, 70
    and system testing, 32
service-oriented application architecture (SOA), 61,
        89
single point of failure, 45, 48, 49, 98, 210
software
    capacity planning for, 235
    cataloging of, 77
    construction of, 6, 83, 181–182
    to detect technological system failures, 24
    elasticity of, 71
    establishing baseline for, 65
    reuse of, 165, 169
    in technical analysis, 123
    upgrades to, 33

software architecture design
  delays in, 184
  vs. development, 3, 6
  substantiation of (*see* design substantiation)
  and system failures, 23–29
software architecture development
  vs. design, 3, 6
  duration of, 192
  scope of, 191
  stakeholders in, 188
  system failures in, 17, 23, 29–31
  testing in, 240
  time/budget constraints in, 8
  and verification, 83
  waterfall vs. iterative approaches to, 182–183
software as service (SaS), 126
software asset distribution, 24, 28
software cataloging, 24
software configuration management (SCM), 65
software development life cycle (SDLC), 65
software engineer, in design substantiation, 187,
      193, 194
software entropy, 183, 192
software modeling, 6–7, 30
software module testing, 192, 193
software simulation, 7, 240
source code
  defects in, 13, 16, 29
  design of, 3, 6, 65, 179, 194
  in design substantiation, 186
  in performance measurement technologies, 240
  and system-level behavior, 164
  testing of, 31, 192
star network topology, 42, 77, 90, 97, 108, 131,
      135, 141
statelessness, 61
stress testing
  function of, 6, 197, 199
  methodology for, 227–233
  and pressure points, 207, 210, 214, 218, 223–227
  as verification process step, 9, 180
structural pressure points, 200, 201–214, 224, 225,
      228–229, 244
structural signature, 202
sub-architectures
  classifying, 108–114, 128–138
  definition of, 102
  discovery, 103–107, 120, 122–128, 140
  overlapping, 138, 140
  structural pressures of, 211–214
  in technical analysis, 119, 120
  in unified business categorization, 115–117,
      138–144
system(s)
  cascading behaviors in, 164, 212, 215–216
  definition of, 9–10, 170
  deployment of, 33

  federated, 24, 28–29
  maintenance of, 33, 34
  scalability of, 24, 28, 235
system fabric
  and application dependencies, 76–77
  and capacity planning, 237
  definition of, 39
  pattern types, 40–53, 202
  and structural pressures, 206–211
  in technical analysis, 119, 120
  tools for analyzing, 56
system failure
  and circular message route fabric pattern, 48
  classification of, 16–21
  definition of, 13
  and environment-level behaviors, 164–165, 199
  examples of, 14–16
  factors in, 11–12
  operation-level, 33–34
  software development-level, 29–31
  technological, 23–29
  testing-level, 31–32
system integration, 24, 28, 33
system-level behavioral decomposition, 170–172
system-level pressure points, 215–216, 224
system load testing, 32
system of systems, 23
system testing, 32

T
technical analysis
  case study, 120–122
  function of, 102, 119
  profiling in, 123–128
  sub-architecture discovery in, 120, 128–138
technical capability, 119, 120, 140–141, 221
technical profiling, 120, 122–128, 138
technical specifications document, 237
technical views, 120, 138
  vs. business views, 145
technological system-level failures, 17
  detecting, 24–25, 28–29
  examples of, 26–27
  types of, 23–24
technological volatility, 156–157, 218, 221–222
technology development, 7
testing
  in capacity planning, 63
  in design substantiation, 192–193
  pre-production application readiness, 63–64
  in software development, 240
  types, 31–32
  See also stress testing
testing-level system failures, 17, 31–32
thick client applications, 57
tight coupling, 71, 76, 89, 94, 96, 112–114, 165
top-down change initiatives, 7

topology mapping, 67–70, 238
transport layer, 80
two-way message exchange, 72–73

U
unit testing, 31, 192, 193
user interface
  in application architecture, 59
  role in system failure, 21
user provisioning (administration), 34, 60

V
volatility pressure points, 200, 218–222, 225, 227,
  228, 244

W
waterfall software development, 182
Web applications, 57, 69
workload management, 98